CHICAGO PUBLIC LIBRARY
HAROLD WASHINGTON LIBRARY CENTER

R0003432549

R00034 32549

S0-AAF-941

ML3060.W35
v.II

Cop.2

MUS BOOK

WELLESZ
Studies in Eastern
Chant   11.25

AUG 1973

AUG 1975

THE CHICAGO PUBLIC LIBRARY

MUSIC DEPT.

FORM 19

STUDIES IN EASTERN CHANT
Volume Two

STUDIES IN EASTERN CHANT

General Editors

EGON WELLESZ
and
MILOŠ VELIMIROVIĆ

VOLUME II

Edited by

MILOŠ VELIMIROVIĆ

London
OXFORD UNIVERSITY PRESS
NEW YORK   TORONTO
1971

Oxford University Press, Ely House, London W. 1

GLASGOW NEW YORK TORONTO MELBOURNE WELLINGTON

CAPE TOWN SALISBURY IBADAN NAIROBI DAR ES SALAAM LUSAKA ADDIS ABABA

BOMBAY CALCUTTA MADRAS KARACHI LAHORE DACCA

KUALA LUMPUR SINGAPORE HONG KONG TOKYO

ISBN 0 19 316318 7

© Oxford University Press 1971

ML
3060
.W35
v.II
c2

783.5
W459n
v. 2 cop.2
MR.

*Printed in Great Britain
by Billing and Sons Limited, Guildford and London*

THE CHICAGO PUBLIC LIBRARY

NOV 19 '71 B

Contents

v

List of Plates

(all between pages 22 and 23)

The Editors wish to express their gratitude to the British Academy for the generous grants which assisted the publication of this volume.

A Note on the Origins of the
'Monumenta Musicae Byzantinae'
(1931–1971)

In 1930 H. J. W. Tillyard and I received an invitation from Carsten Høeg to come to Copenhagen in July as guests of the Rask-Oersted Foundation to review together the present state of research in Byzantine music and to discuss what should be done to give a wider scope to these studies. It may be remembered that Tillyard's first contribution, 'Greek Church Music', had been published as early as 1911 in *The Musical Antiquary*. In the same year he published his important article 'A Musical Study of the Hymns of Casia' in *Byzantinische Zeitschrift* xx, and in 1912 'The Acclamation of Emperors in Byzantine Ritual' in the *Annual of the British School at Athens* xviii. My own contributions began in 1915 with an investigation into the origin of Early Christian chant, followed by the discovery of the key to the rhythmical interpretation of the Middle Byzantine notation in 'Zur Entzifferung der byzantinischen Notenschrift', published in *Oriens Christianus* N.S. vii, 1918.

Carsten Høeg had written an essay on 'La Théorie de la musique byzantine' in the *Revue des études grecques* (1922), and had followed up our publications on Byzantine musical notation.

Even during the first session our talks went much further than we had anticipated; they showed how valuable it was to exchange our views, to examine impartially all arguments and to carry on discussing every point until a solution was found. Tillyard opened the discussion on problems of palaeography, particularly on the Martyriai, I myself on questions concerning the rhythmical interpretation of the musical signs and on the rôle of Byzantine music in the sphere of the music of the Eastern Churches. Høeg, as a philologist of high standing, dealt with the necessity of a textual critical edition of the theoretical treatises. Thus the terms of reference for dividing up the field of studies emerged of their own accord, and their limits were drawn by common consent.

The main topic of our discussions was the transcription of Middle Byzantine neumes. After having thoroughly checked the theoretical sources, the method which I hitherto had employed was accepted. In order to simplify, however, the shape of the melodic line, we decided to exclude the use of semi-quavers and to print only quavers and crotchets since the added rhythmic signs gave sufficient indication how these notes should be sung.

Carsten Høeg proposed to start a series of publications. To this end he got in contact with Professor Blinkenberg and Professor Drachmann, both of the Royal Danish Academy, who showed warm interest in the project. The following report was drafted, submitted to the Royal Danish Academy and published in the *Acta Musicologica* Vol. iii, fasc. 4, pp. 175–7:

From the 15th. to the 19th. July, 1931, a conference took place in Copenhagen at the invitation of the Rask-Oersted Foundation, which is concerned with research into Byzantine music. Professor H. J. W. Tillyard (Cardiff University) and Professor Egon Wellesz (Vienna University) took part in the discussions, which were prepared by Professor Carsten Høeg (Copenhagen University).

The following resolutions were taken unanimously:

1. For further studies of Byzantine music a series of publications were regarded as being of primary importance. They consist of two groups:

   I. Monumenta Musicae Byzantinae.

      1. Complete Facsimilia editions of two or three of the most important liturgical manuscripts with musical signs.

      2. An Evangelion with ekphonetic signs.

      3. A palaeographical atlas showing all phases of Byzantine musical notation, and of the cantillation signs occurring in the Evangelion, the Prophetologion, and the Apostolos.

      4. A collection of the theoretical writings.

   II. Supplementa.

      1. Shorter studies (monographs) will be published concerning the chief problems of Byzantine music. In addition the music of the other Eastern Churches will be treated by the most competent scholars.

2. Systematic catalogues shall be prepared up to about
    A.D. 1500, arranged according to the various liturgical
    books, as well as

3. transcriptions of the melodies into modern notation
    with commentary and formal analyses.

    The undersigned have declared themselves ready to
    undertake the editorship of these publications.

2.   Photographs of important studies will be taken and collected
to facilitate comparative studies. The scope will be limited at first
to the year 1500, so that the framework of the enterprise will not be
stretched too far.

3.   After joint consultation a system for transcribing Byzantine
Chant was drawn up.

4.   Research will be in line with the newly intensified interest in
liturgical music in countries of the Greek Orthodox Church through
the publication of the treasures of its past. The conference hopes
that its work will find support in these countries through gramo-
phone records, by setting up a register of hymns and their music, and
also by the study of music of the transitional period to the new era.

Carsten Høeg   H. J. W. Tillyard   Egon Wellesz
Copenhagen University   Cardiff University   Vienna University

Copenhagen, 19th. July, 1931.

Work began immediately. Høeg, with a grant from the Carls-
berg Foundation, went to Athens, Mount Athos, Jerusalem, and
Mount Sinai and photographed Lectionaria with ecphonetic
signs, musical manuscripts with neumes, and theoretical
treatises, and sent copies of the photographed Codices to
Tillyard and me.

The first results of our collaboration were: 1) the facsimile
edition of the Sticherarium Cod.Vindob.thoel.gr.181, (1935);
2) Tillyard's 'Handbook of the Middle Byzantine Musical
Notation' Subsidia I, 1 (1935); and 3) my 'Die Hymnen des
Sticherarium für September' Transcripta, Vol. I (1936).

From the very beginning it has been our aim to bring the
studies in Byzantine music in line with those on Gregorian
chant, thus widening the field of studies in medieval music. We

wanted to provide reliable transcriptions in order to make available the melodies of the Byzantine Church and later on those of the other Eastern Churches. Thanks to Høeg's unflinching energy, which remained unbroken even when his health was failing, at least some of the task which we had hoped to fulfil has been achieved.

E. W.

I

Egon Wellesz

OXFORD, ENGLAND

H. J. W. Tillyard—In memoriam

HENRY Julius Wetenhall Tillyard died on 2 January 1968, at the age of eighty-six. With his death a friendship and collaboration ended which had lasted forty-five years. In a letter from Birmingham, dated 20 February 1922, he wrote: 'As far as I can see we are in agreement about the Round System on all essential points: for, our versions, though written slightly differently, sound alike.' He then went on to talk about the early and the late system of notation and added: 'Perhaps you will be so kind as to hand on this small subscription for the "Mittagstisch der Professoren" to the right person.' (It was the worst period of starvation in Austria after the first War, and welfare institutions in Great Britain and the United States provided food for the members of the University who had lost all their fortune in the devaluation of 10.000 Kronen reduced to one.) The letter characterizes the scholar and the man: generous in accepting the views of others, generous in helping where help was needed.

Byzantine studies are now in the limelight; even those in music find recognition. When Tillyard began to show active interest in Byzantine chant he found great difficulties in having his articles published. He began to work in 1904 in Rome and his teacher was Dom Ugo Gaisser of the Greek College who had just completed his study *Les 'Heirmoi' de Paques*. From Rome Tillyard went to Athens where he stayed at the British School. Here he worked under J. Th Sakellarides, mainly on the later phase of Greek Church music. His interest in deciphering the earlier phases of Byzantine musical notation was aroused and in 1907 he went for the first time to Mount Athos. A friend of mine, Sir Reader Bullard, a former British Ambassador, told me that he well remembered Tillyard. Bullard was a young attaché when a scholar came to his office for a *laisser-passer* to study manuscripts on Mount Athos. It was an unusual demand in those days and it gave Sir Reader Bullard great pleasure to facilitate Tillyard's journey. The outcome of the expedition was considerable; let me mention only the essay on '*The Acclamations of Emperors in Byzantine Ritual*' in the *Annual of the British School at Athens* (1912), which shows his brilliant and penetrating mind already at that early stage of research.

In 1916 I began to study Byzantine musical notation and Tillyard's articles—alas only those published before the outbreak of the War—aroused my interest. At about 1921 we began to exchange letters about the problems which occupied us and instantly a feeling of mutual understanding and friendship arose. During all the forty-five years of close collaboration there was not a single moment of tension about varying views, perhaps because our disagreements were never of an essential nature.

In those days we never expected that our interpretation of the notation should find approval among those who regarded it as a kind of stenography. It was in 1923 that Tillyard received a book by K. A. Psachos, expounding that theory. The sender was Professor Carsten Hoëg in Copenhagen, who had read Tillyard's study on the hymns of Casia in the *Byzantinische Zeitschrift*. Tillyard discussed the matter with me. We were of the same opinion and he wrote two articles in *Laudate* (1924 and 1925) and one in *Byzantinische Zeitschrift* (1925) refuting Psachos's theory.

All the time we had to publish our studies in short articles in various Journals and Annals. However, Tillyard succeeded in writing a concise book on *Byzantine Music and Hymnography* (1923) and I my *Aufgaben und Probleme auf dem Gebiete der byzantinischen und orientalischen Kirchenmusik* in the same year. But it was impossible to present as much music as we felt necessary in order to show the wealth of Byzantine chant.

Support came unexpectedly from Carsten Hoëg, an outstanding philologist, who began to study the Byzantine treatises on musical theory. In a letter to us, dated 27 January 1931, he wrote that the question of including music had been raised at the International Congress of Byzantine Studies at Athens in October 1930. He had worked out a programme for further studies. In order to interest his colleagues at the Royal Danish Academy and the Union Académique Internationale in the scheme, he wanted Tillyard and me to come to Copenhagen and discuss our plans with him. We agreed and met on 15 July 1931 in Hoëg's house. A Danish journalist called it 'the smallest conference in the world,' but in four days we three had not only reached full agreement about the transcription of melodies in interval-notation but also drawn up a detailed plan for the publication of *Monumenta Musicae Byzantinae*. The Danish Academy accepted our scheme and appointed us as Editors. Tillyard was in his happiest mood: for the first time he had found the recognition he deserved. I too felt happy about the prospect of working in future under more favourable conditions. For now the Director of the National Library in Vienna gave me a room in the building and let me fill the shelves with books from the vast treasure of that library. On the initiative of Hoëg the new institute where I worked with my pupils was declared in the regulations as the 'siège scientifique' of the *Monumenta*. From now on we visited each other frequently. In the autumn of 1932 Hoëg and I went to Cardiff and stayed with Tillyard, in 1934 Tillyard came to Vienna. Not only we, but also our families joined in our friendly relations.

In 1938 I settled in Oxford. Hoëg and his friend Kirsopp Lake arranged a meeting at the British Academy, where Tillyard joined us. The meeting was under the chairmanship of Sir Frederick Kenyon, Secretary of the British Academy, who took great interest in our work and gave us invaluable advice and support whenever we needed it. The outbreak of the War made it impossible for us to get in contact with Hoëg. In 1941 Thomas Whittemore, Director of the Byzantine Institute in Boston, came to London. He proposed to publish during the War an American series of the *Monumenta*. Since at that time the United States were not yet at war, we accepted his proposal on condition of Hoëg's approval, which Whittemore promised to obtain. Thus it happened that my *Eastern Elements in Western Chant* and Tillyard's *Twenty Canons* were printed as volumes I and II of the *American Series*. Unfortunately, Whittemore had not complied at once with our request to inform Hoëg of our arrangement. Later events made it impossible, and when we met Hoëg after the end of the war we had to explain the new

situation. Tillyard and I were deeply impressed by all that
Hoëg had suffered since we had last seen him—a buoyant
young man, looking even younger than his years. Now what
he had gone through as one of the leaders of the Danish resistance had left its marks on his face. Yet his optimism was unbroken and work on the *Monumenta* began unabated. We met
nearly every year and the number of volumes published gives
proof of our activity. We had a particularly successful meeting
in 1956 in Oxford, but soon after this we heard that Hoëg had
suffered a severe heart attack. He recovered and continued
working very hard. We received an invitation for a meeting on
a larger scale in August 1958 in Copenhagen. When Tillyard
and I saw him, we knew that this would be the last time we
should be with him.

Hoëg died on 4 April 1961. Tillyard and I drew nearer to
each other, our correspondence became even more frequent
and also our mutual visits. Another link was the admiration of
my pupils and friends for Tillyard; they all went to Cambridge
and came back enriched by his advice, his help, and his kind-
ness. Once, when I was impatient about an article of a colleague
who with great emphasis went into unnecessary minutiae, he
remained silent for a moment, smiled and said: 'But we had
the fun.'

On 17 November 1967, Tillyard and his wife moved from
their house in Cambridge to a flat in Saffron Walden. Two days
later I got a letter. He described the comfort of living 'under
the same roof with our daughter and son-in-law'; and he
continued: 'This is a picturesque little town 15 miles S.E. of
Cambridge, rather hilly with good air. We are most fortunate
in having such a refuge for old age."

It is good to know that there Tillyard had a few happy
weeks, and that the end came quickly.

2

David Wulstan

OXFORD, ENGLAND

The Origin of the Modes

MISLEADING ideas about modality are common in literature dealing with many types of music. As a result, misconstructions have been put upon folk-music, plainchant, and even upon Medieval and Renaissance polyphony.[1] The gap between theoretical ideas on this subject and reality is perhaps even wider than is usual for musicography generally; this situation is not entirely due to modern writers, however, for confusion began in earnest in early medieval times. A certain amount of blame is due also to Classical theorists who did not stress sufficiently, or were not interested in, the difference between the art and science of music. Although many enlightened modern scholars have repeatedly drawn attention to the facts conflicting with the popular notion of modality, their work has had little apparent effect. It seems useful, therefore, to go over some of the ground once more and to add a certain amount of new material, particularly since the circumstances of the origin of the modal system put the later developments in context.

Modal ethos

According to Plato,[2] Egyptian pictorial art and music were rigidly governed according to fixed laws; unalterable tradition rather than the self-expression of the individual artist dictated the form and content of art. This testimony is particularly

---

[1] The widespread failure to acknowledge the necessity for *musica ficta* in Renaissance music for fear it should lose its so-called 'modality' is a typical example.

[2] Laws II, 656: καὶ παρὰ ταῦτ' οὐκ ἐξῆν οὔτε ζωγράφοις οὔτ' ἄλλοις ὅσοι σχήματα καὶ ὁμοῖ ἄττα ἀπεργάζονται καινοτομεῖν οὐδ' ἐπινοεῖν ἀλλ' ἄττα ἦ τὰ πάτρια, οὐδε νῦν ἔξεστιν, οὔτ' ἐν τούτοις οὔτ' ἐν μουσικῇ ξυμπάσῃ.

5

valuable since, seeing the effects this doctrine had upon their art, we can evaluate by implication what it might have meant in musical terms. This immediately calls to mind the Byzantine method of formulistic construction admirably exposed by Wellesz[3] and gives particular sense to the well-known phrase of Ben Sira:

Law on the music / song investigator(s)

חוֹקְרֵי מִזְמוֹר עַל־חוֹק

The investigator of the song of the Law

(ἐκζητοῦντες μέλη μουσικῶν)

(Ecclus. 44, 5) which may be translated 'such as adapted music according to tradition'. There is here a paranomasia between the verb 'to seek' or 'dig out' and the phrase 'according to rule' or 'tradition' (for this reason the B text seems preferable; the Scrolls *et. al.* have קוֹ for חוֹק, the meanings being similar). It would be quite wrong to translate the line as 'such as composed music', for modern composition is an entirely different proposition; to render the phrase 'such as found out musical tunes' is preferable, if not entirely happy.

The force of the hierophantic tradition in the art of the Egyptians can be measured by the effect of the reforms of the Eighteenth dynasty: even given the new artistic freedom, the painter or sculptor found it difficult not to use the old forms and clichés. It is interesting to see, however, that when making a representation of something that lay quite outside the formal run of things, he was evidently able to express himself within an entirely new concept of naturalism in both form and colour.[4] Examples of this kind are as startling as they are rare, so strong was the force of tradition. For the purpose of art was not self-expression, but the depiction of an *alter ego* which had a separate existence in itself.

To these animists the force of such images was potent and could be used to good or evil ends. The tomb sculptures showing the good life amidst plenty, the ritually 'killed' objects (such as the broken musical instruments which, too, had a soul) helped to ensure the dead person whom they accompanied a happy passage through Judgement to the Fields of Peace. But

---

[3] Discovery of the principle of formulae first stated in 'Der Serbische Oktoichos und die Kirchentöne' *Musica Sacra* 1917, pp. 17-19; 'Die Armenische Messe und ihre Musik' *Jahrbuch Peters*, 1920, pp. 11f.; Cf. also *A History of Byzantine Music and Hymnography*, 2nd ed. (Oxford, 1961), pp. 325f.
Cf., particularly, the tombs of Neḥt and Menna: Thebes, Tombs 52 & 64.

the Ramesside 'execration pots' were for quite another purpose: inscribed with imprecations against one or other of the tribes inimical to the Egyptians, they had only to be shattered to bring the enemy to its knees. (Cf. Jer. 19, 10–11). The firm belief in such animism puts the Jewish prohibition against the making of images in context. It is interesting, however, that no such embargo was laid upon music. It is evident that Moses (we can perhaps trust Philo's[5] statement that he was instructed in music by Egyptian priests) thought that the magical powers of music could be harnessed.

Belief in the power of music can be inferred from a number of passages in the Old Testament and non-Canonical writings. Elisha conjured up water with the aid of a musician (I Kings 3, 15), while David was able to do something by his music to calm Saul's violent temper (I Sam. 16, 23f). The psalmist was alarmed because 'the drunkards make songs upon me' (Ps. 69, 13; cf. also Job 30, 9; Lam. 3, 14 and 63) and Sira warned the unwary from contact with enchantresses 'lest they inflame thee with their mouths' (Ecclus. 9, 4 Hebr). The writer of the section of the Dead Sea Scrolls known as 'David's Compositions' (11QPs[a] Dav. Comp.) credited him with four songs 'for singing over the stricken'. All these passages are connected by the use of one or other cognate word in the Hebrew, from the root NGN, 'to strike' hence: מְנַגֵּן (musician: I Kings 3, 15 etc.); נֹגְנִים (special type of musician: Ps. 68, 26); נַגֵּן (to sing in a particular manner: Ps. 33, 3 etc.); מַנְגִּינָה, נְגִינַת (taunt-song Ps. 69, 13 etc.); נְגִינָה (type of chanting: Ps. 4, 1 etc.). Later uses: † מְנַגֶּנֶת (enchantress: Ecclus 9, 4); נְגִינוֹת שִׁיר (type of song: Ecclus 47/9); נְגִינוֹה (music, in general: 1 QS X9 etc.); but נַגֵּן (to enchant: 11QPs[a] Dav Comp. 5). In the Mishna נְגִינָה still has the connotation 'affliction, breaking, defeat'. In later Hebrew it means inter alia 'musical accent.'

Because of the primary meaning of the root it has been assumed that the musical sense of the word indicates the striking or plucking of a lyre. The early Versions and the contexts show that there is no reason for this supposition. Only one passage (centred on I Sam. 16, 23) mentions an instrument: this specifies that David intoned *with his hand* as though this were

[5] *De Vita Mosis*, I, 23. Cf. Acts 7, 22.

B

unusual.[6] All these cognate words have the shades of meaning present originally in such epithets as 'charming' and 'enchanting' ($\sqrt{}$*carmen* and $\sqrt{}$*cantus*).

It is probable that the root 'to strike' must be taken as meaning 'to strike down'. An interesting parallel re-inforcing this view is the Arabic *qāfiya* which means simply 'a poem'. Originally, however, it meant a satirical poem, a song of derision against an enemy. Its root, *qafā*, means 'the base of the skull', a blow to which paralyses or kills the enemy.[7] So too *ngînah* came eventually to mean simply 'chant' or at least a specialized form of chant.

Returning, however, to the more primitive meaning of $\sqrt{}$*NGN* 'to enchant', it is obvious that the practitioners of the magic arts had to be careful not to confuse the functions of incantation, and therefore not to confuse the chants themselves; there is no better illustration of this point than the story of the Hindu demon who intoned an evil spell against a god with whom he was disenchanted. He misplaced a single accent, and the incantation recoiled fatally upon himself.[8] With this in mind it is interesting to note that in medieval Hebrew *ngînāh* appears in the sense of 'mode'.[9] Though it cannot be ascertained how early this meaning appeared, there is a strong presumption that there is a connection between the shades of meaning 'spell'—'cantillation'—'mode'. Thus the 'modes' were likely to have been separate classes of chants or spells which it was important to distinguish. Hence the particular emphasis on 'ethos' that is continually found in classical authors.[10]

Though we cannot hope to know a great deal about the early modes, we can be fairly sure that the eventual adoption of an eight-mode system was due, as Werner pointed out, to calendar considerations.[11] Just as the *octoëchos* was a system governed by an eight-week cycle, the Babylonian cantors had to be skilled in

[6] This might be explained on the assumption that the *kinnôr* was normally played with a plectrum: see Sachs, *The History of Musical Instruments* (New York 1940), p. 108. Some form of hand movements might alternatively be indicated by this passage: Cf. Egyptian *hsl-m-drt* 'Sing with the hand'.

[7] Cf. Goldziher *Abhandlungen zur Arabischen Philologie* I (Leiden 1896), pp. 83-105.

[8] Cf. Stuart Piggott, *Prehistoric India* (London, 1950) p. 255.

[9] e.g. Ibn Tibbôn in Farmer, *Sa'adyah Gaon on the Influence of Music* (London, 1943), pp. 64f.

[10] Cf. Plato, *Laws* iii, 700 and Aristeides Quintilianus, *De Musica* 19, 11f.

[11] *The Sacred Bridge* (New York, 1959), pp. 373f.

an eight-day liturgy.[12] An indication that this might have been the case in Biblical times is afforded by the coincidence of the superscription 'to the eighth [mode]', *al-haššemînîṭ* (psalm 12), with the fact that this psalm was used on the eighth day of Sukkôth. It is possible that the term *'ălāmôṭ* indicates the first mode; this and the eighth (both of which figure in the super-scriptions to the psalms) occur side by side in II Chron. 16 as though they were perhaps the first and the last; alpha and omega, as it were. In this context they seem to indicate instru-mental tunings, thus the relationship between modes and tunings requires consideration.

Tunings and modes

The Greek tunings (τόνοι), known from Ptolemy and others, were the descendants of the ἁρμονίαι and νόμοι; but it is clear that these theoretical scales were not the only identity of the ἁρμονίαι and certainly not of the νόμοι, the nature of which is uncertain.[13] However, from references in Plato and elsewhere, it seems that the 'nomes' were distinguishable by their ethos.[14] Thus each 'nome' was probably identified originally by its mimetic function, the chants of each no doubt being formulistic-ally similar. The medieval Latin word for 'melodic formula', written or sung, was neuma. The presence of cognate Semitic words (e.g. Heb. *nᶜîmāh*; Arab. *nagma*), having similar meanings, makes the usual and improbable derivation of neuma from two entirely different Greek words (νεῦμα and πνεῦμα) unnecessary, and also points to the probability that νόμος (=nome) was not the same word as νόμος (=law), but a homonym derived from a Semitic root.[15]

Though singers might be quite content to perform without

---

[12] Cf. Langdon, 'Calendars of Liturgies and Prayers', *American Journal of Semitic Languages* xlii (1915), p. 112.

[13] Cf. Winnington-Ingram, *Mode in Ancient Greek Music* (Cambridge, 1936), still the standard work on the subject.

[14] Plato, *Laws* vii, 800 etc.; cf. also Ps.-Plutarch, *De Musica* 6f. For Heb. *nᶜîmāh* = music, cf. Ecclus. 45, 9.

[15] The precise form of both words was clearly due to 'popular etymology'; the same phenomenon is no doubt responsible for the concept of the nome as 'law-giver' evident in the passages cited above (n. 14). The change from ᶜ (originally pronounced *ġ* in this word) to *o* is not so surprising when it is remembered that *omicron* is the Phoenician sign for ᶜayin. In Ugaritic texts long *o* is written as ᶜayin; cp. also Heb. ᶜ*amorah* = Gk Γομόρρα. Cf. Driver, 'Semitic Writing', *The Schweich Lectures of the British Academy* (London, 1948), p. 155.

regard to theoretical considerations, makers of wind instruments
and tuners of stringed instruments had to know how to set their
scales. Hence, perhaps, the conflict between auletic and aulodic,
kitharistic and kitharodic nomes arose;[16] for however variable a
scale pattern could be for a singer, it had to be fixed when
applied to instruments. In such circumstances practice must
bow to theory. Just as today pianists assume that G♯ and A♭
are the same notes, the codifications of melodic practice that
we know as the τόνοι must bear the same relation to the ἁϱμονίαι:
a theoretical fixing of notes for instrumental purposes for the
performance of musical formulae whose intonation is naturally
mutable and not fixed. It is important, therefore, not to confuse
scales or tunings with modes.

Recently discovered tablets have revealed the scales used on
Babylonian stringed instruments.[17] In view of what has been said
above, this information must not be taken as a direct indication
of the nature of the Near-Eastern modal system. At present
there are four tablets (five, if one duplicate is included) known
to contain musical terminology relating to tunings. One (CBS
10996) has the names of intervals in terms of the distance
between the two strings by which they are bounded; these
string-names are identified with the help of another tablet
(U 3011) which in addition has some of the interval names
mentioned in CBS 10996. The names of the intervals are fourteen in number, seven pertaining to distances of a third or
sixth (invertible) and seven referring to 'primary' intervals of a
fifth or fourth. The quality of the interval is irrelevant to the
nomenclature, i.e. it is described similarly whether it is a major
or minor third/sixth or a perfect or tritonic fourth/fifth; the
interval name simply indicates the distance between two strings,
however tuned. A third tablet (B.M. fragment 7/80) uses these
same names to identify scales; while a fourth (KAR 158, viii)
shows that these terms could also be used to classify songs. This
latter use might be an indication of the Babylonian 'modes'.
However, this seems unlikely: one reason is that of the songs
classified in KAR 158, viii, only a certain number fall into the
system covered by these 'modal' names; secondly, only seven

16 Cf. Plato, *Laws* iii, 700; Ps.-Plutarch *De Musica* 3f.
17 Discussed in Wulstan, 'The tuning of the Babylonian Harp', *Iraq* xxx/2 (1968),
pp. 215f.

'modes' or scales are named—as is well known, eight is the regular number of 'modes', while seven is the maximum possible number of diatonic octave-species. The first objection is hardly conclusive, for no modal system can ever honestly embrace all the chants of a repertory, but the second is something of a crucial point.

It is true that seven is a number of magical significance,[18] but it seems likely that this is coincidental to the fact that there are only seven possible diatonic octave-species. On the other hand, eight modes cannot be explained away on purely musical grounds, and thus it seems likely that the number of modes was arrived at primarily for magical reasons.[19] It is interesting to note that the Ptolemaic system reconciles the seven octave-species with only four (again a number known to be magically significant) mode-names to which are added three *hypo*-species to complete the number.[20] In all probability the Hebrew harp-tunings, which seem also to have been eight in number, resolved the problem in the same way, by representing one of the modes by a species duplicated at the octave.

The Babylonians, however, seem to have taken another solution, that of classifying songs by the tunings required rather than by their modal qualities; this interpretation is, of course, arguable. But this conclusion is reinforced to a certain extent by one of the striking similarities of the Babylonian system to that of Ptolemy: the 'starting-notes' of the Babylonian scales are in the same order as in the 4×2 sequence of names in the Greater Perfect System (Dorian, hypo-Dorian, Phrygian, etc.). The order of the scales also follows the order of the planets in the 'days of the week' sequence,[21] which supports Werner's supposition of a calendar connection with modal or scalar theory.[22] The following example shows the Babylonian scales with their names:

---

[18] Cf. Heb. שֶׁבַע 'seven' and שָׁבַע 'to swear'.

[19] Cf. I Chron. 26, 5: 'Pᶜūltay was the eighth, for God blessed him.'

[20] Ptolemy, *Harmonics* 11, shows that an eighth τόνος cannot be added to these. But the fact that he mentions an eighth τόνος (the Hypermixolydian) shows that for him there existed a dilemma: there are more 'modes' than τόνοι. Another obvious indication of the dilemma is the wildly conflicting nomenclature amongst Classical authors. Cf. Winnington-Ingram, *op. cit.*

[21] Cf. Wulstan, *op. cit.*, p. 225.

[22] Cf. n. 11.

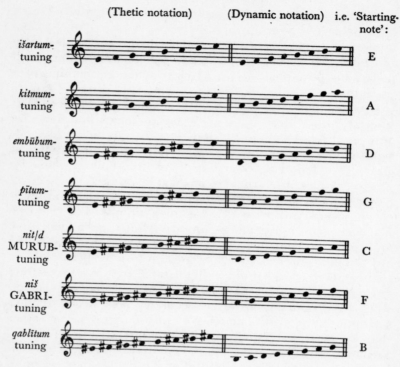

(Thetic notation)   (Dynamic notation)   i.e. 'Starting-note':

išartum-tuning ... E

kitmum-tuning ... A

embūbum-tuning ... D

pītum-tuning ... G

nit/d MURUB-tuning ... C

niš GABRI-tuning ... F

qablītum tuning ... B

There are further points of contact between the Babylonian and Greek systems which strongly suggest that the latter is descended from the former.[23] A connection can also be assumed between the Jewish and Christian systems. The work of many scholars, particularly Idelsohn and Werner, has established many correspondences of detail, and thus it is natural to suppose a general similarity of organization. This is one reason why it may be supposed that there were eight modes in the Hebrew system. It is possible, however, that the division of the Byzantine modes into 4 × 2 was made with reference to the Classical system, though there is no evidence of any further similarity of substance. Certainly the groups of formulae by which the eight can be recognized, though they may have relatively constant final notes for each ἦχος, cannot be shown to be organized according to scales.

[23] e.g. *qablītu* ('middle'); cp. μέση.

The psalm-tone formulae are admirably dealt with by Strunk in his article 'The Antiphons of the Octoechos'.[24] Strunk shows how twelve of the *ἀναβαθμόι*, antiphons based on the 'Psalms of the Ascents'[25] were sung according to a modal ordering. This is particularly interesting in the light of the Dead Sea Psalm scroll,[26] which groups these same twelve psalms together. This is suggestive. The scroll is grouped in a liturgical, rather than Biblical, order. Since there are properly fifteen Psalms of the Ascents,[27] the correspondence of the number allocated in the Hebrew and Greek sources seems unlikely to be coincidental.

Modes and scales

The pieces of evidence discussed so far point to the origin of the modes as classes of spells, distinguished by function and formulistic identity, whose organization was linked with the calendar and planets. To a certain extent in conflict with the nature of the modes was the necessity to fix tunings on instruments such as the harp; but although some theorists may have equated such tunings with modes, there is no evidence that practical musicians ever assumed more than a slight correspondence.[28] Theoretical writings concerned with limmas and commas must be regarded in a different light from the vaguer but more tantalizing references to practical matters. For it was in *νόμοι* and *neumae* that the stuff of music lay, rather than in Pythagorean doctrine.[29] However disparate the theory, practi-

---

24 In the *Journal of the American Musicological Society* xiii (1960), p. 50. Cf. also the same author's 'Intonations and Signatures of the Byzantine Modes', *Musical Quarterly* xxxi (1945), pp. 339f.

25 Heb. *šîrê hama'alôt*.

26 *11QPs*[a] ed. Sanders, *The Psalms Scroll of Qumrân Cave 11* (Oxford, 1965).

27 Pss. 120-135 (Heb. and Eng.); Pss. 119-134 (Gk. and Vulg.)

28 Cf. Arabic *āṣābi* and *maqāmāt*: one a set of finger scales, the other a set of modes (again, later theorists associated the *maqāmāt* with scales). Wright (*Galpin Society Journal* xix (1966), p. 40, has re-examined the *āṣābi*, though confusing them with modes. Interpreted so that 7 + 1 species result from his findings, the order of the scales seems to be *a g b d c e g f*; this tetradic order appears to be independent of classical Greek theory, though analogous. Similarly the notes associated with the planets are different, though in the same relative order. It may be, therefore, that Arabic theory contained Near-Eastern elements not derived from Greek sources.

29 Cf. Plato's remark about the theorists of his day attempting to perceive smaller and smaller intervals on the lyre (*Republic*, 531), or the more scathing remark of Heracleitus in Frag. XVI (Bywater): πολυμαθίη νόον ἔχειν οὐ διδάσκει· Ἡσίοδον γὰρ ἂν ἐδίδαξε καὶ Πυθαγόρην αὐτίς τε Ξενοφάνεα καὶ Ἑκασταῖον. (Cf. also Frag. XVII.)

cal links between early Greek music on the one hand and Semitic and Christian music on the other cannot be ruled out.

As long as music was learnt by ear, or from notation which had no rigid scalar basis, instrumental participation was the only substantial problem of modality. With the advent of diastematic notation, however, tones, semitones, and microtones had to be fixed on paper, and therefore there was added impetus towards making scales out of modes. It is true that some early experiments in notation (cf. Montpellier MS. H 159) had room for microtones; but eventually it was thought undesirable to have more than one shifting note, the B, which could be either 'soft' or 'hard'. Diastematic notation was to have far-reaching consequences, for it began a trend which led eventually to the alteration of melodies for a number of reasons, particularly those which had accidentals that could not be accommodated theoretically.

The three main characteristics of a mode were, as is evident from the facts presented above, (i) its ethos, (ii) its formulistic identity and (iii) the scale or tuning upon which theoretically it can be based. These considerations, it is reasonable to suppose, were originally in descending order of importance. With the decline in significance of the first quality, the second of these characteristics would become pre-eminent. When the music became systematized due to the use of diastematic notation, the third and hitherto insignificant element assumed prime importance; and so the order of priorities became inverted. How gradually this happened may be judged from the theoretical writings of the time. Guido still speaks in the eleventh century of the calendaric and ethical character of the modes, and yet the twelfth-century John Cotton, who also attributes ethos to the modes, instructs the singer to look at the end of a chant in order to identify the mode.[30] Earlier writers, however, considered the beginning to be as important, particularly the ninth-century Aurelian, who discussed the structure of melodic formulae.[31] Slightly later, Regino, like Aurelian, draws a distinction between chants of the Antiphon type and those of the Responsory type, the latter requiring reference to the end for the purposes of modal recognition.[32]

[30] Gerbert, *Scriptores Ecclesiastici de Musica* (St. Blaise, 1784)—henceforward *GS*— II, 12 and II, 251.   [31] *GS* I, 44.   [32] *GS* I, 231.

So the identification of the mode began to rest less on the characteristic formulae with which it was associated, and more on the final note of the chant. The reason for this was simple. While theorists had increasing regard for the scalar characteristics of a mode, at the same time they had to look for a further distinguishing feature in addition to the scale itself. This was because of what has already been referred to as the Ptolemaic dilemma: there are only seven possible octave-species; if eight modes are to be represented by seven scales, one such scale must serve twice. But then in order to distinguish between the identical pair of scales, different characteristics (of final and 'dominant') must be ascribed to each. This was easily achieved, for there was a ready-made means for this in the Byzantine 4 × 2 ('authentic' and 'plagal') grouping which was adopted in the *maneriae* system. There is certainly a tendency for melodies of each ἦχος to end on a regular final (though there were at least two regular finals to each ἦχος), and there are often recognizable *loci* about which these melodies revolve. In making general tendency a law, and assuming the mode-scale equivalence, however, unwarranted distortions and extensions of the tone pattern of the Byzantine system were perpetrated, if such a 'system' could be said to have existed.

By the use of the concept of fixed finals and dominants, seven species can be extended into eight 'modes' (or indeed any number up to fourteen, which was eventually done by Glarean). This was effected by Hermannus Contractus.[33] Already the mode-scales had been given respectable classical names; Contractus added the Hypomixolydian (having peremptorily rejected the Hypermixolydian). That the classical names were not used modally, and that in any case the order of species was the reverse of the medieval nomenclature (named erroneously by τόνοι), is an indication of the worth of this procedure. Thus by a progression of half-truths culled from classical and Byzantine sources, the eight-scale system evolved.[34]

Now if scales are directly identified with modes, and are virtually the sole means of distinction (except for the duplicated

---

[33] Ed. Ellinwood, *Musica Hermanni Contracti* (New York, 1936).

[34] The Byzantine octoechos is first paralleled in the West by Alcuin (*GS* I, 26), but the application of the τόνος names to modes first occurs in *Alia Musica* (*GS* I, 125). The theorist of *GS* I, 119 complains: 'modi or tropi they now call tones'.

scale differentiated by alternative 'finals') three correlatives follow: hardly any accidentals (perhaps one—the B♭ or B♮) can be admitted; each melody cannot greatly exceed the range of its scale; and the melody should not lie too far inside it. The consequences can readily be seen in the sources of the period.[35] The tonarius of Berno explains how to avoid the *defectus neumarum* (lack of chromatic notes) by transposition into a position where the chromatic notes are disguised as B♭ or B♮. Numbers of melodies exhibiting such transposition exist; but this solution did not commend itself to theorists such as Ps-Odo, who combats irregularities of this nature, including excessive range, by melodic alteration.[36] Evidence of such alteration is frequently to be seen, but a third method of dealing with the problem of accidentals is normally invisible: that of omitting in writing what was supplied by *musica ficta* in practice. It cannot be doubted that this solution was employed, judging by the number of parallel texts which make use of transposition instead, not to mention the earlier versions that have the chromatic notes written in.[37]

Once the idea of modal scales had taken hold, modality could be reckoned, theoretically at least, as an equivalent of diatonicism. A reluctance to write accidentals is evident even in secular music, which leads commentators to ascribe '*modal*' characteristics here, too.[38] But from the music and occasional theoretical passages, it is obvious that the situation was equivocal. On the one hand the re-introduction of one of the oldest chants, the *Tonus Peregrinus*, was frowned upon as a new-fangled thing.[39] The Cistercian and Cluniac reforms, expunging chromaticism and altering the ranges of chants, also directed attention to the final notes and even reciting notes which were

[35] *GS* II, 62.
[36] *GS* I, 252.
[37] A number of interesting examples of alteration, chromatic notes etc., together with references to literature on the subject are given by Apel in his *Gregorian Chant* (London, 1958), pp. 161-72, though we need not share his puzzlement at 'modal ambiguity' evinced by some of the examples. See also Appendix.
[38] Cf. the famous 'À l'entrada del tens clar', part of which was transposed in Paris B.N.fr. 20050 to avoid accidentals; the correct form of the tune is evident from the motet 'Veris ad imperia' in Florence B. Laur. plut xxix 1. See also Wulstan (ed.), *An Anthology of Carols* (London, 1968), Nos. 9, 15, and 30 and the notes thereto.
[39] Cf. *GS* I, 52; *GS* I, 218.

changed in order to accord with the scalar-modal theory.[40] Yet on the other hand, the majority of manuscripts show that musicians and scribes seem to have had little inclination to keep their house in order (indeed the Ambrosian MSS. never attempted a modal classification); while even theorists still talked of ethos and discussed the characteristic modal *neumae*.

For polyphonic music of the Middle Ages and the Renaissance a similar situation existed. In practice, *musica ficta* and transposition gave composers freedom to express themselves independently from the theoretical ideas of 'modality'.[41] Nevertheless, theorists strove indefatigably (then as now) to classify polyphony modally, even though it is ludicrous to ascribe scalar-modality to more than one line. That their task was difficult is understandable; even Tinctoris, having clutched at the straws of *commixtio et mixtio modorum* had to admit that modality was really attributable to one line only.[42] Pietro Aron lamely described how to detect a mode in 1525,[43] in spite of the fact that a fit of practicality had previously (in 1523) led him to appeal[44] for all accidentals to be written out, not left to the singers. The most amusing example of the attempts to preserve theory in the face of practice was the invention of extra modes by Glarean in order that no music should be left modeless.[45] But the detailed consideration of modal theory in connection with polyphony and even harmonic music is outside the scope of this article. It must suffice to say that the 'breakdown of the modal system' that was coeval with the rise of tonality was rather the breaking down of an equivocation. Moreover, since the careful organization of accidentals and adherence to key centres of the tonal period was trammelled compared with the harmonic freedom of the polyphonic era, it is fanciful to

---

[40] Cf. Wagner, *Einführung in die Gregorianische Melodien* (Leipzig, 1911-21) II, 449; Bomm, *Der Wechsel der Modalitätsbestimmung in der Tradition der Messegesänge im IX bis XIII Jahrhundert* (Leipzig, 1929). See also Appendix.

[41] On *musica ficta* see, for example, Lowinsky, *The Secret Chromatic Art of the Netherlands Motet* (New York, 1946), and Bray, 'English Sixteenth-century *Musica Ficta*' (*Plainsong and Mediaeval Music Studies*, 1970). On transposition, cf. Wulstan, 'The Problem of Pitch in Sixteenth-century English Vocal Music', *Proceedings of the Royal Musical Association* 93 (1966-7). On the 'tones' cf. Hendrie, 'The Keyboard Music of Orlando Gibbons' *ibid*, 89 (1962-3), p. 11.

[42] *Liber de natura et proprietate tonorum* (*GS* IV, 16).

[43] *Trattato . . .* (Facsimile, Utrecht, 1966).

[44] *Il Thoscanello.*

[45] *Dodecachordon* (1547, ed. Miller, *American Musicological Society*, 1965).

attribute this deliberate narrowing of resources to a release from a 'strict modal system' which was at best illusory.

Conclusion

The idea of ordering music within a modal system appears to be well over two millennia old. Increasingly misunderstood, this system has preoccupied theorists from the Middle Ages to the present day. In spite of such misconceptions, and procrustean efforts to bring some of the music into line with these notions, the force of practical tradition is seen to have been more than a match for theory.

The history of the modes still poses many unsolved problems. In Antiquity a great deal more information is needed to add to our meagre knowledge of their evolution. In the chant we need to know how far 'chromaticism' was within the integrity of the modes, and how accidentals were added in practice. The enormous influx to the West of Byzantine monks and musicians from Asia Minor after the Turkish conquests, and from Byzantium itself at the fall of the city, evidently confirmed the use of accidentals in the chant. On behalf of part-music, similarly, the umbrella of 'modality' as a shelter from the gentle rain of sharps and flats must be abandoned, followed by research into what tonal schemes were really employed. All this is another way of saying that we want to know how the music sounded, and how to perform it—a not unreasonable ambition.

Specimens of 'Modal' Alteration

A. Manuscript versions of the hymn 'Pange lingua .... corporis' showing alteration and transposition to avoid chromaticism

(a)

Munich Cod. 22022 (Wagner, *op. cit.* III, p. 477): *d* scale; **e* given, ÷*e♭* avoided.

(b)

Munich Cod. lat. 17701 (*ibid*, p. 478): *e* scale; * no ♯ for *f*,
÷*f* avoided.

(c)

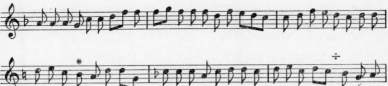

Sarum version ed. Frere, *Hymn-Melodies* . . . (Plainsong and
Mediaeval Music Society, 2nd Ed., 1943): *a* scale; the use of
♭♮ and ÷♭♭ would give rise to *e♮ and ÷*e♭ in the *d* scale,
or *f♯ and ÷*f♮ in the *e* scale.

B. Alteration of final note and of accidentals

(a)

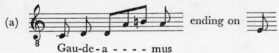

ending on

Gau-de - a - - - - mus

Saint-Yrieix (*P.M.* XIII: cf. Suñol: *Introduction à la Paléographie Grégorienne*

[Tournai, 1935], p. 264).

usual reading:

(b)

ending on

Gau-de - a - - - - mus

Introit *Gaudeamus* as seen in *Liber Usualis*

The *Commemoratio Brevis* (GS I, 230) *c.*900, contains a tonary
giving different reciting-notes from those found in, e.g., GS II,
243. See also Suñol *Introduction à la paléographie musicale grégor-*

ienne (Tournai, 1935), p. 263 for evidence of the alteration of reciting-notes in accordance with the new theory. But cf. also Wagner, *op. cit.*, p. 445, for regional variants which might, however, be mistaken for modal alteration.

C. Alteration of range

(a)

si - cut pas - - - - - - - - ser er - - - - - - ep - - - ta   est

Paris Cod. lat. n.a. 1235 (Wagner *op. cit.* II, p. 456)

(b)

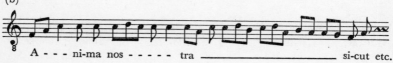

A - - - ni-ma nos - - - - - tra _____ si-cut etc.

Swiss (Cistercian) M.S., 13th cent. (Wagner *ibid.*, p. 457).

ADDENDA

Since I wrote this article, musical notation has been found to exist at Ugarit. This notation (*c.* 1300 B.C.) is related to the tablets already discussed, and makes use of the tunings set out on p. 12; KAR 158, viii is therefore simply a list of songs and their tunings, as anticipated. Prof. H. G. Guterbock will publish a preliminary article in *Études Archeologiques Offertes à Claude F. A. Schaeffer....* (Paris 1969), and I shall publish transcriptions shortly in *Music and Letters*.

In connection with the early octoechos systems it should have been mentioned that Armenian chant makes use of an eight-mode ordering in which the modes are chanted in sequence day by day. Each week, therefore, Sunday bears a different mode. It is most likely that it was in this fashion that the daily ordering of modes developed into the Byzantine hebdomadal pattern; it might be added that the daily sequence of modes survives even in Byzantine use at Easter.

3

Christos J. Bentas

The Treatise on Music by John Laskaris

WHILE most of the Byzantine composers of music are known by
their names and little if anything is known about them as persons, John Laskaris is, at present, relatively well documented as
a person. On the basis of data from Venetian Archives one now
has a vivid picture of the flamboyant character and of some
aspects of the life of Laskaris.[1] Amongst other things he was the
author of a treatise on music. One copy of his treatise has been
located in a manuscript in the National Library in Athens and
another copy (though it remains uncertain at the time of writing
whether this is an exact copy) in a manuscript in Rome.[2]
Laskaris' treatise has never before been published.

The theoretical treatises about music by Byzantine writers
have so far been unavailable in an English translation, though
a few of them have been published in the original Greek.[3] In
view of this, at the suggestion of Prof. Velimirović this writer
has undertaken to prepare English translations of some of them.
The treatise by Laskaris is the first to be chosen, due to the
availability of the text on a microfilm of the manuscript,
MS 2401 from the National Library in Athens. The microfilm
was kindly placed at this writer's disposal by Professor Velimirović. Besides the full text and its translation, this writer is
offering a few comments in hope that they may provoke a dis-

---

[1] Cf. Miloš Velimirović, 'Two Composers of Byzantine Music: John Vatatzes
and John Laskaris', in *Aspects of Medieval and Renaissance Music—A Birthday
Offering to Gustave Reese*, edited by Jan La Rue (New York, 1966), pp. 818-31.

[2] *Ibid.*, pp. 823-4; cf. D. Lorenzo Tardo, *L'Antica melurgia bizantina* (Grottaferrata,
Roma, 1938), p. 148.

[3] For instance in Tardo's book cited in n. 2 above.

cussion which will ultimately lead to the clarification of a
number of moot points in the complex problems of the theory
of Byzantine music.

The text and its translation read:

Athens, Nat. Lib., MS 2401, fol. 223r.

Ἡ ἑρμηνία καὶ παραλλαγὴ τῆς μουσικῆς τέχνης.

Ἑτέρα παραλλαγὴ τῆς μουσικῆς τέχνης, σοφωτέρα καὶ ἀκριβεστέρα
εἰς ἄκρον. πονηθεῖσα δὲ καὶ συνταχθεῖσα παρὰ Ἰωάννου τοῦ Λάσκαρι.
ἐναντία μὲν τῆς πρώτης, καὶ οὐκ ἐναντία. ἐναντία γάρ, πρὸς τοὺς μὴ
εἰδότας ὡς γέγραπται. εἰς δὲ τοὺς ἐντέχνως κατέχοντας αὐτὴν ἀκρι-
βῶς, βεβαίωσίς τε μᾶλλον καὶ ἀναπλήρωσις, καὶ μεγίστη ἡδύτης
ἐντεῦθεν ἀναφανεῖσα τῇ τέχνῃ, καὶ τὰ ἐν αὐτῆς ἰδιώματα, σαφέστερα
καταγγέλουσα. ἀποδεικνύουσα δὲ ἅπασαν τῶν τεσσάρων ἠχῶν, τὴν
ὑπόστασίν τε καὶ κίνησιν, καὶ τῶν τεσσάρων πλαγίων ἠχῶν αὐτῶν,
ἔν τε ἀναβάσει καὶ καταβάσει. ἐν μὲν τῇ ἀναβάσει τοῦ ἤχου ἐκ τῶν
πλαγίων, διφώνους τε τριφώνους καὶ τετραφώνους ἀποτελοῦσι, καὶ
εἰς τοὺς πλαγίους αὐτῶν καὶ ἄλλους καταλήγουσιν. ἐν δὲ τῇ καταβάσει
αὐτῶν ἐκ τῶν κυρίων εἰς μέσους ἐκπίπτουσι καὶ παραμέσους. εἰς
πλαγίους τε καὶ παραπλαγίους, καὶ εἰς αὐτὸ τὸ θεμέλιον καταλήγουσι.
γέγραπται γάρ, ὅτι κύριοι ἦχοι εἰσὶ τέσσαρες, καὶ τέσσαρες πλάγιοι,
καὶ κύριοι μεν εἰσίν, ὁ πρῶτος, ὁ δεύτερος, ὁ τρίτος τε καὶ ὁ τέταρτος.
πλάγιοι δέ, ὁ πλάγιος τοῦ πρώτου, ὁ πλάγιος τοῦ δευτέρου, ὁ πλάγιος
του τρίτου ἤγουν ὁ βαρύς, καὶ ὁ πλάγιος τοῦ τετάρτου. ἔχουσι δὲ
οἱ κύριοι ἦχοι, καὶ μέσους ἐν ταῖς κατιούσαις, ὁμοίως καὶ οἱ πλάγιοι
μέσους ἐν ταῖς ἀνιούσαις, οὓς λέγομεν διφώνους. ὁ μέσος γὰρ τοῦ
πρώτου, ἐστὶν ὁ βαρύς.

καὶ ὁ μέσος τοῦ δευτέρου, ὁ πλάγιος τοῦ τετάρτου. καὶ ὁ μέσος
τοῦ τρίτου, ὁ πλάγιος τοῦ πρώτου. καὶ ὁ μέσος τοῦ τετάρτου, ὁ
πλάγιος τοῦ δευτέρου. ἔχουσι δὲ καὶ οἱ πλάγιοι ἦχοι ὡς προείπωμεν,
διφώνους ἐν ταῖς ἀνιούσαις.

fol. 223v.

ὁ πλάγιος τοῦ πρώτου, ἔχει δίφωνον τὸν τρίτον. καὶ ὁ πλάγιος τοῦ
δευτέρου, ἔχει δίφωνον τὸν τέταρτον. καὶ ὁ πλάγιος τοῦ τρίτου ἤγουν
ὁ βαρύς, ἔχει δίφωνον τὸν πρῶτον. καὶ ὁ πλάγιος τοῦ τετάρτου, ἔχει
δίφωνον τὸν δεύτερον. ἔχουσι δὲ καὶ τινα ἰδιώματα οἱ μέσοι ἀδόμενοι
ἐκ τῶν κυρίων, ὅτι σχηματίζονται καὶ ἀλλοιοῦνται εἰς παραμέσους.
καὶ οἱ πλάγιοι, εἰς παραπλαγίους. οἱ δὲ παράμεσοι τῶν κυρίων,
εἰσὶν οὗτοι.

παράμεσος πρώτου, ὁ πλάγιος τοῦ δευτέρου, ὁ δὲ παράμεσος τοῦ
δευτέρου, ἐστὶν ὁ βαρύς. καὶ ὁ παράμεσος τοῦ τρίτου, ὁ πλάγιος

1. (a) Tillyard with Egon Wellesz and Carsten Hoëg in Copenhagen, 18 July 1931

(b) Tillyard shortly before his death

2. Folio 224, Athens National Library MS 2401 (see p. 24)

3. The 'Palauzov Copy' of the Synodikon of Tsar Boril. The second musical piece, folios 2 verso and 3 recto (see pp. 69-73)

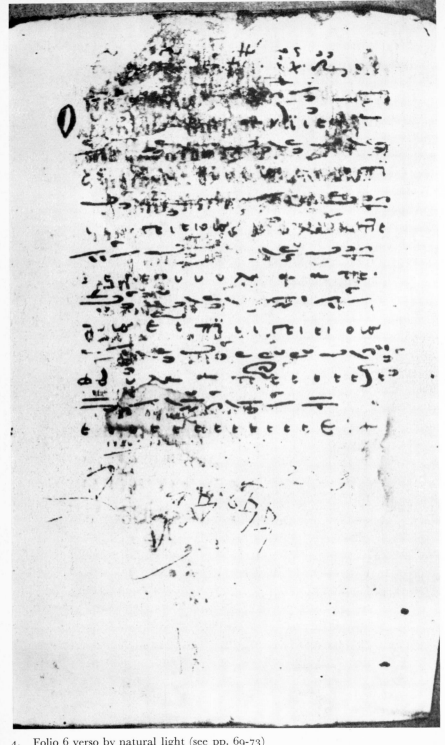

4. Folio 6 verso by natural light (see pp. 69-73)

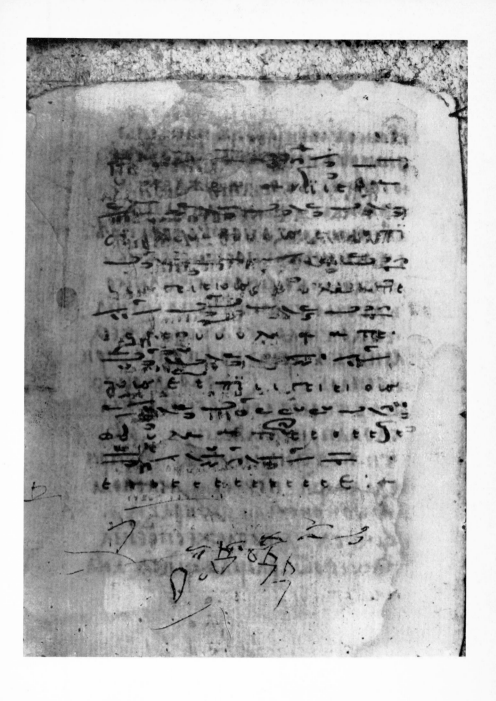

5. Folio 6 verso by infrared light (see pp. 69-73)

6. Folio 6 verso as reconstructed (see pp. 69-73)

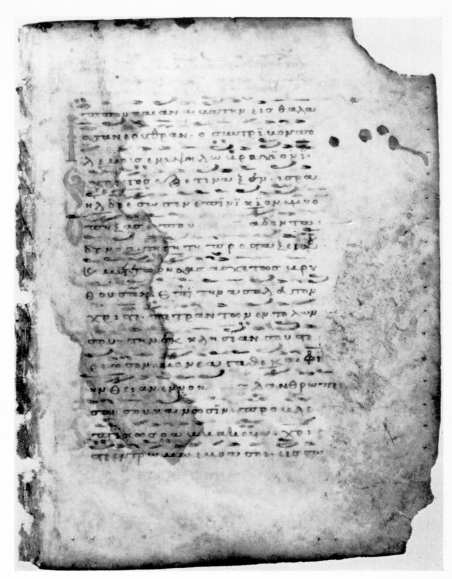

7. The Dearden manuscript, recto (see pp. 100-102)

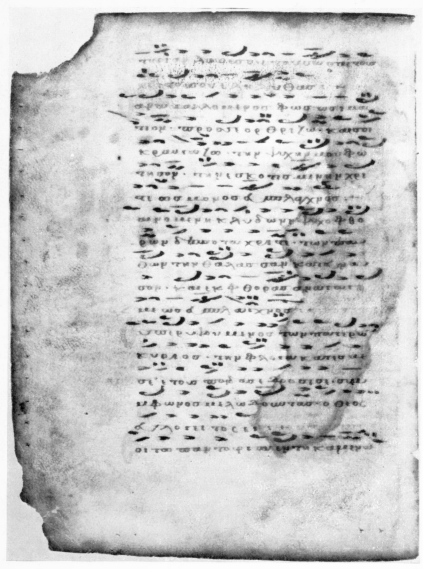

8. The Dearden manuscript, verso (see pp. 100-102)

τοῦ δευτέρου, καὶ ὁ παράμεσος τοῦ τετάρτου, ὁ πλάγιος τοῦ πρώτου.
παραπλάγιοι δὲ τούτων εἰσὶν οὗτοι.

παραπλάγιος πρώτου, ὁ πλάγιος τοῦ δευτέρου. καὶ παραπλάγιος
τοῦ δευτέρου, ὁ πλάγιος τοῦ πρώτου. καὶ παραπλάγιος τοῦ τρίτου, τὸ
λέγετο(ς), καὶ παραπλάγιος τοῦ τετάρτου, ὁ πλάγιος τοῦ τρίτου,
ἤγουν ὁ βαρύς. ἔχουσι δὲ τοῦτοι, καὶ τριφώνους καὶ τετραφώνους.
οὕς καὶ παρακυρίους λέγομεν. ἐξ αὐτῶν γὰρ καὶ νάοι γεννῶνται, καὶ
πρωτόβαροι, καὶ τετράφωνοι. τοῦτο γὰρ γίνωσκε ὦ ἀκροατά, ὅτι
τρεπτικώς <ος> ἐστὶν ὁ ἦχος. καὶ διὰ τοῦτο οἱ κύριοι εἰς πλαγίους
τρέπονται, καὶ οἱ πλάγιοι εἰς κυρίους τὸ ἀνάπαλιν, καθὼς καὶ ὁ
ἁγιώτατος μαΐστωρ Ἰωάννης ὁ Κουκουζέλης, ἐν τῇ σοφωτάτῳ
μεθόδῳ αὐτοῦ τῇ παραλλαγῇ, τοῦτο ὑπέδειξεν. ἐν μὲν τῇ ἀναβάσει
διὰ τοῦ ὀλίγου, τοὺς πλαγίους κυρίους ἀπέδειξεν. ἐν δὲ τῇ καταβάσει
διὰ τοῦ ἀποστρόφου, τοὺς κυρίους πλαγίους πάλιν ἀπέδειξε. καὶ
ταῦτα μέν, περὶ τούτων.

The Explanation and Modulation of the Musical Art

This is another modulation of the musical art, more wisely
devised and more exact in every detail, worked out and drawn
up by John Laskaris. It is both contrary to the first one and not
contrary. It is [appears] contrary to the first one for those
[readers] who did not understand it as it was written; but for
those who possess full artistic and exact knowledge of it, it is
rather a verification and a supplement, as it revealed itself as a
great delight by virtue of [a command of] its skill, having clearly
indicated its peculiarities by showing the whole essence and
movement of the four [main] Modes and of their four Plagal
Modes, both in ascent and descent. In the ascent of a Mode
from the Plagal ones, one obtains the di-phonic, tri-phonic, and
tetra-phonic ones and these terminate into their Plagal ones
and other [Modes]. In descent from the Main Modes, these
result in Mediant and Para-Mediant Modes, Plagal and Para
Plagal ones, and these terminate on their own fundamentals.
For it was written that there are four Main and four Plagal
Modes and that the Main Modes are Mode I, Mode II, Mode
III, and Mode IV, while the Plagal ones are, Mode I Plagal,
Mode II Plagal, Mode III Plagal that is the Barys, and Mode
IV Plagal.

The Main Modes, in their descent, have Mediant Modes.
Likewise the Plagal Modes, in their ascent, have Mediant

Modes which we call di-phonic. The Mediant Mode of Mode I is the Barys Mode; the Mediant of Mode II is Mode IV Plagal; the Mediant of Mode III is Mode I Plagal; and the Mediant of Mode IV is Mode II Plagal. As we have previously stated, the Plagal Modes also have their di-phonic Modes in their ascent: Mode I Plagal has as its di-phonic Mode the Mode III; Mode II Plagal has Mode IV as its di-phonic Mode; Mode III Plagal, i.e. Barys, has Mode I as its di-phonic Mode; and Mode IV Plagal has Mode II as its di-phonic Mode.

The Mediant Modes have certain peculiarities when they are sung [in derivation] from the Main Modes: they are formed and changed into Para-Mediant [Modes], and the Plagal ones into Para-Plagal [Modes]. The Para-Mediant Modes of the Main ones are the following: The Para-Mediant of Mode I is Mode II Plagal; the Para-Mediant of Mode II is the Barys; the Para-Mediant of Mode III is Mode II Plagal; and the Para-Mediant of Mode IV is Mode I Plagal.

The Para-Plagal of these are the following: The Para-Plagal of Mode I is Mode II Plagal; the Para-Plagal of Mode II is Mode I Plagal; the Para-Plagal of Mode III is the [Mode] Legetos; and the Para-Plagal of Mode IV is Mode III Plagal, i.e. Barys.

These also have the tri-phonic and tetra-phonic Modes which we call Para-Kyrioi and from these are then derived those [called] Naoi, Protobaroi and the tetra-phonic [Modes]. Know this, O listener, that the Mode is changeable; and that for this the Main Modes change [modulate] into the Plagal ones, and the Plagal into the Main ones again, just as the Master John Koukouzeles, of Blessed Memory, has shown in his wisest method of modulation. For he has demonstrated that in ascending by means of an Oligon, the Plagal Modes are [made] into Main ones and that in descending by means of an Apostrophos the Main ones become Plagal. So much then, for these matters.

*   *   *

Following the text of this treatise, on fol. 224 r there is a diagram of twenty circles, in five rows of four circles. (See Plate 2.) Within each circle are the martyriai for three modes presumably representing some of the relationships discussed in the treatise. Some parts of the diagram are relatively clear whereas others are less so. Basically, the first two rows of four circles each, totalling eight circles, are devoted to the Main Modes and each of the Modes is given two circles. The first of two circles for the Main Modes contains the martyriai of the Mode and its Mediant and Para-Mediant (the scheme does not seem to correspond to the textual listing of these Modes). The second of the two circles contains the martyriai of a Main Mode and its Plagal and Para-Plagal Modes. The third row of four circles depicts the di-phonic relationship of each of the Plagal Modes. The fourth row does the same for the tri-phonic Modes and the last row for the Tetra-Phonic Modes. There are discrepancies between the text and the diagram which, in the absence of comparative materials, cannot be resolved at this time.

The documented existence of the concepts of Mediant and other types of Modes raises some interesting points, not the least of which is the extension of the basic concept of a Mode in Byzantine chant of the fifteenth century (and perhaps earlier as well?) and an even more intriguing point, namely modulation from one Mode into another if not an outright transposition of a Mode. The relationship of Plagal and Authentic (i.e. Main) Modes appears to be more varied and suggests the possibility of (at least theoretically if not in practice) more than one type of tonal units, i.e. tetrachords and pentachords, in the organization of Modes. Some time ago, during the academic year 1961/62, this writer had an opportunity of discussing similar problems with Dom Bartolomeo di Salvo, and notes taken on those occasions, together with the publication of this treatise, suggest that discussion should be re-opened on the nature as well as structure of Modes in Byzantine Music. It is this writer's belief that the tonal fabric of Byzantine music did not utilize conjunct tetrachords but only disjunct tetrachords and that a Mode could have more than one 'tonic' depending on the position of the tetrachord in the gamut. While the 'central gamut' from d to d' presents this concept clearly enough, the tonal ranges above and below the 'central gamut' reveal these differences in a more conspicuous manner, as the appended scheme demonstrates. In preparing this scheme no chromatic changes have been introduced, resulting in different structures of tetrachords depending on the position of the tetrachord. It is obvious that much more work is necessary in order to determine whether tetrachords ought to remain uniform regardless of their position in the gamut.

	Plagal modes	Solmization syllable	Relative pitch	Authentic modes	
	MODE PLAGAL IV	mi	(e″)	MODE IV	A
P	,, BARYS (PL. III)	re	(d″)	,, III	U
L	,, PLAGAL II	do	(c″)	,, II	T
A	,, ,, I	si	(b′)	,, I	H
G	,, ,, IV	la	(a′)	,, IV	E
A	,, BARYS (PL. III)	sol	(g′)	,, III	N
L	,, PLAGAL II	fa	(f′)	,, II	T
	,, ,, I	mi	(e′)	,, I	I
M					C
O	,, ,, IV	re	(d′)	,, IV	
D	,, BARYS (PL. III)	do	(c′)	,, III	M
E	,, PLAGAL II	si	(b)	,, II	O
S	,, ,, I	la	(a)	,, I *starting note	D
					E
I	,, ,, IV	sol	(g)	,, IV	S
N	,, BARYS (PL. III)	fa	(f)	,, III	
	,, PLAGAL II	mi	(e)	,, II	I
D	,, ,, I	re	(d)	,, I	N
E					
S	,, ,, IV	do	(C)	,, IV	A
C	,, BARYS (PL. III)	si	(B)	,, III	S
E	,, PLAGAL II	la	(A)	,, II	C
N	,, ,, I	sol	(G)	,, I	E
T	,, ,, IV	fa	(F)	,, IV	N
	,, BARYS (PL. III)	mi	(E)	,, III	T

(Central Gamut brackets the rows from "IV re (d′)" down to "I re (d)".)

These remarks do not exhaust by any means all implications of the treatise by Laskaris nor of the appended scheme. On the contrary, they are intended as an invitation for discussion, so that eventually some of the least studied aspects of Byzantine music may be elucidated.

A few remarks about the translation

Byzantine treatises on music are notoriously difficult to translate. As examples, the following remarks are restricted to two terms only: 'parallage' and 'phone'.

The first of these words—'parallage'—has been translated as 'modulation'. Its actual meaning is still uncertain. The term appears in medieval manuscripts, possibly meaning a kind of practice of expressing various intonation formulae in diagrammatic fashion. The term may perhaps also express the idea of 'solmization.' The decision to translate as 'modulation' has been based on the fact that in the treatise 'parallage' describes a transition from one Mode into another without effecting the type of changes peculiar to the use of *phthorai*. It should be added that in the Chrysanthine practice (19th century) 'parallage' denotes a performance utilizing solmization syllables as a device while instructing students of music.[4] In such singing the actual text is not used.

The second term—'phone'—poses a number of problems and is capable of several interpretations. It may be translated as 'note', 'tone,' 'sound' and even 'interval.' This last is especially apt for terms such as 'tetra-phonic' where the reference is clearly to a distance of four tones, i.e. the interval of a fifth.

Other terms, like 'legetos,' 'naos,' 'proto-baros' etc. require special study before specific suggestions about their meaning can be made.

[4] Chrysanthos, *Theoretikon mega*, No. 43-49, pp. 16-19.

4

Markos Ph. Dragoumis

ATHENS, GREECE

Some Remarks on the Traditional
Music of the Greeks of Corsica

IN the mid-seventeenth century, the Maniot town of Vitylos was
the scene of a feud between the two great local clans, the Iatriani
and the Stephanopouli. A male member of the Stephanopoulo
clan abducted an Iatrian girl who was engaged to Liberakis
Yerakaris, one of the most formidable Greek pirates of the time.
In revenge, Yerakaris joined the Turks, who were attempting
to conquer Mani, and helped them to build a fortress on a site
dominating Vitylo. From there he conducted daily raids against
the town, carrying away and killing any member of the Stephanopoulo clan he could get hold of. The Stephanopouli were
therefore compelled to look for a new home. After several
months of vain search their representative arrived in Genoa.
There the authorities offered him lands in Corsica, which had
been in Genoese hands since 1347. He then returned to Vitylo,
a French ship was chartered, and on 3 October 1675 the
Stephanopouli with three hundred kinsmen and allies, seven
hundred and thirty souls in all, departed for Corsica. They
arrived there on 14 March 1676, after a stay of one month in
Genoa. In Genoa the immigrants signed an agreement with the
local authorities, the main points of which were that they
would become Uniats (i.e. submit to the Roman Church and
practice their religion in the manner observed by the ex-
Orthodox of Sicily and the Kingdom of Naples), that they would
accept as their Governor an official appointed by the Genoese
state, and that whenever it should be considered necessary they
would serve in the Genoese army or navy.

In Corsica there are still about three hundred inhabitants descended from the Maniots who emigrated there in 1676. Most of them live in Cargese, and although only very few (about ten) still speak Greek, all are aware of their Greek origin. Cargese was built in 1775 on the western coast of the island, towards the north of its capital Ajaccio, and was originally inhabited only by Greeks. Since 1830, however, its population has included several native Corsicans. Very near Cargese are the ruins of Paomia, Revinda, and Salogna, the earliest Greek settlements in Corsica. These villages were destroyed in 1731 by native Corsican bandits after the fierce Battle of Paomia. During the forty-five year period from the Battle of Paomia to the foundation of Cargese the Greeks of Corsica lived in Ajaccio.[1]

Cargese has two churches, one for the native Corsicans, and another for the Greeks. The latter was completed in 1872 and is named St. Spyridon. The vicar of St. Spyridon, Father Chappet, is French, but speaks fluent Greek, since he lived for many years in Constantinople and Athens. The services and the Liturgy are sung in Greek from a prayerbook which was edited by Father Chappet with a Latin transliteration on one page and a French text on the other. The hymns are chanted by a blind precentor and a choir of about six or seven women.[2]

Characteristic examples of the music which is sung in St. Spyridon were recorded by Mr. Vayiakakos, the author of a fine study on the Cargesians, during a visit he made to Cargese in 1963. The following is a brief description of the liturgical music of the Cargesians, based on Vayiakakos' recordings, which I had the opportunity to hear in 1965.

Both the precentor and the choristers of St. Spyridon have soft and pleasing voices and do not sing through the nose as most Greek precentors do. This is probably due to the influence which the French manner of singing has exerted on the Cargesians. The music they sing is diatonic, does not employ irra-

---

[1] Χρονογραφία περί τῆς καταγωγῆς τῶν ἐν Μάνῃ Στεφανοπούλων (Athens, 1865); N. Phardys, "Ὕλη καί σκαρίφημα τῆς ἐν Κορσικῇ Ἑλληνικῆς Ἀποικίας (Athens, 1888); P. Stephanopoli, Histoire des Grecs en Corse (Paris, 1900); G. Blanken, Les Grecs de Cargèse (Corse), Tome I: Partie linguistique (Leyden, 1951); P. Leigh Fermor, Mani (London, 1958), 99-111; D. Vayiakakos, 'Οἱ Μανιάται τῆς Κορσικῆς,' Parnassos, VII (1965), 25-46.
[2] Vayiakakos, loc. cit., 41ff.

tional (non-tempered) intervals, and seems to be more closely
related to medieval Byzantine music than to the music of the
modern Greek Church (Neo-Byzantine chant). This certainly
holds true for the first antiphon of the Liturgy of St. John
Chrysostom. The medieval Byzantine version (A)[3] is an inflected monotone on *b*, which goes once up to *d'* and twice down
to *a*. The Cargesian version (B) is almost identical, although it
should be pointed out that it utilizes in two cases the major
third below *b* (i.e. *g*). The Neo-Byzantine version (C)[4] is also
an inflected monotone, but in this case the reciting note is *d'*
instead of *b*, and the range *b—e^{b'}* instead of *a—d'*. It is noteworthy, however, that although C has far fewer claims to
similarity with A than B, it is, all the same, a variant of A,
since they both start with an ascending-descending melodic
movement of a minor third, and finish on the same note with
which they start.

Ex. 1

Let us turn now to the secular music of the Cargesians.
Nicholas Phardys[5] (1853-1901) in his book on Cargese[6] writes
that in the late nineteenth century the Cargesians seemed to
remember the tunes of only four of their own traditional folk
songs. Further, he states that he was able to note all four and

---

[3] Cod. Athens 2047 (15th c.), fols. 135r and v.
[4] *Μουσικὴ Συλλογή*, III (Constantinople, 1909), 15.
[5] Greek physician, classical scholar and musician who spent two years in Cargese
(1885-6) working as a schoolmaster and studying the local history and customs.
[6] Phardys, *op. cit.*, 169ff.

that he would publish them at some other time. This he never did because of his premature death.

For more than half a century after Phardys's death the whereabouts of the above tunes was unknown. Recently, however, three of them were discovered by the present writer in the Gennadeion Library. They were in an autograph manuscript of Phardys, which also contains some of his unpublished articles, and the music of about fifty folk-songs from his native island of Samothrace.

These three tunes from Cargese, together with a fourth one recorded there by Vayiakakos in 1963 are, as far as I know, the only surviving specimens of Cargesian secular music. The three 'Phardys' tunes are given in Exx. 2–4. In the manuscript they are written in Chrysanthine notation. Here, however, they have been transcribed into staff notation for those who may not be familiar with the other system. The 'Vayiakakos' tune is given in Ex. 5. It was sung to the collector by Justine Volymaki, a Cargesian lady, who in 1963 was in her seventies. The transcription was made by the present writer.

Examples 2 and 3 are carols for the feast of St. Lazarus,[7] and were sung on the morning of the feast or on the following morning by groups of young boys outside the houses of the villagers.[8] The text[9] of the first carol refers to the festivities of the day. The second carol has two texts.[10] The use of the first or the second one depended on whether the carollers had received a reward for singing Ex. 2 (sweets or fruit), or whether they had been told to go away. The first text praises the householder and his family, while the second addresses a string of abuse to them. Ex. 4 was meant to be sung during intimate convivial occasions, and its text[11] is one of the many variants of a medieval Greek ballad, the so-called 'romance of Charzianis'. This, according to Baud-Bovy,[12] originated in the twelfth century in either Rhodes or Aegina. Its subject is usually the following: a young man seeks the hand of a girl who refuses his offer. He then resorts to sorcery in order to win her heart. Eventually he

---

[7] The Feast of St. Lazarus is movable and is invariably celebrated on the day before Palm Sunday.

[8] I have drawn the following information from Blanken, *op. cit.*, 292-5.

[9] Phardys, *op. cit.*, 178.

[10] *Ibid.*, 178-9.   [11] *Ibid.*, 169-70.

[12] S. Baud-Bovy, *La Chanson populaire grecque du Dodécanèse* (Paris, 1936), 197.

Ex. 2

Κα-λη-σπέ-ρα σας, κα-λή χρο-νί-τσα, ἦρθ᾽ ὁ Λά-ζα-ρος, ἦρ-θαν τά Βά-για

Ex. 3

Πα-δά πού κα - λαν - - - τί - σαμε, κα - - λά μᾶς ἀ-πε - ρά-σουν,

— κα-λά νά πᾶν τά ἔ-χῃ τους, καί τά πο-δέ-λοι - πά τους.

Ex. 4

Μαύρ᾽ ἦ-ταν ᾽κεῖ-να μαῦ- - -ρε μου, στά πέ-ρα πα-να- - θύ-ρια,

μέσ᾽ ἕν δρο-μί μέσ᾽ ἕν στρα-τί, μέσ᾽ ἕ- -να σταυ-ρο - -δρό-μι.

Ex. 5

marries her, but she is badly treated by her parents-in-law and dies shortly after the marriage. Ex. 5 was not associated with any particular text as were the other tunes. It was sung to pairs of fifteen syllable verses in iambic metre improvised during parties. Incidentally, the missing 'Phardys' tune was meant to be sung to similar verses. Thus, if it were discovered, it would probably prove identical.

None of the above tunes seem to have originated in Cargese,

except, perhaps, Ex. 5. Ex. 2 is the most widely known. It is almost identical with the tune of a medieval 'chanson de geste'[13] (see Ex. 6), and it appears time and again in Greek 'Lazarus' carols[14] (see Ex. 7).

Ex. 6

Ex. 7

Ποῦ ἦ-σουν Λά - ζα - ρε,   ποῦ ἡ φω - νή σου,

ὅ-που σ᾽ ἔκ - λαι - γαν,   οἱ ἀ - δελ - φοί σου.

Ex. 4 has so far been located in five Greek islands,[15] though in each instance it is associated with a different text, none of which has anything in common with the Charzianis ballad. The following version is from Rhodes.[16]

Ex. 8

Καί τά Κε- φα- λω- - νί-τι- κα στή Ρό-δον εἶν ρα-γ - μέ-να,
καί καρ-τε- - ροῦ-σιν   τόν και-ρό νά φύ-γουν τά καη᷉ - μέ-να,

Δός τοῦ πέ-ρα δός τοῦ   πέ-ρα, δός τοῦ φους-τα-νιοῦ σ᾽ ἀ - έ - ρα.

Ex. 3 resembles a tune set to a text in the native Corsican dialect[17] (see Ex. 9), but it is hard to say whether it is genetic-

[13] W. Wiora, *Die vier Weltalter der Musik* (Stuttgart, 1961), 176.
[14] A. Sigalas, Συλλογή Ἐθνικῶν Ἀσμάτων (Athens, 1880), 501.
[15] Cf. S. Baud-Bovy, *Chansons du Dodécanèse*, I (Athens, 1935), 195-6; H. Pernot– P. le Flem, *Mélodies populaires grecques de l'Ile de Chio* (Paris, 1903), 45; A. Remandas–P. Zacharias, Ἀρίων (Athens, 1917), 25; N. Mavris–E. Papadopoulos, Κασιακή Λύρα (Port Said, 1928), No. 61; G. Rigas, Σκιάθου Λαϊκός Πολιτισμός (Thessaloniki, 1958), 104.
[16] S. Baud-Bovy, *op. cit.*, 195-6.
[17] X. Tomasi, 'Corsica'—*Recueil de chansons populaires de l'Ile de Corse* (Corsica, 1912), 18-19.

Ex. 9

ally related to it. Corsica and Greece belong to the same cultural area, and within such an area the independent creation of similar melodic forms is frequent.

Ex. 5 may have originated in Cargese, though the only argument in favour of this assumption is that I have never come across it in the collections of Mediterranean folk music which I have seen.

The close connection which exists between the sacred and secular music of the Greeks of Corsica and Greece itself proves that the process of assimilation of the Greek element in Corsica was exceedingly slow. However, the sad fact that less than ten individuals in Cargese still speak Greek, shows that the systematic collection of the traditional music of this isolated Greek community must not be delayed.

5

Enrica Follieri

ROME, ITALY

The 'Initia Hymnorum Ecclesiae Graecae' Bibliographical Supplement

WITH the publication of the fifth and last volume of the *Initia Hymnorum Ecclesiae Graecae* in April, 1966, a project on which I had begun work in 1956 was completed.[1] This collection is already known and has been reviewed several times[2] and I have spoken about it on more than one occasion at recent Congresses of Byzantine Studies.[3] My purpose in returning once more to this subject is to facilitate the use of this working instrument for those who may wish to make use of it in their researches.

What the 'Initia' contains

The *Initia Hymnorum Ecclesiae Graecae* is an alphabetically

---

[1] H. Follieri, *Initia Hymnorum Ecclesiae Graecae*, I-V (pars prior—pars altera) (*Studi e Testi*, 211-15bis) (Vatican City, 1960-6).

[2] H.-G. Beck in *Byzantinische Zeitschrift* [=BZ], 55 (1962), 101-2; and 59 (1966), 372-3; P. Canart in *Revue d'histoire ecclésiastique*, 57 (1962), 350-2; J. Darrouzès in *Revue des Études Byzantines*, 20 (1962), 245; I. Dujčev in *Byzantinoslavica*, 22 (1961), 340-1; F. Halkin in *Analecta Bollandiana* [=AB], 79 (1961), 178-9 and 85 (1967), 247-8; O. Parlangèli in *Paideia*, 16 (1961), 167-8 and 18 (1963), 204-5 and 21 (1966), 168-70; N. Tomadakes in Ἐπετηρὶς Ἑταιρείας Βυζαντινῶν Σπουδῶν [=EEBS], 30 (1960), 567-8 and 34 (1965), 349-50. For the mention of supplements see: M. Naoumides, "Ὑμνογραφικὰ κείμενα εἰς παπύρους καὶ ὄστρακα,' in *EEBS*, 32 (1963), 60-93; also N. Tomadakes, *ibid.*, 23-5 (for hymnographic compositions published in the rare periodical Νέα Φόρμιγξ, in the years 1921-2).

[3] E. Follieri, 'Sulla preparazione di un incipitario della poesia liturgica bizantina,' *Akten des XI. Internationalen Byzantinistenkongresses 1958* (Munich, 1960), 160-4; *eadem*, 'Problemi di innografia bizantina,' *Actes du XIIe Congrès International d'Études byzantines*, II (Belgrade, 1964), 311-25. At the Thirteenth Congress of Byzantine Studies held at Oxford in September 1966, I presented a brief communication which has not been published. The contents of that paper have been taken up again and enlarged in this article.

arranged collection of the *incipits* of the *troparia* which constitute
the Byzantine liturgical hymns. ,The hymns taken into consideration are those composed mainly prior to 1453 and published in printed volumes as late as 1958. The principles that I
have followed in the compilation of this collection are given in
the Preface to the first volume and were also explained in my
communication to the Munich Congress of 1958, at which I
first announced the work.[4] I propose to confine myself here to
recalling that apart from the initia of the troparia, I have collected the beginnings of the *heirmoi* and the metrical *synaxaria*
and the indications of acrostics contained in the liturgical books
used in the Greek Church according to two editions, the Roman
edition of the Propaganda Fide[5] and a Venetian edition[6], as
well as in monographs, anthologies, various collections, and
periodicals.

The texts listed have all been published and the bibliographical references (in abbreviations) are to printed publications
(sometimes more than one for the same text) in which the
particular troparion appears, either alone or as a part of a
larger hymn. Unpublished texts are, therefore, normally excluded from this repertory, but it must be noted that in exceptional cases I have included a certain number of unpublished
texts on the basis of the lists of unpublished liturgical hymns
compiled by Metropolitan Sophronios Eustratiades and published by him in the periodicals Ἐκκλησιαστικὸς Φάρος and Νέα
Σιών. Eustratiades mentions only the *incipits* which, in listing
all the hymnographic material contained in these periodicals,
I have incorporated in the *Initia*; but I have noted such entries
with an asterisk indicating that in the cited bibliography the
troparion was not printed in full, but only its first words. In the
cases of these unpublished hymns and also for those in the
famous Patmos codices of Romanos (described by the Greek

---

[4] See *above*, n. 3.

[5] Εὐχολόγιον τὸ μέγα, ἐν ʿΡώμῃ, 1873; ʿΩρολόγιον τὸ μέγα, ἐν ʿΡώμῃ, 1876;
Μηναῖα τοῦ ὅλου ἐνιαυτοῦ, I-VI, ἐν ʿΡώμῃ, 1888-1902; Παρακλητικὴ ἤτοι
Ὀκτώηχος ἡ μεγάλη, ἐν ʿΡώμῃ, 1885; Πεντηκοστάριον χαρμόσυνον, ἐν
ʿΡώμῃ, 1883; Τριῴδιον κατανυκτικόν, ἐν ʿΡώμῃ, 1879.

[6] Εὐχολόγιον τὸ μέγα, ἐν Βενετίᾳ, Φοῖνιξ, 1862; ʿΩρολόγιον τὸ μέγα, Βενετία,
Φοῖνιξ, 1895; Μηναῖα, I-XII, Βενετία, Φοῖνιξ, 1895; Παρακλητικὴ ἤτοι
Ὀκτώηχος ἡ μεγάλη, ʿΕνετίησιν, ῞Αγιος Γεώργιος, 1871; Πεντηκοστάριον,
ʿΕνετίησιν, ῞Αγιος Γεώργιος, 1875; Τριῴδιον κατανυκτικόν, Βενετία, Φοῖνιξ,
1876.

scholars, students of Professor Tomadakes) my reference is to the listings in printed texts rather than in the manuscripts.

What the Initia does not contain

Manuscripts, rich as they may be with hymnographic material, are omitted from my collection, which is limited to supplying investigators of codices with a basic repertory. For this reason catalogues of manuscripts in which many liturgical hymns are listed, usually only briefly quoting the *incipit* have not been taken into consideration. For example, among the well-known works of this kind which I have not included are: Dmitrievskij's collection of liturgical codices,[7] Papadopoulos-Kerameus' description of the Jerusalem manuscripts,[8] the catalogue of the Grottaferrata manuscripts compiled by Antonio Rocchi,[9] and the catalogues of a considerable group of Greek manuscripts in the Vatican compiled by Ciro Giannelli.[10] These entries in the catalogues (which I intend to record in a future supplement) must not be left out of consideration by anyone proposing to publish hitherto unpublished hymns.

Lacunae to be filled

In the process of the preparation of the *Initia* all publications to which I had access in 1959 were examined including also printed works which appeared during 1958. Any publication since that year is therefore missing in the *Initia Hymnorum* and this is by no means a small lacuna if one considers, for example, the new important editions of the hymns by Romanos the Melodos, for which, besides the continuation of the Athens edition,[11] there is now an Oxford edition by Paul Maas and C. A. Trypanis[12] and a Paris edition of J. Grosdidier de Matons.[13] Moreover, many liturgical hymns, and in particular *kanons*, have been published singly or in groups and among those responsible for these new editions I must include myself, since I have published more than twenty *kanons* and have another ten in the press. It is, of course, inevitable that a reper-

[7] See bibliography, No. 17.
[9] See bibliography, No. 58.
[11] See bibliography, No. 64.
[13] See bibliography, No. 26.

[8] See bibliography, No. 47.
[10] See bibliography, Nos. 22, 23.
[12] See bibliography, No. 30.

tory such as the *Initia Hymnorum Ecclesiae Graecae* is bound to promote the study and the publication of unpublished texts. This in itself renders it little by little out-of-date.

This fact makes it essential to compile supplements. My present plan is to prepare one within the next ten years. This supplement would include the *incipits* from all the editions that have appeared since 1958, and contain additions to the original bibliography of the *Initia*, in which certain publications have not been mentioned; such as, for example, the *akolouthia* in honour of John Mauropus edited by Sophronios Eustratiades and later on by Silvio Giuseppe Mercati, each of them in miscellaneous collections.[14] Further, the *kanons* written by Demetrios Chomatianos for St. Clement of Ochrid published in 1898 by Balasčev,[15] the hymn attributed to Andrew of Crete for the Ὑπαπαντή edited by the Archimandrite Amphilokhij in a rare publication which appeared in 1870 in Moscow,[16] some hymns by Joseph the Studite published in Μακεδονικά,[17] various *kanons* published in the Athonite series Ἁγιορειτικὴ Βιβλιοθήκη[18] and in a periodical 'à tirage confidentiel', Ῥωμανὸς ὁ Μελῳδός, edited by Eustratiades.[19] The entire valuable series of the *Monumenta Musicae Byzantinae*, in which the texts are taken into consideration from the musical point of view, ought not to be missing in a repertory of this kind.[20]

While awaiting the future supplement, it appears to me that a supplementary bibliography, though brief, would be useful. I have therefore added it at the end of this article. Certainly even

---

[14] S. Eustratiades, "Ἰωάννης ὁ Μαυρόπους Μητροπολίτης Εὐχαῖτων,' in Ἐναίσιμα . . . (Athens, 1931), 405-37 (see bibliography, No. 19); S. G. Mercati, 'Ufficio di Giovanni Mauropode Euchaita composto dal nipote Teodoro,' in *Mémorial Louis Petit* (Bucharest, 1948), 347-60 (see bibliography, No. 38). This edition was brought to my attention together with some other publications by Professor H.-G. Beck in *BZ*, 55 (1962), 102.

[15] See bibliography, No. 7. I owe this information to the scholarship and the courtesy of Professor I. Dujčev who also kindly placed this rare publication at my disposal.

[16] See bibliography, No. 4.

[17] Vol. 2 (1941-52), 25-88; see bibliography, No. 97. I owe this information to Professor H.-G. Beck, *loc. cit.*, and to an oral communication from Professor E. Mioni.

[18] See bibliography, No. 89.

[19] Brought to my attention by Rev. F. Halkin, *AB*, 85 (1967), 248. See bibliography, No. 107.

[20] See bibliography, No. 41. Other publications which refer to Byzantine Music are given at numbers: 11, 27, 49, 60, 61, 62, 70.

this is not complete,[21] and I shall therefore be extremely grateful to all those who will be kind enough to inform me of the lacunae and of new publications and so enable me to make the supplement as complete as possible.

The list of hymnographers, the concordance tables and the hagiographical—liturgical index

It is my hope that in spite of its shortcomings the *Initia* will render useful services. In order to facilitate its use by students, the fifth volume is equipped with a list of hymnographers,[22] and with tables of concordances for the Roman and Venetian editions of the Greek liturgical books used, including indications for the days of the church calendar and correspondence with the respective pages. Furthermore, the second part of the same fifth volume, published separately from the first (which can be purchased separately from the rest of the work), is supplied with an index of saints and of the commemorations in the Byzantine liturgical year in relation to the hymnography. This index, which I had not originally planned, was compiled at the

---

[21] There must be added, for example, the catalogues of Greek manuscripts in which there are references to liturgical hymns, here only represented by Nos. 8, 17, 22, 23, 46, 47, 55, 57, 58; the starting point for this research is the valuable work by Abbé M. Richard, *Répertoire des bibliothèques et des catalogues de manuscrits grecs* (Paris, 1958²), with its first supplement, *Supplément 1958-1963* (Paris, 1964). There is also a great number of *akolouthiai* published in individual editions, often quite rare. This copious bibliographical material has been listed by Mgr L. Petit, *Bibliographie des acolouthies grecques* (Brussels, 1926); a supplement to this has been issued by S. Eustratiades under the title "*Ἁγιολογικά*" in *EEBS*, 9 (1932), 80-122. This must not, however, be placed indiscriminately in the *Initia*, because it is useless to register the *akolouthiai* which are simple extracts from the *Menaia*, and it is necessary, given the general principles adopted, to exclude all hymns composed after 1453.

[22] The names of authors included in this list are those given in printed editions (see ref. in vol. V, *pars prior*, p. 250: 'Hymnographorum nomina ad fidem editionum proferuntur'). The numerous problems of attribution and of homonyms, as well as a number of other points, could not be resolved or even tackled here. Only in some now well-clarified instances has a correction been added to the identifications given by some editors. For instance, under *Ἰωάννης ὁ Δαμασκηνός* after SR IX 713 it has been noted in parentheses 'sed vere *Ἰωάννης ὁ Μαυρόπους*'; under *Σωφρόνιος Ἱεροσολύμων* after SR IV 126-225 has been added 'perperam, pro *Ἰωσήφ*'. Numerous references link the relative indications to the homonymous hymnographers on whose real identity and on whose œuvre editors frequently disagree. Much still remains to be done in this field with the help of the manuscript tradition and the formal and stylistic examination of the texts; the *Initia* can here provide only a bibliographical starting point.

D

suggestion of Professor Agostino Pertusi and Reverend R.-J. Loenertz. I was able to accomplish this thanks to the benevolent understanding of Reverend A. Raes, the Prefect of the Vatican Library. The preparation of the index considerably delayed the appearance of the fifth volume and I should like to express my regrets to all those who waited for so long for the completion of this work.

In conclusion it should be pointed out that the three parts (diverse in character and in size) into which the work is divided —the true and proper collection of the *initia*, the list of hymnographers and the hagiographical-liturgical index—all drawn up on the basis of the same bibliographical material, supplement one another and are to be used in a parallel way in the course of research. For instance, anyone interested in a hymnographer should begin his research with the indications referring to him in the list of hymnographers. Then, having traced the hymns that are listed under that name, he should search for all the editions through the series of *initia*. It would thus be possible, for instance, to observe that some hymns have been attributed to other authors as well or have been re-used for other saints.

When there are several bibliographical indications for a single *initium*, it would be just as well not to restrict oneself to consulting only one; this can be safely done only for the official liturgical books of the Greek Church. All other indications can add some new fact, particularly where modern studies are concerned. It will not always be easy to gain access to some of the publications mentioned in the *Initia*. In this respect, though, it must be remembered that I had the privilege of working in Rome in the Vatican Library and in the library of the Pontifical Institute for Oriental Studies, both of which are well supplied with rare books and periodicals. For every bibliographical problem it is always possible to write to these libraries or, if need be, directly to me, and I shall be very happy to assist whenever possible.

* * *

P.S. The appended bibliography was completed in February 1968.

SUPPLEMENTARY BIBLIOGRAPHY

BOOKS

1. *Actes du XIIe Congrès International d'Études byzantines, Ochride, 10—16 septembre 1961*, I—III (Beograd, 1963-4).
   (See: I, 137-50, 249-67, 366-73, 382-3; II, 311-25, 565-9, 576-82.)

2. Agapios [Landos] (*Ἀγάπιος μοναχὸς ὁ Κρής), Θεοτοκάριον ὡραιότατον καὶ χαρμόσυνον ... μετατυπωθέν τε καὶ διορθωθὲν ... παρὰ τοῦ ἱεροδιακόνου Σπυρίδωνος Παπαδοπούλου. Ἐνετίῃσιν, παρὰ Νικολάῳ Γλυκεῖ, 1775*.

3. *Akten des XI Internationalen Byzantinistenkongresses, München 1958*, (München, 1960).
   (See: pp. 539-55.)

4. Amfilokhij, arkhimandrit, *O neizdannykh kanonakh v služebnoj febral'skoj grečeskoj minei konca X věka* (Moskva, 1870).

4a. Amfilokhij, arkhimandrit, *Paleografičeskoe opisanie*, I-IV (Moskva, 1879-80).
   (See: II, 7-19, 75-78; III, 1-4, 40-41, 65-69, 73-76, 119, 122-3; IV, 3-10, 25-32, 46-51.)

4b. *Analecta Hymnica Graeca e codicibus eruta Italiae Inferioris*, Ioseph Schirò consilio et ductu edita.
   I.—Ada Debiasi Gonzato, *Canones Septembris* (Roma, 1966).

5. *Atti del Convegno sul tema: La Persia e il mondo greco-romano, Roma 11-14 aprile 1965* ('Problemi attuali di scienza e di cultura,' Quaderno 76, Roma, Accademia Nazionale dei Lincei, 1966).
   (See: pp. 227-42.)

6. *Atti del Convegno internazionale sul tema: L'Oriente cristiano nella storia della civiltà, Roma 31 marzo—3 aprile 1963; Firenze 4 aprile 1963* ('Problemi attuali di scienza e di cultura,' Quaderno 62, Roma, Accademia Nazionale dei Lincei, 1964).
   (See: pp. 251-71.)

7. Balasčev, G., *Kliment episkop Slověnski* (Sofia, 1898).

8. Beneševič, V. N., *Opisanie grečeskikh rukopisej monastyrja Svjatoj Ekateriny na Sinaě*, I, III/1 (St. Peterburg, 1911-17).
   (See: I, 134-74; III/1, 1-19).

9. Bouvy, E., *Poètes et mélodes. Étude sur les origines du rythme tonique dans l'hymnographie de l'Église grecque* (Nîmes, 1886).
   (See *passim*, e.g.: 260-62, 268, 276, 309 etc.)

10. Cantarella, R., *Poeti bizantini*, I-II (Milano, 1948).
   (An anthology. See: I, 39, 67-71, 72-73, 76-81, 83, 86-93, 100-21, 125, 128-42, 222, 242-4.)

11. Chourzamanes, E. Ch., *Ἦχος πρῶτος. Σύντομος εἱρμολογικός*, I-II (*Ἀθῆναι*, 1961-2).

12. *Collectanea Vaticana in honorem Anselmi M. card. Albareda a Bibliotheca Apostolica edita*, I-II ('Studi e Testi,' 219-20, Città del Vaticano, 1962).
   (See: I, 337-57.)

13. Colonna, M. E., *Gli idiomeli di Andrea Libadeno* (Napoli, 1959).

14. Daniel, H. A., *Thesaurus hymnologicus sive hymnorum canticorum sequentiarum*

circa annum MD usitatarum collectio amplissima, I-III (Lipsiae, 1855).
(See: III, 5, 17-20, 47-97, 101-23, 125-38.)

15. Del Grande, C., *L'inno acatisto in onore della Madre di Dio* ('Il Melagrano,' 32-33, Firenze, 1948).

16. Dmitrievskij, A., *Bogosluženie v russkoj cerkvi v XVI věkě* (Kazan, 1884). (Some material, e.g. on p. 133.)

17. Dmitrievskij, A., *Opisanie liturgičeskikh rukopisej khranjaščikhsja v bibliotekakh pravoslavnago vostoka:* I. *Τυπικά* (Kiev, 1895); II. *Εὐχολόγια* (Kiev, 1901); III. *Τυπικά* (Petrograd, 1917).

18. *Εἰς μνήμην Σπυρίδωνος Λάμπρου* (*'Εν 'Αθήναις*, 1935). (See: 162-9, 170-6, 255-8.)

19. *'Εναίσιμα. Τιμητικὸς τόμος ἐπὶ τῇ ἐπιστημονικῇ 35ετηρίδι τοῦ Μακ. 'Αρχιεπισκόπου 'Αθηνῶν Χρυσοστόμου* (*'Εν 'Αθήναις*, 1931). (See: 405-37.)

20. Eustratiades, S., *'Αγιολόγιον τῆς 'Ορθοδόξου 'Εκκλησίας* (n.p., n.d. [Athens, 1960]).

21. Eustratiades, S., *'Ρωμανὸς ὁ Μελῳδὸς καὶ ὁ 'Ακάθιστος* (*'Εν Θεσσαλο-νίκῃ*, 1917).

22. Giannelli, C., *Codices Vaticani Graeci*. Codices 1485-1683 (in Bibliotheca Vaticana, 1950). (See: *Initia operum quae inedita vel minus nota visa sunt*, pp. 455-66.)

23. Giannelli, C. †—P. Canart, *Codices Vaticani Graeci*. Codices 1684-1744 (in Bybliotheca Vaticana, 1961). (See: *Initia operum quae inedita vel minus nota visa sunt*, pp. 155-70.)

24. Giovanelli, G., *S. Bartolomeo Juniore confondatore di Grottaferrata* (Badia greca di Grottaferrata, 1962). (See: pp. 87-98.)

25. Grenfell, B. P.—A. S. Hunt, *The Amherst Papyri*. Greek, I. Theological Fragments (London, 1900). (See: pp. 43-44.)

26. Grosdidier de Matons, J., *Romanos le Mélode, Hymnes*. I-IV ('Sources chrétiennes,' 99, 110, 114, 128, Paris, 1964-7).

27. Koschmieder, E., *Die ältesten Novgoroder Hirmologien-Fragmente* ('Abhandlungen der Bayerischen Akademie der Wissenschaften, phil.-hist. Klasse, N.F., H.35, München, 1952; H.37, München, 1955).

28. *Late Classical and Mediaeval Studies in honor of A. M. Friend, Jr.* (Princeton, 1955). (See: 82-87.)

29. Livadaras, N. A., *Τὸ πρόβλημα τῆς γνησιότητος τῶν ἁγιολογικῶν ὕμνων τοῦ 'Ρωμανοῦ* (*'Αθῆναι*, 1959) [= TRM IV, *Παράρτημα*].

30. Maas, P.—C. A. Trypanis, *Sancti Romani Melodi Cantica*. Cantica genuina (Oxford, 1963).

31. Maltzew, A.v., *Liturgikon. Die Liturgien der Orthodox-Katholischen Kirche des Morgenlandes* (Berlin, 1902). (Some material, e.g. p. 319n.)

32. Maltzew, A.v., *Menologion der Orthodox-Katholischen Kirche des Morgenlandes*, I-II (Berlin, 1900-1). (Some material, e.g. in I, 220, 226.)

33. Maltzew, A.v., *Oktoichos oder Parakletike der Orthodox-Katholischen Kirche des Morgenlandes*, I-II (Berlin, 1903-4).
    (Some material, e.g. in I, 35, 38, 107, 117, etc.)

34. Mateos, J., *Le Typicon de la Grande Église*, I-II ('Orientalia Christiana Analecta,' 165-6, Roma, 1962-3).

35. Mearns, J., *The Canticles of the Christian Church Eastern and Western in Early and Medieval Times* (Cambridge, 1914).
    (See: 15-24).

36. Meersseman, G. G., *Der Hymnos Akathistos im Abendland*, II ('Spicilegium Friburgense,' 3, Freiburg, 1960).
    (See: p. 34.)

37. *Mélanges Eugène Tisserant*, I-VII ('Studi e Testi,' 231-7, Città del Vaticano, 1964).
    (See: II, 103-69; III, 47-76, 175-207.)

38. *Mémorial Louis Petit* ('Archives de l'Orient Chrétien,' 1, Bucarest, 1948).
    (See: 347-60.)

39. *Le Millénaire du Mont Athos (963-1963), Études et Mélanges*, I-II (Chevetogne—Venezia, 1963-4).
    (See: I, 135-43.)

40. Miller, E., *Manuelis Philae Carmina*, I-II (Parisiis, 1855-7).
    (See: II, 319-33.)

41. *Monumenta Musicae Byzantinae*, several series:

    Série principale (Facsimilés)

    I. Høeg, C.—H. J. W. Tillyard—E. Wellesz, *Sticherarium (Codex Vindobonensis Theol. Graec. 181)* (Copenhague, 1935).
       (See: 29-35, 37-66.)

    II. Høeg, C., *Hirmologium Athoum (Codex Monasterii Hiberorum 470)* (Copenhague, 1938).
       (See: 19-24, 25-27, 28.)

    III/1. Tardo, L., *Hirmologium Cryptense (Codex Cryptensis E.γ. II)* (Roma, 1951).
       (See: 21, 24, 28-30, 41-95 etc.)

    IV. Høeg, C., *Contacarium Ashburnhamense (Codex Bibl. Laurentianae Ashburnhamensis 64)* (Copenhague, 1956).
       (See: 20-2, 34-5, 42-47.)

    V.A Jakobson, R., *Fragmenta Chiliandarica Palaeoslavica. Sticherarium (Codex Monasterii Chiliandarici 307)* (Copenhagen, 1957).
       (See: 13-25.)

    V.B Jakobson, R., *Fragmenta Chiliandarica Palaeoslavica. Hirmologium (Codex Monasterii Chiliandarici 308)* (Copenhagen, 1957).
       (See: 7-14.)

    VI. Bugge, A., *Contacarium Palaeoslavicum Mosquense* (codex qui olim in Ecclesia Cathedrali Cremlensi Memoriae Dormitionis Deiparae dedicata 9 π inscriptus nunc in Musaeo Historico Mosquensi asservatur) (Copenhague, 1960).
       (See: xiv, etc., xxiii-xxv, 1-10.)

VII. Strunk, O., *Specimina notationum antiquiorum*, Pars suppletoria (Hauniae, 1965).
(See: 22-26, 35-40.)

Subsidia

I.1. Tillyard, H. J. W., *Handbook of the Middle Byzantine Musical Notation* (Copenhague, 1935).
(See: 23, 24, 38-48.)

II. Wellesz, E., *Eastern Elements in Western Chant* (Oxford–Boston, 1947; 2nd ed. Copenhagen, 1967).
(See: 22-23, 27-30, etc.)

III. Palikarova-Verdeil, R., *La musique byzantine chez les Bulgares et les Russes (du IXᵉ au XIVᵉ siècle)* (Copenhague, 1953).
(See: 123, 127, 155-61, etc.)

VII. Raasted, J., *Intonation Formulas and Modal Signatures in Byzantine Musical Manuscripts* (Copenhagen, 1966).
(See: 225-8.)

Transcripta

I. Wellesz, E., *Die Hymnen des Sticherarium für September* (Copenhague, 1936).

II. Tillyard, H. J. W., *The Hymns of the Sticherarium for November* (Copenhagen, 1938).

III. Tillyard, H. J. W., *The Hymns of the Octoechus*, Part I (Copenhagen, 1940).

IV. Tillyard, H. J. W., *Twenty Canons from the Trinity Hirmologium* (Boston, 1952).

V. Tillyard, H. J. W., *The Hymns of the Octoechus*, Part II (Copenhagen, 1949).

VI. Ayoutanti, A.—M. Stöhr—C. Høeg, *The Hymns of the Hirmologium*, Part I (Copenhagen, 1952).

VII. H. J. W. Tillyard, *The Hymns of the Pentecostarium* (Copenhagen, 1960).

VIII. Ayoutanti, A. and H. J. W. Tillyard, *The Hymns of the Hirmologium*, Part III/2—*The Third Plagal Mode* (Copenhagen, 1956).

IX. Wellesz, E., *The Akathistos Hymn* (Copenhagen, 1957).

Lectionaria

I, 1-5. Høeg, C. and G. Zuntz, *Prophetologium* (Hauniae, 1939-62). (See: 39, 41, 45, 53, etc.)

42. Oikonomos, K., *'Υμνῳδῶν 'Ανέκδοτα. 'Εκ τῶν 'Απογράφων τῆς Βιβλιοθήκης τοῦ Μεγάλου Σπηλαίου. 'Αθήνῃσι,* 1840. (At present inaccessible to me; yet see: K. Oikonomos, *Τὰ σῳζόμενα ἐκκλησιαστικὰ συγγράμματα,* I, *'Αθήνῃσι,* 1862, 554-68.)

43. Onasch, K., *Das Weihnachtsfest im orthodoxen Kirchenjahr. Liturgie und Ikonographie* ('Quellen und Untersuchungen zur Konfessionskunde der Orthodoxie,' 2, Berlin, 1958).
(See: 70-89, 202-3, 223-67.)

44. Pandurski, V. I., *Prep. Josif Pesnopisec (Iz istorijata na c'rkovnata himno-*

logija), in 'Godišnik na Dukhovnata Akademija "Sv. Kliment Okhridski",' Tome VIII [XXXIV] (1958-9), pp. 271-313.

45. Pantelakes, E. G., *Κοντάκια καὶ Κανόνες τῆς 'Εκκλησιαστικῆς Ποιήσεως.* (*'Εν 'Αθήναις*, 1923³). (An Anthology.)

46. Papadopoulos-Kerameus, A., *'Ανέκδοτα 'Ελληνικά ('Ο ἐν Κωνσταντινουπόλει 'Ελλ. Φιλολογικὸς Σύλλογος, Μαυρογορδάτειος Βιβλιοθήκη, 'Εν Κωνσταντινουπόλει*, 1884) (See: 97-98, 100.)

47. Papadopoulos-Kerameus, A., *'Ιεροσολυμιτικὴ Βιβλιοθήκη*, I-V (*'Εν Πετρουπόλει*, 1891-1915).
(See: I, 81; II, 85, 111, etc.)

48. *Πεπραγμένα τοῦ Θ' Διεθνοῦς Βυζαντινολογικοῦ Συνεδρίου, Θεσσαλονίκῃ, 12-19 'Απριλίου 1953, Α'-Γ' ('Αθῆναι, 1955-1958).*
(See: B', 118, 140-9, 220-8; Γ', 184-7, 277-87.)

49. Petresco, J.-D., *Les idiomèles et le canon de l'office de Noël* (*d'après des manuscrits grecs des XI*ᵉ, *XII*ᵉ, *XIII*ᵉ *et XIV*ᵉ *s.*) ('Études de paléographie musicale byzantine,' 1, Paris, 1932).

50. Phountoules, I. M., *'Ο ἅγιος 'Αλέξανδρος ὁ ἐν Λέσβῳ ('Λεσβιακὸν 'Εορτολόγιον,'* 2, *'Αθῆναι*, 1960).
(See: 49-73.)

51. Phountoules, I. M., *Οἱ ἅγιοι Γεώργιοι ἀρχιεπίσκοποι Μυτιλήνης ('Λεσβιακὸν 'Εορτολόγιον,'* I, *'Αθῆναι*, 1959).
(See: 13-15.)

52. Phountoules, I. M., *Οἱ ὅσιοι αὐτάδελφοι Δαβίδ, Συμεὼν καὶ Γεώργιος οἱ ὁμολογηταί ('Λεσβιακὸν 'Εορτολόγιον,'* 3, *'Αθῆναι*, 1961).
(See: β'—ιγ'.)

53. Pitra, I. B., *Iuris ecclesiastici Graecorum historia et monumenta*, I-II (Romae, 1864-8).
(See: II, 248, 249, 281-7, 300, 354, 363-5.)

54. *Polychronion. Festschrift F. Dölger zum 75. Geburtstag* ('Corpus der griechischen Urkunden des Mittelalters und der neueren Zeit,' Reihe D, Band I, Heidelberg, 1966).
(See: I, 266-86.)

55. Porfirij [Uspenskij], arkhimandrit, *Putešestvie v Meteorskie i Osoolimpijskie Monastyri v Fessalii* (S.- Peterburg, 1896).
(See: 526-8.)

56. *Proceedings of the XIIIth International Congress of Byzantine Studies, Oxford, 5-10 September 1966*, edited by J. M. Hussey, D. Obolensky, S. Runciman (London, 1967).
(See: 255-80.)

57. Roberts, C. H., *Catalogue of the Greek and Latin Papyri in the John Rylands Library, Manchester*, III.—*Theological and Literary Texts* (Manchester, 1938).
(See: 28-35.)

58. Rocchi, A., *Codices Cryptenses seu Abbatiae Cryptae Ferratae* (Tusculani, 1883).
(See: 286-410, 411-38.)

59. *Studia Patristica.* Papers presented to the Second International Conference on Patristic Studies held at Christ Church, Oxford, 1955, I-II

('Texte u. Untersuchungen zur Geschichte der altchristlichen Literatur,' 63-64, Berlin, 1957).
(See: II, 47.)

60. Thibaut, J.-B., *Monuments de la Notation Ekphonétique et Hagiopolite de l'Église Grecque* (St. Pétersbourg, 1913).
(See: 71, 72, 74-83, 88-92, 97-115, 129-47, 3*-11*.)

61. Thibaut, J., *Panégyrique de l'Immaculée dans les chants hymnographiques de la Liturgie grecque* (Paris, 1909).
(See: 9-49.)

62. Tillyard, H. J. W., *Byzantine Music and Hymnography* (London, 1923).
(See: 52-59, 68.)

63. Tomadakes, N. B., '*Η Βυζαντινὴ ῾Υμνογραφία καὶ Ποίησις, ἤτοι Εἰσαγωγὴ εἰς τὴν Βυζαντινὴν Φιλολογίαν*, II ('Αθῆναι, 1965³).
(See: 257-83 and *passim*.)

64. Tomadakes, N. B., '*Ρωμανοῦ τοῦ Μελῳδοῦ ῞Υμνοι, Τόμος τέταρτος*, Α'-Β' ('Αθῆναι, 1959-61).

65. Tomadakes, N. B., *Συλλάβιον βυζαντινῶν μελετῶν καὶ κειμένων*, Α', '*Η ἀκάθιστος ἑορτὴ καὶ ἡ ὑμνολογία της* ('Εν 'Αθήναις, 1964).

66. Trempelas, P. N., '*Εκλογὴ ἑλληνικῆς ὀρθοδόξου ὑμνογραφίας* ('Βιβλιοθήκη 'Αποστολικῆς Διακονίας,' 20, 'Αθῆναι, 1949).
(An Anthology.)

67. Trypanis, C. A., *Medieval and Modern Greek Poetry*, An Anthology (Oxford, 1951).

68. Tzedakes, Th. V., *Κασιανή, ἡ μεγάλη τῆς 'Εκκλησίας Μελῳδός* ('Ηράκλειον Κρήτης, 1959).

69. Valentini, G., *Metrofane, I canoni trinitari* ('Il Melagrano,' 190-1, Firenze, 1957).

70. Wellesz, E., *A History of Byzantine Music and Hymnography* (Oxford, 1961²).
(See: *passim*, e.g. 59, 138, 166, 176, 178, 180, 181, 182-94, etc.)

PERIODICALS TO BE ADDED TO THE BASIC LIST

71. *Acta Antiqua Academiae Scientiarum Hungaricae.* Budapest.
(See: 3(1955), 284; 5(1957), 381-3; 10(1962), 88-95; 11(1963), 407-14; 13(1965), 455-9.)

72. *'Απόστολος Βαρνάβας, 'Εκκλησιαστικὸν Περιοδικόν. 'Εν Λευκωσίᾳ (Κύπρου).*
(See, e.g.: S.II.2 (1930), 103-5. Hitherto only in part accessible.)

73. *'Απόστολος Τίτος. 'Ηράκλειον Κρήτης.*
(Inaccessible at present.)

74. *'Αρχεῖον τοῦ Θρακικοῦ Λαογραφικοῦ καὶ Γλωσσικοῦ Θησαυροῦ. Περιοδικὸν σύγγραμμα ἐκδιδόμενον ὑπὸ ἐπιτροπῆς Θρακῶν. 'Εν 'Αθήναις.*
(See, e.g.: 22(1957), 56, 63, 107, 117, 120, 298; 25(1960), 208.)

75. *Archivio Italiano per la Storia della Pietà.* Roma.
(See: 3(1962), 37-278; 5(1968), 1-200.)

76. Ἄθως ('Ο). 'Αθῆναι.
   (Inaccessible at present.)
77. Atti del (R.) Istituto Veneto di Scienze, lettere ed arti, Classe di Scienze morali e lettere. Venezia.
   (See: 96,2 (1936-7), 23-83; 118 (1959-60), 277-314.)
78. Bogoslovskie trudy, izdanie Moskovskoji Patriarkhi. Moskva.
   (See: 2(1961), 79.)
79. Byzantinoslavica. Prague.
   (See: 25(1964), 1-36.)
80. Βυζαντίς. 'Επιθεώρησις τῶν βυζαντιακῶν σπουδῶν ἐκδιδομένη κατὰ τριμηνίαν ὑπὸ τῆς ἐν 'Αθήναις Βυζαντινολογικῆς 'Εταιρείας. 'Εν 'Αθήναις.
   (See: 1(1909), 517-40.)
81. Classica et Mediaevalia. Revue danoise de philologie et d'histoire. Copenhague.
   (See: 17(1956), 35-46, 116; 22(1961), 167-71, 172-5, 176-81; 23(1962), 302-10.)
82. Δελτίον τῆς 'Ιστορικῆς καὶ 'Εθνολογικῆς 'Εταιρίας τῆς 'Ελλάδος. 'Εν 'Αθήναις.
   (See, e.g.: 4(1892-5), 42-44.)
83. Dumbarton Oaks Papers. Cambridge, Massachusetts.
   (See: 5(1950), 106; 8(1954), 312; 9/10(1955-6), 145-74, 201-2; 16(1962), 356-61, 378-81; 17(1963), 141-42.)
84. Eastern (The) Churches Quarterly. Ramsgate-London.
   (Some material, e.g. 4(1940-41), 315.)
84a. Eastern Churches Review. London.
   (Inaccessible at present.)
85. 'Εκκλησιαστικὸς Κῆρυξ. 'Εν Λάρνακι.
   (See: 1(1911), 727, 728; 2(1912), 443-56, 479-89, 511-17, 588-95, 623-31, 668-74; 3(1913), 23-28, 52-58, 83-87, 115-18, 239-45.)
86. 'Επιστημονικὴ 'Επετηρὶς ἐκδιδομένη ὑπὸ τῆς Θεολογικῆς Σχολῆς τοῦ Πανεπιστημίου Θεσσαλονίκης. 'Εν Θεσσαλονίκη.
   (See, e.g.: 7(1962), 227-43.)
87. 'Επιστημονικὴ 'Επετηρὶς τῆς Θεολογικῆς Σχολῆς τοῦ Πανεπιστημίου 'Αθηνῶν. 'Αθῆναι.
   (See, e.g.: 11(1955-56), 237, 249-51, 258, 272-73.)
88. Γρηγόριος ὁ Παλαμᾶς. 'Εκκλησιαστικὸν Περιοδικόν. 'Εν Θεσσαλονίκη.
   (See, e.g.: 1(1917), 193-207, 269-80, 483-90, 625-34, 641-9, 817-32; 5(1921), 137-42; 6(1922), 314-15, 577-84; 7(1923), 163-7, 289-98; 8(1924), 30-32, 61-65, 256-66, 337-43, 437-42; 10(1926), 76-9; 11(1927), 371-84, 471-3; 12(1928), 372-92; 15(1931), 409-10, etc.)
89. 'Αγιορετικὴ Βιβλιοθήκη. 'Εν Βόλῳ.
   (See, e.g.: 1 (1936-7), Nos. 1, 1bis, 6, 7, 8, 9 pp. 30-42, 10, 11, 12; 2(1937-8), 9-34, 95-100, 111-130, etc.)
89a. Helikon, Rivista di tradizione e cultura classica dell'Università di Messina. Roma.
   (See, e.g.: 6(1966), 705-15.)
90. Jahrbuch der österreichischen byzantinischen Gesellschaft. Wien.
   (See: 3(1954), 161, 164; 4(1955), 2-6; 14(1965), 133-8.)

91. *Jahrbuch für Liturgiewissenschaft*. Münster in Westfalen.
    (See: 2(1922), 4-17; 3(1923), 114-16; 6(1926), 98, 101; 7(1927), 363.)
92. *Journal (The) of Roman Studies*. London.
    (Some material, e.g.: 37(1947), 70-73, 145-51.)
93. *Journal (The) of Theological Studies*. Oxford.
    (See: 47(1946), 201-203; N.S. 16(1965), 463-8.)
94. *Κρητικὰ Χρονικά. Κείμενα καὶ μελέται τῆς Κρητικῆς ἱστορίας. Ἡράκλειον Κρήτης.*
    (See: 15-16, 2 (1961-62), 113-39.)
95. *Κυπριακαὶ Σπουδαί. Δελτίον τῆς Ἑταιρείας Κυπριακῶν Σπουδῶν. Ἐν Λευκωσίᾳ Κύπρου.*
    (See, e.g.: 1(1937), 89-132; 3(1940), 31-50; 4(1940), 65-86, etc.)
96. *Kyrios*. Vierteljahresschrift für Kirchen- und Geistesgeschichte Osteuropas. Königsberg/Berlin.
    (See: 3(1938), 332; 5(1940-41), 12-23; N.S. 2(1962), 172-82; 5(1965), 144.)
97. *Μακεδονικά. Σύγγραμμα περιοδικὸν τῆς Ἑταιρείας Μακεδονικῶν Σπουδῶν. Ἐν Θεσσαλονίκῃ.*
    (See: 2(1941-52), 25-88.)
98. *Marianum*. Ephemerides Mariologiae cura Patrum Ordinis Servorum Mariae. Roma.
    (See: 24(1962), 471, 499, 519, 522-4, 528-32.)
99. *Musical (The) Quarterly*. New York.
    (See, e.g.: 23(1937), 201-9; 28(1942), 190-204; 29(1943), 254-6; 38(1952), 68-79; 39(1953), 223-31.)
100. *Νέα Φόρμιγξ.*
    (Inaccessible at present.)
100a. *Νέον Ἀθήναιον. Ἀθῆναι.*
    (See, e.g.: 5(1964-66), 5-26.)
101. *Ortodoxia*. Revista Patriarhiei Romîne. Bucureşti.
    (See: 13(1961), 55-80.)
102. *Proche-Orient Chrétien*. Revue d'études et d'informations. Jérusalem.
    (See, e.g.: 7(1957), 109, 154; 15(1965), 118-19.)
103. *Rassegna gregoriana per gli studi liturgici e per canto sacro*. Roma.
    (See: 1(1902), 111, 126-31; 4(1905), 385-412; 5(1906), 508-14.)
104. *Recherches de science religieuse*. Paris.
    (Some material, see, e.g.: 19(1929), 266-83.)
105. *Rivista di storia e letteratura religiosa*. Firenze.
    (See: 1(1965), 108.)
106. *Rivista liturgica*. Praglia (Padova)/Finalpia (Savona).
    (See, e.g.: 1(1914-5), 285; 2(1915-6), 209.)
107. *Ῥωμανὸς ὁ Μελῳδός. Θρησκευτικὸν περιοδικὸν σύγγραμμα ἐκδιδόμενον κατὰ μῆνα. Συντασσόμενον ὑπὸ τοῦ Μητροπολίτου πρ. Λεοντοπόλεως Σωφρονίου Εὐστρατιάδου. Ἐν Παρισίοις.*
    (See: 1(1932-33), 12, 25, 28-39, 53-54, 57, 67-94, 106-13, 117-21, 122, 372-410, 413-27, 445-7.)
108. *Studia Catholica*. Nijmegen.

(See, e.g.: 15(1939), 352-74; 16(1940), 108-17, 307-38; 17(1941), 33-46; 18(1942), 292-308; 20(1944), 15-19.)

109. *Studies in Eastern Chant.* [Oxford University Press] London.
  (See: 1(1966), 2-35, 57-64, 80-86, 97-106, 113-129.)

110. Ὁ ἐν Κωνσταντινουπόλει Ἑλληνικὸς Φιλολογικὸς Σύλλογος. Ἐν Κωνσταντινουπόλει.
  (See: 9(1874-75), 129; 10(1875-76), 10-22; 26(1894-95), 40-42, 193; 27(1895-99), 246-62.)

111. Σύμμεικτα. Βασιλικὸν Ἵδρυμα Ἐρευνῶν. Κέντρον Βυζαντινῶν Ἐρευνῶν. Ἐν Ἀθήναις.
  (See: 1(1966), 39-40, 45, 125-36.)

112. *Traditio.* Studies in Ancient and Medieval History, Thought and Religion. New York.
  (See, e.g.: 1(1943), 71; 8(1952), 418-23; 16(1960), 353-63.)

113. *Trudy Kievskoj Dukhovnoj Akademii.* Kiev.
  (See, e.g.: 1906, 1, 237-52.)

114. *Zapiski Imperatorskoj Akademii Nauk po istoriko-filologičeskomu otděleniju* (= *Mémoires de l'Académie Impériale des Sciences de St.-Pétersbourg.* Classe des sciences historico-philologiques). St. Peterburg.
  (See: VIIIe Série, 1,7 (1897), 23-161; 6,1 (1902), 75-86; 7,2 (1905), 79-90; 8,3 (1906), 63; 13,4 (1918), 41, etc.)

115. *Zbornik radova Vizantološkog Instituta.* Beograd.
  (See: 7(1961), 191-5; 8,1 (1963),302; 8,2 (1964), 393-8, 417-26, 451-8; 9 (1966), 258-9, 270, 272, 274, 275.)

PERIODICALS TO BE BROUGHT UP TO DATE

Aevum. Milano.
  Starting with vol. 33 (1959).
Analecta Bollandiana. Bruxelles.
  Starting with vol. 77 (1959).
Ἀρχεῖον Πόντου. Ἐν Ἀθήναις.
  Starting with vol. 19 (1954).
Archivio storico per la Calabria e la Lucania. Roma.
  Starting with vol. 28 (1959).
Archivum Fratrum Praedicatorum. Romae.
  Starting with vol. 29 (1959).
Ἀθηνᾶ. Ἀθήνησιν.
  Starting with vol. 63 (1959).
Bollettino della Badia greca di Grottaferrata. Grottaferrata.
  Starting with vol. N.S. 13 (1959).
Byzantinische Zeitschrift. München.
  Starting with vol. 52 (1959).
Byzantion. Bruxelles.
  Starting with vol. 28 (1958).
Eos. Wratislaviae.
  Starting with vol. 44,1 (1950).

'Επετηρὶς 'Εταιρείας Βυζαντινῶν Σπουδῶν. 'Αθῆναι.
Starting with vol. 29 (1959).
Ephemerides Liturgicae. Roma.
Starting with vol. 73 (1959).
Muséon (Le). Revue d'Études orientales. Louvain.
Starting with vol. 72 (1959).
Νέα Σιών. 'Εν 'Ιεροσολύμοις.
Starting with vol. 54 (1959).
Oriens Christianus. Wiesbaden.
Starting with vol. 43 (1959).
Orientalia Christiana Periodica. Roma.
Starting with vol. 25 (1959).
Revue des Études Byzantines. Paris.
Starting with vol. 17 (1959).
Revue des Études Grecques. Paris.
Starting with vol. 72 (1959).
Sacris Erudiri. Steenbrugge.
Starting with vol. 11 (1960).
Studi Bizantini e Neoellenici. Roma.
Starting with vol. 10 (1963); since 1964 name changed into *Rivista di Studi Bizantini e Neoellenici,* N.S.
Θεολογία. 'Εν 'Αθήναις.
Starting with vol. 30 (1959).
Vizantijskij Vremennik. Moskva.
Starting with vol. N.S. 15 (1959).

6

Simon Harris

LONDON, ENGLAND

The Communion Chants in Thirteenth-Century Byzantine Musical MSS.

THE koinonika, or Communion chants for the Greek Mass, are to be found in their earliest surviving form in a small group of thirteenth-century manuscripts which contain the melismatic repertoire of choral chants for the Byzantine Rite. By comparison with the other major repertoires of Byzantine Chant, this collection, known as the Asmatikon, is very modest in size. Indeed, in several sources its contents are included with those of the Psaltikon, or soloist's book, while even in those which preserve its independence it is usually to be found associated with a fairly large collection of miscellaneous chants. In a number of ways however the Asmatikon is an important collection and has recently attracted a fair amount of attention from scholars.

One of the reasons for its importance is the fact that, apart from a few chants which are to be found in the Psaltikon, the Asmatikon contains all the earliest known chants for the Byzantine Mass. Unlike the music for the Roman Mass, these chants are not arranged in cycles of ordinary and proper chants; in fact, for the Eisodikon, Trisagion, and Cheroubikon the Asmatikon provides only a single unvarying chant. The koinonika, however, form an extensive body of chants which are arranged in two cycles, one of them consisting of a variety of different texts and melodies for the major feasts of the year, the other consisting of cycles of melodies to three texts arranged in an oktoëchos—that is to say according to mode, one setting of each text in each mode. The koinonika therefore conform to the normal Byzantine pattern of a double cycle, seen also in the hypakoai, kontakia, and alleluias, with the important exception that several of the koinonikon texts are provided with six or more different melodies, a unique feature in both the Asmatikon and the Psaltikon.

Besides being small, the Asmatikon repertoire in the thirteenth century is preserved in manuscripts whose original distribution in the Byzantine area was very uneven. The eight or so to be found in Italian libraries all without any doubt originated in South Italy, while only one has so far been discovered from the rest of the area. The fact, however, that the repertoire was generally used throughout the Byzantine world is attested by the existence of three thirteenth-century Slavonic manuscripts, the so-called Uspensky, Blagoveshchensky, and Synodalny Kondakars.[1] The notation of these manuscripts is such that direct transcription from them is impossible, and comparison with Greek sources is likely to remain difficult until the notation is more fully understood. But it seems fairly certain that the koinonikon melodies which they contain are substantially the same as those preserved in Greek sources, and they are therefore of vital importance, at least as historical documents.[2]

The Greek manuscripts containing the Asmatikon repertoire are extremely heterogeneous. Four of them—Grottaferrata $\Gamma.\gamma.$ I, $\Gamma.\gamma.$ VI, $\Gamma.\gamma.$ VII, and the non-Italian source from Mt. Athos, Laura $\Gamma.3$—contain separately compiled Asmatika and follow a roughly similar scheme of arrangement. In all of them the Asmatikon seems to have formed only the first half or less of the whole manuscript, though we can only be sure of this in the case of the two complete ones, $\Gamma.\gamma.$ VII and Laura $\Gamma.3$. MS $\Gamma.\gamma.$ I seems to have lost all but the first forty or so

[1] The Uspensky MS has been published in facsimile by A. Bugge, *Contacarium Palaeslavicum Mosquense*, MMB, Principal Series, Vol. VI (Copenhagen, 1960). The other two MSS are, respectively, Leningrad Public Library, Q.I.32, and Moscow, Historical Museum, No. 777.

[2] The relationship between the Greek and Slavonic manuscripts was outlined by K. Levy in 'The Byzantine Communion Cycle and its Slavonic Counterpart,' *XIIme Congrès International des Études Byzantines* (Ochride, 1961), *Résumés des Communications*, p. 62. In a subsequent publication, 'A Hymn for Thursday in Holy Week,' *Journal of the American Musicological Society*, xvi (1963), Levy has compared the notation of the two traditions in the hymn Τοῦ δείπνου σου, which replaces the koinonikon for Maundy Thursday (pp. 139-45).

folios, but these contain at least three quarters of the Asmatikon, and we have probably lost no more than thirteen or fourteen koinonika from the yearly cycle. What remains of it suggests that it may have been the richest of all the surviving collections; it is the only manuscript to contain all three cycles of koinonika in the oktoëchos, it is the only Italian source for the Cheroubikon, and the richness of its yearly cycle is matched only by that of Messina 129. Although it would be wrong to regard the graffito on f. 17, linking the manuscript with Rossano, as evidence that it was a product of the scriptorium at the Patirion,[3] there is nothing in its contents to suggest that it could not have been compiled for use there. Finally, besides being one of the clearest and best produced of the Asmatikon sources, it is also the most reliable.

Of all the Asmatikon sources, $\Gamma.\gamma$. VI seems to have had the most eventful existence. It survives only as collection of four short fragments which, at some stage in its life, were rebound in an incorrect order, so that fragments 1 and 3 are the remains of the Asmatikon, while fragments 2 and 4 contain kalophonic chants and kontakia, written in a different hand and without red ink. In view of the fact, however, that the size and quality of the paper is the same throughout the manuscript, there is no reason to doubt that the surviving fragments all derive from a single source of the same kind as $\Gamma.\gamma$. VII. Judging from the koinonika that it contains, we can be fairly certain that its original repertoire was more comprehensive than those of $\Gamma.\gamma$. VII or Laura $\Gamma.3$, but not as rich as that of $\Gamma.\gamma$. I.

The arrangement of the three Italian Asmatika is practically identical, the only difference occurring in the position of the Dochai for Easter Week and the Sundays of Lent, which in $\Gamma.\gamma$.I are placed before the Eisodikon, and which have completely disappeared from $\Gamma.\gamma$. VI, if indeed they appeared there at all.[4] $\Gamma.\gamma$. VII in this respect follows the order of Laura $\Gamma.3$, but in most other ways the arrangement of the latter is quite different

---

[3] P. Batiffol, *L'Abbaye de Rossano* (Paris, 1891), p. 68, lists this MS as one having belonged to the Rossano library, and dates the hand of the graffito to the sixteenth century.

[4] See Dom B. di Salvo, 'Asmatikón,' *Bollettino della Badia Greca di Grottaferrata*, N.S. xvi (1962), p. 156. On pp. 144-153 this article contains a most useful comparative table of contents for the four Grottaferrata MSS., $\Gamma.\gamma$.I, $\Gamma.\gamma$.VI, $\Gamma.\gamma$.VII and E.α.XIII.

from that of the Italian manuscripts, as can be seen from the following comparative table:

Γ.γ. VII

I ff. 1-20. An oktoëchos of the whole Asmatikon, including the 8 hypakoai and 16 of the koinonika (the *'Αγαλλιᾶσθε* and *Αἰνετε* texts for Saturdays and Sundays respectively).

II ff. 20-41′ The hypakoai of the yearly cycle of feasts, including the Great Troparia for the Christmas and Epiphany vigils.

III ff. 42-45′ The Dochai for the complete ordinary week.

IV ff. 46-48′ The single Mass chants—Eisodikon, Trisagion, etc., with doxologies. No Cheroubikon.

V ff. 49-51′ The Dochai for Easter Week and the Sundays of Lent.

VI ff. 51′-71 The koinonika of the yearly cycle of feasts.

Laura Γ.3

I ff. 1-8′ The 8 hypakoai of the oktoëchos.
ff. 8′-9 Two settings of the *Πᾶσα πνοή.*
ff. 9-11′ 8 koinonika of the oktoëchos (the *Γεύσασθε* text only for the Lenten celebration of the Liturgy of the Presanctified. The Saturday and Sunday cycles have been lost from the manuscript).

II ff. 11′-23′ The koinonika of the yearly cycle of feasts.

III ff. 25-41 The hypakoai of the yearly cycle of feasts, including the Great Troparia.

IV ff. 41-43 Chants for the Dedication of the Church.

V ff. 44-50 The Dochai for the ferial days of the week, followed by additional troparia and doxologies.

VI ff. 50′-52 The single Mass chants—Eisodikon, Trisagion and Cheroubikon with doxologies.

VII ff. 52′-58 The Dochai for Sunday, Easter Week and the Sundays of Lent, followed by additional miscellaneous chants.

It will be seen from this that the contents of Laura *Γ.3* are both more heterogeneous in character and less tidy in their arrangement than those of the Italian manuscripts, which perhaps suggests that it belongs to an older tradition of arrangement.

The five Italian Psaltika containing Asmatikon chants show a wide variety of both contents and arrangement. The two largest of these, Messina gr. 129 and Vatican gr. 1606, are closely similar in form, arranging both Psaltikon and Asmatikon chants into two comprehensive cycles of an oktoëchos and a Proper. Thus the chants included above in sections II and VI of *Γ.γ*. VII are to be found scattered through the Proper, or yearly cycle, which constitutes the first two thirds of the manuscript; those in section I are in the oktoëchos, which in these manuscripts follows the yearly cycle. The chants found in sections III–V of *Γ.γ*. VII are, however, mostly absent from these manuscripts. Vatican 1606 contains those of section III—the Dochai for the ordinary week, associated with their respective prokeimena—in an appendage to the oktoëchos, but the equivalent part of Messina 129 has been lost. Apart from this Vatican 1606 only has the Trisagion for Solemn feasts, Ὅσοι εἰς Χριστὸν ἐβαπτίσθητε which is to be found among the chants for Christmas Day (f. 44).

The Psaltikon, Grottaferrata *Γ.γ*. V, compiled at the Messina scriptorium and dated 1225, shows yet another system of arrangement. In this, the comprehensive yearly cycle and oktoëchos is restricted to the Psalm formulas, hypakoai, and kontakia, while the alleluias, prokeimena, and koinonika are arranged in separate cycles, but are combined with the hypakoai and kontakia in the oktoëchos. The Asmatic hypakoai are excluded entirely from the manuscript, and in fact the only Asmatic chants represented are a very reduced set of koinonika, including only the Sunday cycle (the Αἰνεῖτε text) in the oktoëchos and very few duplicate text settings in the yearly cycle. In contrast to Messina 129 and Vatican 1606, *Γ.γ*. V is not a stylish production, even though it was copied at the scriptorium of S. Salvatore, but an ill-prepared palimpsest which may well have been destined for use elsewhere.

The two remaining sources for the koinonika, Grottaferrata E.a.XIII and Vatican, Borgia gr. 19, are even shabbier productions. The latter may perhaps be a fragment of a Psaltikon on the model of *Γ.γ*. V, in which only the yearly cycles of the alleluias and koinonika have been preserved. Both text and music are written in a crude, though tolerably legible hand, but this advantage is unfortunately outweighed by the fact that the musical notation of the koinonika is virtually meaningless. Like *Γ.γ*.V the repertoire of koinonika is a very reduced

E

one, containing few duplicate text settings. Moreover, although the manuscript probably originally contained an oktoëchos, the existence of three settings of the Αἰνεῖτε text at the end of the yearly cycle, none of which can be definitely identified with other known settings of the text, suggests that not even the Αἰνεῖτε melodies were included in the oktoëchos, and that the surviving collection of koinonika may therefore be complete.

Like Γ.γ. V and Borgia 19, E.a.XIII is a messy palimpsest, but in its arrangement it bears no resemblance to either manuscript. It appears to be complete, and contains two cycles—an oktoëchos and a yearly cycle—of hypakoai and koinonika only, though a few miscellaneous chants are added at the end. Unlike all the other manuscripts containing a comprehensive cycle, the oktoëchos here precedes the yearly cycle; and, more curiously still, while the oktoëchos contains both Psaltic and Asmatic hypakoai, the yearly cycle has only the Asmatic series. Apart from that of Borgia 19, the koinonikon repertoire of this manuscript is by far the smallest, with only the Αἰνεῖτε melodies in the oktoëchos and fifteen melodies in the yearly cycle, two of which are alternatives added at the end, and a third an obviously late addition in a kalophonic style.

This, therefore, is the complete list of sources for the koinonika, apart from one or two isolated copies of chants in other Italian Psaltika.[5] The most striking feature of the collection is its variability from manuscript to manuscript. Altogether there are rather more than sixty melodies, but no source contains the whole collection, the largest being Messina 129 with a repertoire of fifty-six. At the other end of the scale is E.a.XIII with a complete collection of twenty-three chants. It is true that Byzantine musical manuscripts do show a fair amount of variability in their contents, but this is clearly most exceptional, and is probably due at least partly to the existence of duplicate settings of the same texts. For it seems that while some communities tried to compile a comprehensive collection of these melodies, others were content with single settings. Moreover, the variability of the repertoire is paralleled both by a variability

---

[5] Messina gr. 120 contains two koinonika—those for Virgins and for Easter Sunday (ff. 10′ and 155); Grottaferrata E.β. I has the Asmatic hypakoe and koinonikon for the Dormition (f. 136′). Otherwise both these manuscripts contain only Psaltikon chants.

in the detailed arrangement of the koinonika in the yearly cycle, and by detailed divergences about precisely which settings of a text were to be sung on a particular feast. A careful comparison of the sources therefore is likely to reveal a fair amount about the development of the koinonikon repertoire, and about the different communities to which these manuscripts belonged.

But perhaps the most important feature of the koinonika is the information that they yield about the melodic tradition of the Asmatikon. Ever since transcriptions of the melismatic repertoire have been attempted, scholars have been puzzled by the enormous number of apparent mistakes or corruptions contained in the original texts, many of which are supported by all, or nearly all sources. An example of one such corruption in the Psaltikon is given by Wellesz in the introduction to his transcription of the Akathistos Hymn.[6] In the third line of the first oikos, the first note appears to be a third lower than the previous cadence on *g*; but the intervening mode signature is of the first plagal mode which would indicate that either the drop of a third should in fact be a drop of a fourth, or that if the line begins on *e*, an *f sharp* should be added in transcription, since a first plagal mode formula appears a tone above its correct position. In this particular case, Wellesz adopts the reading of a manuscript which, in effect, starts the new line a fourth below the previous one, but with a different melodic phrase.

There are three possible ways of approaching this problem. One is that, followed above, of correcting the melodic line by shifting it to the correct pitch; a second is to leave it as it stands, but to add no accidentals and instead to alter the preceding mode signature to one that is more plausible; the third is to alter nothing, and to add suitable accidentals to the transcription in order to preserve the correct interval values.

Clearly, the first of these methods provides the most satisfying solution, provided, of course, that there is sufficient manuscript evidence to suggest that it can be followed. But equally clearly, this procedure becomes completely arbitrary when there is no manuscript evidence to support it, firstly

---

[6] E. Wellesz, *The Akathistos Hymn, MMB, Transcripta* ix, pp. lx-lxi. The passage in question is line 3 of the first Oikos of the hymn, transcribed on page 5, 11.4-6 (εἰπεῖν τῇ Θεοτόκῳ).

because we do not know whether our correction is justified at all, and secondly because, even if it is, we have no means of deciding with certainty where it should be made.

The second procedure, however, seems to me even less satisfactory. It might be held that to refrain from inserting accidentals into a melody, where there is some doubt about the interval qualities, constitutes a properly non-committal procedure. It does nothing of the kind; though Byzantine notation fails to distinguish between tones and semitones, to refrain from inserting accidentals is to provide an editorial interpretation of the chant as much as to put them in. If we are really to make true sense of the melodies, this is precisely the sort of problem which it is the editor's job to solve; and simply to alter the relevant mode sign to one that seems more plausible looks very like an evasion of this responsibility, followed by a move to make the evasion look tolerably respectable.

The fact is, however, that in certain chants in the Psaltikon,[7] and in a truly alarming number of Asmatikon melodies, one of these procedures has to be followed if we are not to use accidentals in transcription, since there is no manuscript evidence of actual mistakes. In other words, there does seem to be strong manuscript evidence that melodic formulae could be transposed to different pitches relative to each other, and still retain their original interval qualities.

A full examination of this evidence would only be possible in a lengthy discussion of a sizeable number of melodies in transcriptions collating all available sources.[8] In the meantime, however, we can try to define the issues that are involved. The most important of these issues seems to me to be why we avoid the use of accidentals.

The Byzantine Papadikai, being handbooks of notation rather than theoretical works, provide very little information about Byzantine musical theory. What they do tell us suggests that it certainly did not attain the sophistication of Western theory, and probably remained quite rudimentary.[9] We know

[7] Some of these are described by C. Thodberg in *The Tonal System of the Kontakarium*, Hist. Filos. Medd. Dan. Vid. Selsk. 37, n. 7 (Copenhagen, 1960).

[8] I have already prepared a transcription of the koinonika, in an introduction to which I have dealt more fully with transcription problems than is possible here.

[9] O. Strunk in 'The Tonal System of Byzantine Music,' *The Musical Quarterly*, 28 (1942), pp. 190-204, gives a clear account of Byzantine musical theory, such

that, although the octave was recognized as an important interval, the fifth was in practice equally important, and that interval patterns were thought to repeat sufficiently exactly at the fifth for it to be possible for finals of a mode to lie a fifth apart. Thus Mode I could have finals on both *d* and *a*, which implied that melodic phrases associated with the first mode could occur at either pitch. This, by itself, suggests that melodic formulae might occur at two separate pitches a fifth apart within a single chant, and even perhaps that the transposition of sections of a chant up or down a fifth was not unacceptable to Byzantine musicians. Certainly, we cannot take the silence of the Papadikai on the subject of transposition as conclusive evidence that it was not practiced, either at the fifth or at some other less likely interval. For what emerges most clearly from them is that no definite species of scale over a whole octave had developed in Byzantine theory as it had at a very early stage in the West.

In Western theory on the other hand, we find an established scale of fixed notes in theorists of the tenth century—in fact before even a fully diastematic notation had been evolved. In this context, transposition would have been theoretically impossible if it involved an exact reproduction of interval values since it would have led to the use of notes which literally did not exist. This is precisely the reason given by Odo of Cluny for certain emendations which he recommends in the case of chants in which semitones fall in the wrong places; and by making such recommendations, Odo suggests that even in the West some melodic traditions required the use of accidentals which were intolerable to the theorist.[10] But if, in spite of the existence of a fixed scale whose semitones were clearly defined and beyond which chromatic notes were not even allowed an existence, unauthorized accidentals could occur at least in some oral traditions, how much more likely is it that they will occur

---

as it was. Of his two main sources, the Codex Chrysander, previously used by O. Fleischer (*Die Spätgriechische Notenschrift*, Neumenstudien III, Berlin, 1904) mentions the octave and the fifth as the two main intervals; the other, Vatican, Barberini gr. 300, seems to describe a modal system based wholly on the interval of a fifth (cf. L. Tardo: *L'Antica Melurgia Bizantina*, Grottaferrata, 1938, pp. 158 and 160).

[10] An English translation of this important passage is to be found in O. Strunk, *Source Readings in Music History* (New York, 1950), pp. 110-12.

in a melodic tradition whose notation did not even distinguish between tones and semitones, and whose theory, such as it was, gives no indication of an awareness of accidentals, let alone that they can cause problems? Considered in this light, the argument that because Western chant did not employ accidentals, transcriptions of Byzantine chant should not do so either, sounds most unconvincing. For it could be argued equally persuasively that because there is some evidence that the lack of accidentals in Western chant is due, at least partly, to deliberate suppression, the fact that there is no evidence of such suppression in Byzantine traditions should lead us to expect that occasional accidentals should probably appear in our transcriptions.

We therefore should admit that on this issue at least Western theory is an unreliable guide, and Byzantine theory offers no guidance at all. It follows that the only way of deciding the issue is from the musical manuscripts themselves.

Byzantine musical manuscripts do not distinguish between tones and semitones; but they do provide us with means by which we can infer this distinction, and in the majority of cases there is little doubt whether a tone or a semitone is intended. These means are the use of mode signatures both at the beginning and during the course of a chant, and the association with these of a number of clearly defined melodic formulae. If an incorrect signature, therefore, has been inserted we can usually tell that it is incorrect by the following melodic phrase. In the Psaltikon, these medial signatures occur throughout most chants with very great frequency, but in the Asmatikon, and in particular, in the koinonika, they are sparingly used, sometimes not even appearing once in the course of a substantial chant.[11] In most chants, however, a relatively narrow and well-defined range of melodic formulae is used making transcription a good deal easier and more certain than might at first be thought.[12]

---

[11] An example of such a melody is the koinonikon for Ascension, 'Ανέβη ὁ Θεός, in the course of which none of the five Italian MSS gives a medial signature.

[12] There are a few koinonika which do not adhere very closely to this repertoire of formulae—notably the long setting of Σῶμα Χριστοῦ (for Easter Sunday), found in Γ.γ. V and four other Italian manuscripts, and the extremely long Εἰς μνημόσυνον setting in Laura Γ.3 and three Italian MSS. Because of this stylistic difference, these chants are much more difficult to transcribe with certainty than other koinonika.

What does emerge clearly from attempts to transcribe the koinonika, is that in about a third of the chants melodic formulae, with or without mode signatures, are, at some point during the course of the chant, displaced, usually by a fourth or a second. The same phenomenon has been observed in the Psaltikon; but what makes the evidence of the Asmatikon so important is the extraordinary degree of unanimity between the manuscripts from South Italy. For in many of these cases of displacement, or transposition, there is no hint in any of the Italian manuscripts of the existence of an alternative reading— a fact which is made doubly significant by the fact that there is none of the fluidity in the Italian melodic tradition that is to be found in the Psaltikon. The result is that, whereas many of the melodies in the Psaltikon, notably the kontakia, have a melodic tradition of such complexity as to make collation almost impossibly complicated, the Asmatikon melodies can be collated quite easily.

The South Italian melodic tradition is, however, a local one, differing quite considerably from that of Laura Γ.3. Whether the latter belonged to a single, uniform tradition like that of South Italy, or whether the mainland of Greece had an Asmatic tradition more like that of the Psaltikon, is unlikely to be known until another Asmatikon source is discovered in this area. But since many of the differences between Laura Γ.3 and the South Italian manuscripts are slight, it seems unlikely that many wide divergences occurred elsewhere. The difference between the traditions is in fact a curious one; there is scarcely any difference between the length of the melodies and often exactly the same notes occur in both, but they are simply grouped or phrased differently. The resulting effect is that the version of Laura Γ.3 sound more florid—or more fluid—that of the South Italian sources more rigid. The main reason for this is that the South Italian manuscripts have more cadences, most of which tend to be on the mode final, while the cadences in Laura Γ.3 are both fewer and more varied. This is particularly noticeable in several chants in the fourth mode, in which cadences on the mode final (g in transcription) occurring in the South Italian tradition are replaced by cadences a tone higher in Laura Γ.3, as can be seen in the following koinonikon for St. Michael and All Angels (8 November):

The simpler and more flexible style of Laura *Γ*.3 in this and many other passages suggests that it may have an earlier origin than the South Italian style. But if this is so, it means that the greater insistence on the mode final in many of the South Italian melodies is no more than a correction of an earlier contrary tendency, and that if we are to gain a true picture of the koinonika in the thirteenth century we must transcribe both versions separately and compare them.

Several facts emerge from doing this which throw light on the subject of transposition. The most important is that, in a significant number of melodies, sections of the chant appear at different pitches in the two versions. In nearly all these cases, the transposed section is preceded in the South Italian version by a mode signature, but not in Laura *Γ*.3, which strongly suggests that, in these cases, the transposition was deliberately introduced in the South Italian tradition. The following case is from the koinonikon of the third plagal mode for the Liturgy of the Presanctified:

γγο κυ ου υ γγυ ρι χι ου ι ι ος δ΄ α γι α γγα να χα χα

α χα χα ου α α λε ε ε ε ε ου ε ου εγγε εγγε χε χε ου

ε ε ε ε ου ε ε να νε ου ε ε ε λου ι αγγα γγα

It will be seen here that the transposition of the middle section of the melody is preceded *and* followed by an appropriate mode signature in *Γ.γ.*1 which must have served to underline the alteration to the melody. But, more important than this, the alteration looks very like the correction of a version that was considered either wrong or uncomfortable to sing. The implication is that, right or wrong, *both* versions were actually sung.

Many other instances can be found in the koinonika of corrections or alterations of this kind both by the South Italian tradition as a whole and by individual manuscripts within it. A number of these alterations were a good deal less successful than the one shown above. In the koinonikon for Virgins we find considerable confusion in the South Italian version as the following example shows:

Undoubtedly some of the versions given above are unsatisfactory and would be rejected for purposes of transcription, but it is equally clear that the confusion cannot simply have arisen from scribal errors. On the contrary it looks very like a musical confusion over the pitch relationship of two halves of a chant.

The two examples given above strongly suggest that transposition was practised, at least in South Italy, and many similar cases in the koinonika show that, if it was, that it was not restricted to a few chants. Laura Γ.3 moreover affords abundant evidence that elsewhere, sections of chants were transposed, though since the melodic versions that it contains appear to have an earlier origin than those in South Italy, this cannot be demonstrated from comparisons with Italian manuscripts.

The issue of transposition cannot of course be settled from two cases, but it can be shown from them that positive evidence on the subject does exist, and must be taken into account when the melodies are transcribed.

But perhaps the most important reason for us to revise our present assumptions that transposition is inadmissible is the fact that the arguments used in defence of this assumption are self-defeating. For if we interpret apparent transpositions as scribal errors, we must find some convincing reason why so many errors of this kind could have persisted in so many sources without correction. The most ingenious explanation for this is that which attributes them to the changeover from a non-exact to an exact notation at the end of the twelfth century. It is, of course, quite possible that many mistakes occurred in this way, but so far, no concrete evidence for such mistakes has yet come to light, and in the melismatic repertoire, unless more paleobyzantine sources are discovered, such evidence is not likely to be forthcoming. There is also a further difficulty. We should expect manuscripts written in Middle Byzantine notation and copied from a manuscript in Coislin notation to date only from the early part of the thirteenth century. By, let us say, 1240, it seems reasonable to suppose that most of these errors would have been eradicated, and that manuscripts dating from the last two decades of the century, such as the Codex Ashburnham 64, would have contained very few, if any, of these mistakes. For if they *were* simply copyists' errors, they would have been easy enough to correct.

The fact that so many of them were not corrected has led to the further theory that the singer did not trouble to have them corrected since he already knew the melodies by heart. Again, this sounds initially convincing, but the implications are dangerous. If melodies really were sung by heart to the extent that manuscript versions were completely ignored, and therefore left uncorrected, we should have to conclude that all manuscripts are too unreliable for us to transcribe from them with any degree of certainty; and in practice this would mean that an editor has *carte blanche* to alter whatever he fancies, since his transcriptions are unlikely to be accurate, however closely he follows his sources.

The alternative objection is that the melodies, as they are preserved in thirteenth century manuscripts, are corrupt— that is to say, through having been mislearnt and altered by singers for so long, they had degenerated so much that a modern editor is at liberty to restore them to what he takes to be their original form.

There is, it is true, plenty of evidence of mislearning and alteration in the koinonika. Indeed the variations that occur between Psaltikon manuscripts, and the existence of two separate Asmatikon traditions clearly indicates that manuscripts were still only records of an oral tradition. But to ignore all evidence of transposition in the hopes of thereby restoring melodies to their original form is surely to go to extreme lengths in the pursuit of an unrealistic objective. There is evidence in the earliest typika that some koinonika were in existence three hundred years before our earliest sources. The processes of transposition, alteration and substitution which can be discovered from comparisons of different sources could have completely transformed melodies during such a period. However corrupt the thirteenth century sources may be, therefore, they are the only ones with which we can deal, and if we are to transcribe them at all we must take them as we find them.

It is, after all, not difficult to imagine how transposition might have occurred in the first place. Byzantine notation gives no indications of an absolute pitch standard, and many initial mode signatures give no indication of the point in its total range at which a melody begins. The chances of an untrained voice beginning too low or too high are therefore considerable, and even if a singer could manage a complete chant at a given pitch, he might well decide that the total range was inconveniently restricted, and that the second half could be sung more conveniently a fourth or fifth higher or lower. This seems to me the most likely explanation for the presence among the koinonika of melodies, like the koinonika for Virgins and for the Transfiguration, of particularly extended ranges. And it may be therefore that later corrections—or miscorrections— were made for the sake of convenience rather than of modal purity.[13]

[13] Since the completion of this article, another important source for the koinonika has come to light in northern Greece. The manuscript, from Kastoria and known as Kastoria 8, is a thirteenth-century Asmatikon with contents very similar to those of Lavra *Γ*. 3. A full description of its most interesting features is being prepared by Prof. O. Strunk. As regards the koinonika, the melodic tradition which it preserves is substantially different both from that of Lavra *Γ*. 3, and from that of the South Italian manuscripts. In certain ways, however, it agrees more closely with the latter, and this is especially true where evidence for transposition occurs.

7

Stefan Lazarov

SOFIA, BULGARIA

The Synodikon of Tsar Boril and the Problem of Byzantino-Bulgarian Musical Relations*

AMONG the documents of the Middle Bulgarian literature of the thirteenth century the Synodikon of Tsar Boril merits special attention. It contains historical references about the Council of Trnovo, convoked in 1211 to deal with the problem of the Bogomils and also about the establishment of the Patriarchate of Trnovo in 1235. In addition, it contains the text of an anathematization of the Bogomils and other heretics and detractors of the dogmas of the Church and acclamations in honour of Bulgarian rulers, queens, patriarchs, and noblemen. The whole work, however, is based on a translation of a Greek Synodikon. Under this designation (τὸ συνοδικὸν = collection, assembly) one finds in the Byzantine literature a special liturgical and dogmatic work dedicated to the defence of Orthodoxy. The type appeared for the first time in the eighth century, in the period of iconoclastic struggles, and became fixed in 843 at the occasion of a Council in Constantinople at which the victory of the Orthodox Church over the iconoclasts was celebrated. The significance of these documents, largely distributed from the ninth century on, is of great importance for the history of Byzantine culture.[1] The Bulgarian Synodikon, which carries the name of the

---

* Translated by Miloš Velimirović.
[1] Uspenskiĭ, F. I., *Ocherki po istorii vizantiĭskoĭ obrazovannosti* [Essays on the History of Byzantine Civilization] (St. Petersburg, 1892), pp. 7-8, 364.

nephew and of the usurper of the throne of the first three rulers of the Assan dynasty—Boril (1207–17), was compiled at the Tsar's own orders. That same Tsar convoked the Council of 11 February 1211 to deal with the Bogomils, and presided at its session. The oldest and unchanged sections of this Synodikon are those which were translated from Greek and which deal with the Council. The section containing the report about the establishment of the Trnovo Patriarchate, though of a slightly later date, is also an unvarying element of this Synodikon. Other sections of the manuscript were completed and developed during the following two centuries. Judging on the basis of two preserved copies, one from the fourteenth and the other from the sixteenth centuries, the Synodikon of Tsar Boril was conceived for practical purposes. The text of the Synodikon was to be read in churches during the first week of Lent, a recognition of the importance of spoken delivery of the text for its absorption by the faithful. It would be extremely difficult to find in the whole Bulgarian ecclesiastical literature another such document in which the nuances of intonation and of enunciation and other oratorical devices are so carefully annotated by means of remarks, such as: разлагом, велми г[лаголю]ще, and where even the indications of the speed of the delivery are so noted. These remarks, not hitherto studied in detail, represent an element of great interest for their musical significance.

Of even greater significance for musicological studies are the four texts with musical notation, which may be found in the oldest segment of the translated texts in the fourteenth-century manuscript, the so-called 'Palauzov Copy', which is at present in the Division of Manuscripts and Old Printed Books in the National Library 'Saint Cyril and Methodius' in Sofia, with the call-number 289(55). These texts are to be found respectively on folios: 2r, 2v-3r, 4r-4v and 6v. The Russian scholar T. D. Florinsky[2] and the well-known Bulgarian linguist B. Tsonev[3] were the first ones to pay attention to these texts. Both of these scholars agreed on their Greek origin and Florin-

[2] Florinskiĭ, T. D., *K voprosu o bogomilakh* [About the question of Bogomils], in *Sbornik uchenikov Lamanskogo* [Collection of Studies by the students of Prof. Lamanskiĭ] (St. Petersburg, 1883), p. 36.

[3] Tsonev, B., *Opis na rŭkopisite i staropechatnite knigi na Narodnata Biblioteka v Sofiia* [Description of Manuscripts and of Old Printed Books in the National Library in Sofia] (Sofia, 1910), p. 196.

sky associated them with the excommunication of heretics. The
Russian scholar M. G. Popruzhenko, who was also a professor
at the Sofia University and the author of the best available
study on this Synodikon of Tsar Boril, described it in detail and
demonstrated the purely practical reasons for this compilation.
Popruzhenko also cited the Greek texts[4] and state that 'upon
the reading of certain sections of the text of this Bulgarian
Synodikon, the singers stepped forward to sing in Greek those
sections which had just been read in a Bulgarian translation'.[5]
The same author considers it also strange that a Greek text
with its musical notation should appear in a Slavic document,
this being a curious phenomenon from several points of view:
paleographical, ecclesiastical, archeological and liturgical.[6]
The eminent French scholar Father J.-B. Thibaut was the first
musicologist to show an interest in these musical texts. In his
well-known study *Étude de musique byzantine. La notation de St. J.
Damascène ou Hagiopolite*, published nearly seventy years ago,
when enumerating ten valuable manuscripts, he listed in the
fifth place: 'Une belle copie du Synodique de Boris faite au
XIVe siècle (aujourd'hui conservée à la Bibliothèque nationale
de Sophia). Ce document est très précieux au point de vue de
l'histoire musicale des byzantins. Le texte du Ms., qui est en
slave, est parsemé de chants papadiques avec notation et texte
grecs, d'où nous pouvons conclure que les jugo-slaves n'ont pas
suivi l'exemple des sévéro-slaves, mais ont préféré la notation
damascénienne.'[7] Thibaut also published a facsimile of the
third musical text[8] to which he appended his transcription into
modern musical notation.[9] In another study of his, dedicated to
the notation of Kukuzeles, Thibaut represented some of the
neumes from the Synodikon in his paleographical chart, yet
without any further explications.[10] The facsimile reproduction
of the third musical text was published once more by the same

4 Popruzhenko, M. G., 'Synodik tsaria Borila,' in *Bŭlgarski starini* [Bulgarian
Antiquities], viii (Sofia, Bulgarian Academy of Sciences, 1928), p. xvii.
5 *Ibid.*, p. xviii.   6 *Ibid.*
7 Thibaut, J.-B., 'Étude de musique byzantine. La notation de St. Jean Damascène
ou Hagiopolite,' *Izvestiia Russkogo arkheologicheskogo instituta v Konstantinopolie*
[Bulletin of the Russian Archeological Institute in Constantinople], iii (1898),
pp. 140-1.   8 *Ibid.*, Plate No. 1.   9 *Ibid.*, p. 176.
10 *Idem*, 'Étude de musique byzantine. La notation de Koukouzélès,' *Izvestiia . . .*,
vi (1900), p. 370.

author in his book *Origine byzantine de la notation neumatique de l'église latine*.[11]

Approximately half a century later, the eminent Bulgarian scholar, Mme R. Palikarova-Verdeil, who resided in Paris, dedicated a whole chapter to the Synodikon in her book *La musique Byzantine chez les Bulgares et les Russes*.[12] Her main points can best be summarized in her own words: 'Le fait que les chants étaient écrits en grec dans un document officiel bulgare, mentionnant la présence des représentants les plus notoires de l'État et de l'Église, prouve que l'emploi du grec dans les chants était fréquent à l'époque. Les Bulgares, pendant un siècle et demi de liberté, sont donc restés aussi soumis à l'influence de la musique byzantine que pendant leur esclavage. . . . Ce manuscript est très important non seulement pour les Bulgares, car il montre leur complète dépendance musicale envers les Byzantines, mais également pour les Grecs, car il offre un échantillon de la notation byzantine du XIIIᵉ siècle, époque à laquelle les chants ont été composés. Le Synodik est un de ces manuscrits qui possèdent une notation intermédiaire entre la médiobyzantine et la néobyzantine, ce qui confirme la conviction de beaucoup de chercheurs que cette dernière est apparue progressivement. . . . Ce manuscrit montre que les Bulgares du XIVᵉ siècle adoptaient en même temps que les Byzantins les réformes de leur système musical.'[13]

Both of these scholars then agree on the point that the Synodikon of Tsar Boril is a document which, for the period under consideration, demonstrates the musical hegemony of the Greeks over the Bulgarians. Is this really so? Without an *a priori* acceptance or rejection of the conclusion of J.-B. Thibaut and of Mme Verdeil, we shall try to examine the essence of the four musical texts.

The appearance of texts with musical notation is itself quite significant. They were written with the same black (now faded to a brownish hue) and red ink with which the Slavic texts of this manuscript were written, and thus are harmoniously incorporated at their respective pages into the total body of the

---

[11] Paris, 1907, Plate 12. Through an unusual misprint the manuscript is referred to as 'Synodique de Paris,' p. 104.

[12] Published in the '*Monumenta Musicae Byzantinae*' series *Subsidia*, iii (Copenhagen, 1953).

[13] *Ibid.*, pp. 214-15.

F

manuscript. Although the rather homogeneous Bulgarian uncial script cannot be compared directly with the more recent Greek minuscule, and even less with the musical signs, it is still possible to reach the certain conclusion that the manner of writing is in all instances the same. This can be demonstrated, for instance, by a comparison of the ways in which some accents and abbreviations in the Bulgarian text are written with the notation of the neumatic signs *ison, petaste* and *klasma* in the musical texts.

The textual content of the first three musical pieces is revealed in advance by the Bulgarian texts, namely the Greek texts repeat what had just been read in Bulgarian.

The first piece with the neumatic notation has, in Greek: Θέρος καὶ ἔαρ. Σὺ ἔπλασας ταῦτα. Μνήσθητι ταύτης. which is preceded by: Лѣто й вѣснѫ създа ꙗ помѣни сїа. (this Bulgarian text is cited after the sixteenth-century copy, the so-called 'Drinov Copy' MS 432/634/, due to the fact that the folio which is supposed to have contained it is lacking in the 'Palauzov Copy'). The text in question is derived from Psalm 73, verses 17 and 18.

The second piece has the following text in Greek: Διὰ σταυροῦ τε καὶ τῶν πρὸ τοῦ σταυροῦ καὶ μετὰ τὸν σταυρὸν παθῶν τε καὶ θαυμάτον αὐτοῦ. which is preceded by Кр͗та ради же й прѣжде кр͗та й по кр͗тѣ (*fol. Ꙃr:*) стр͗темь и чюдесмь его. ('For the Cross and before the Cross and after the Cross with its sufferings and its miracles.') A note in front of the musical setting contains the specific indication that these are to be sung by the singers. The Greek text was never before read in full by any of the scholars who studied this manuscript.

The third musical piece has the following text in Greek: Αὔτη ἡ πίστης τὴν οἰκουμένην ἐστήριξεν preceded by a more elaborate Slavic version: Сй вѣ′ра ап͗лска, сй вѣ′ра ѿчска сй вѣ′ра православныхъ, сй вѣ′ра въселенжа оутвръди. (The Greek text: 'This faith strengthened the universe' whereas the Slavic texts has 'This apostolic faith, this faith of ancestors, this faith of the Orthodox ones, this faith strengthened the universe'.) Another note in front of the musical setting contains the indication that 'this too is sung by the singers.'

The fourth text reads: Οὐράνιε βασιλεύς τοὺς πιστοὺς φύλαττε ('Celestial King, protect the faithful') and has no Slavic equivalent preceding it. Its content, however, reminds one of the well-known prayer Βασιλεῦ ἐπουράνιε ('Rex coelestis') which has its place in the Vespers services.

All this indicates that the musical settings in the Synodikon of Tsar Boril are organically linked with the literary exposition and that the presence of music is not accidental. Let it be repeated that the musical settings are to be found in the translated part of the oldest section of the manuscript.

All musical pieces in the Synodikon are set in the Fourth Mode and their intonation signs (martyries) belong to two types. Among the thirty neumes utilized in the Synodikon, nineteen are cheironomic. Their high number already demonstrates that one is faced with a transitional stage between the Middle-Byzantine notation and the Neo-Byzantine notation, a point already stressed by Mme Verdeil. In my essay on the musical notation in the Synodikon[14] I have discussed this intermediary stage of the notation in this document comparing it with a Middle-Byzantine Sticherarion from the twelfth-thirteenth centuries, presently in the Ecclesiastical Museum in Sofia, and with the Neo-Byzantine 'Codex Rilensis' from the first half of the eighteenth century, MS 5569 in the Library of the Rila Monastery, which I discovered and was able to use in my studies.[15]

Thus in the Synodikon only a few of the neumes appear in graphic variants, as is the case with the Dyo Kentemata (No. 4 in the appended scheme), Kratema (No. 16) and Tromikon (No. 26) and these variants are not significant; the Ison (No. 12) appears in a variant as if it were combined with an Oligon (No. 1), whereas Elaphron (No. 9) has also a 'pointed' shape which can be found only in the fourth piece and seems to have been written in by a different hand. The neumes No. 27 and No. 28 are, respectively, Tromikon-Synagma and Tromikon-parakalesma (the latter resembles greatly the Psephiston-Parakalesma). The neume No. 30 has not been identified. As can be seen from the scheme of neumes on p. 75, it is similar

---

[14] Lazarov, St., 'Sinodikŭt na tsar Boril kato muzikalno-istoricheski pametnik,' [The Synodikon of Tsar Boril as a document for History of Music], *Izvestiia na Instituta za Muzika pri BAN* [Annual of the Institute for Music at the Bulgarian Academy of Sciences], vii (1961), pp. 15-19.

[15] *Ibid.*, pp. 67-8 where the facsimile reproductions of these two manuscripts were published for the first time.

in shape to the Neo-Byzantine Parakalesma as found in the Codex David Raidestinos in the Library of the Russian Archeological Institute in Constantinople, from the fourteenth century (after Thibaut)[16] indicated A in the scheme. It also resembles a kondakarian neume of the twelfth century in its Greek and Slavic variant as found in the MS Q.n.I.32 (Blagoveshchenski Kondakar) in the Public Library in Lenigrad (see B in the scheme),[17] and to a certain extent it also resembles a kondakarian neume in the now lost fragment from Chartres of the ninth century (?), as depicted under C.[18] It is doubtful that it has any resemblance to the sign D which appears in the Trephologion from the Monastery Zografou on Mount Athos.[19] Neume No. 30 is to be found only in the first and the fourth pieces in the Synodikon and it always appears in conjunction with three isons with a characteristic rhythm.

The first piece (Ex. 1) with neumatic notation in the Synodikon can be easily transcribed within the framework of its Mode provided that in the complex of neumes above the second syllable from the beginning, the Petaste is not treated as a voiceless ('a-fonos') sign but be counted here and elsewhere for both its agogic and its intervallic values. If this point were not heeded the transcription would end one tone lower and outside the Fourth Mode. In order to elucidate the validity of such a graphic form of the neume in question and also to make sure that nothing was missing in the slightly damaged sections of the manuscript, the first, second, and fourth pieces were photographed by means of infra-red photography, with the kind assistance of the experts in the Scientific and Technical Section of the People's Militia in Sofia. In this first piece the infra-red photograph did not reveal anything missing, leaving us with the supposition that the scribe had preference for some graphic forms and the way he wrote them down.

In transcribing the second piece into modern notation, I had assumed that the combination of Petaste+ Kentema in the third line may have been a scribal error and consequently transcribed

---

16 See note 10 above, Plate No. 2.
17 Uspenskiĭ, N. D., *Drevnerusskoe pevcheskoe iskusstvo* [The Old-Russian Art of Chanting] (Moscow, 1965), Plates ix and x.
18 Verdeil, *op. cit.*, p. 122.
19 Sobolevskiĭ, A. I., M. Lisitsyn, V. Metallov and A. V. Preobrazhenskiĭ, *Zografskiĭ trifologiĭ* [The Trefologion from Zografou] (Petrograd, 1913), Plate 5.

SCHEME OF NEUMES

I	II	III	IV
—	⌒	⌒◡	•• , ʺ	＼
1	2	3	4	5
⊂	ꜱ	ꜱꜱ	⌒⌒	ꜱ
6	7	8	9	10
×	⌣ ⌣	◡	//	⌐
11	12	13	14	15
⌒ ⌒	⌣	＼	～	⌣
16	17	18	19	20
⌐	⌒	ꞃ	⌣	⌐
21	22	23	24	25
ꜱꜱ	⨍	⨍	ꜱ	⌒
26	27	28	29	30

		a/		
⌒	⌒	⌒ b/	⌒	⌒
30	A	B	C	D

Ex. 1

it as a third (instead of a fourth) upward.[20] However, the infra-red photograph revealed at the end of that same line the con-tours of a group of neumes which clarified what was problematic (Marked No. 3 and with parentheses in the photograph: see Plate 3). The other easily reconstructed places are marked No. 1 and No. 2.

The third musical piece is the best preserved one. Thibaut's transcription differs from this one mainly in that he used the quarter-note as the basic unit of transcription and not the eighth-note here utilized. Further, by not bracketing the inserted syllable -χε- which is frequently encountered in melis-

[20] Lazarov, *op. cit.*, pp. 29-33.

Ex. 2

matic settings, he misread the word οἰκουμένην as οἰκοῦ μεχάνην (Sic!).

The fourth musical piece is on a folio which is considerably damaged (Plate 4). This particular page appears to have stuck to the following one (7r) and as a consequence both the text and the neumatic notation became smudged. The text lines appear to have been retouched twice at a later date and not very skilfully at that. In my previous study[21] I had suggested some reconstructions of the neumes, based more on intuition than on

[21] *Ibid.*, pp. 39-44.

Ex. 3

factual grounds. Now, with an infra-red photograph, many of the signs not seen clearly earlier became quite legible (Plate 5). Still, the reading of some neumes presents difficulties and remains uncertain, such as the second Oxeia in the first line (numbered 3 in the scheme) and another Oxeia in the third line (numbered 4) in front of a Tromikon which is now quite perceptible. All other neumes are easily reconstructed. In the line with the designation of the Mode, after the first two words 'τοῦ αὐτοῦ', it is possible, though with difficulty, to recognize letters which seem to read ἐθε which, I am assuming, may represent an abbreviation of ἐθελοντί meaning 'if desired.' The sign immediately following is the 'gamma' = Γ′ which has the numerical value of 3 and which, according to my assumption, seems to indicate that this whole text could be sung three times.[22] (See Plate 6 for the complete reconstruction.)

Ex. 4

The melismatic style of these pieces suggests that they may be considered prototypes for the 'papadike-style' of chanting. This fact unquestionably supports the thesis of Mme Verdeil

[22] Gardthausen, V., *Griechische Paleographie*, Bd. II (Leipzig, 1913), p. 345; Cf. Montfaucon, B. de, *Palaeographia graeca* (Paris, 1708), p. 345.

that the papadike style of chanting and the Neo-Byzantine notation represent the end result of a long evolutionary process. In this respect, this document presents an example of unusual interest.

Concerning the structure of each of these four melodies it is of interest to note that the Mode and its peculiar variants can be established without difficulties. This can best be demonstrated by using the method of Béla Bartók.[23] The literary texts are not syllabic verses and can, therefore, be considered as heterometric lines of text in which one has to take into account all supplementary (even inserted) syllables. The results of such an analysis are as follows:

FIRST PIECE

$$\_ \_ \_ \_ \ \underline{g^1} \ //$$
$$\_ \_ \_ \_ \_ \ \underline{d^2} \ ///$$
$$\_ \_ \_ \_ \_ \ \underline{g^1} \ ///$$

5, 6, 6, g¹. ⌐I.⌐ ⑤

1 2 3 4 5 6 7

Melody of 3 lines with a heterometric stanza of 3 lines

Tonic   g¹

Dominant   d²

Uppermost note f²

Tonal pivots   g¹, d²

Mode   Ionian
variety   hypophrygian

SECOND PIECE

$$\_ \_ \_ \_ \_ \_ \_ \ \underline{d^2} \ //$$
$$\_ \_ \_ \_ \ \underline{b^1} \ //$$
$$\_ \_ \_ \_ \_ \_ \_ \_ \ \underline{d^2} \ ///$$
$$\_ \_ \_ \_ \_ \_ \_ \_ \_ \_ \ \underline{g^1} \ ///$$

7, 4, 8, 10. g¹ ⑤ ⌊3⌋ ⑤

1 2 3 4 5 6 7

Melody of 4 lines with a heterometric stanza of 4 lines

Tonic   g¹

Dominant   d²

Uppermost note f²

Tonal pivots   g¹, d², b¹

Mode   Ionian
variety   hypophrygian

[23] Bartók, B., *Melodien der rumänischen Kolinde* (Wien, 1935).

THIRD PIECE

_ $\underline{g^1}$ /_ _ _ $\underline{c^1}$ ///

_ _ _ _ c^2 _ $\underline{a^1}$ //

_ _ _ $\underline{g^1}$ ///

FOURTH PIECE

_ _ _ _ _ _ _ _ $\underline{b^1}$ //

_ _ _ _ _ _ _ _ $\underline{e^1}$ //

_ _ _ $\underline{e^1}$ ///

_ _ _ _ _ _ _ _ _ _ $\underline{g^1}$ ///

5, 6, 4. g^1 $\boxed{IV}$ $\lceil 2 \rceil$ 9, 8, 4, 11 g^1 $\lceil 3 \rceil$ $\lfloor VI \rfloor$ $\boxed{VI}$

IV V VI VII 1 2 3 4 5   VI VII 1 2 3 4 5 6

Melody of 3 lines with a heterometric stanza of 3 lines	Melody of 4 lines with a heterometric stanza of 4 lines
Tonic g^1	Tonic g^1
Dominant c^1	Dominant e^1
Uppermost note d^2	Uppermost note d^2
Tonal pivots g^1, c^1, a^1, c^2	Tonal pivots g^1, e^1, b^1.
Mode variety Ionian hyperlydian	Mode variety Ionian undetermined

The musical notation is written out, on the whole, rather clearly. An experienced reader cannot confuse signs with one another. The scribe appears to have been well versed in writing the more recent minuscule of the Greek as well as the musical neumes, which, however, he did not represent in a calligraphic way. The writing seems to have proceeded with the utmost economy of space which, at times, resulted in a crowding of some neumes (like the Apostrophos and Hyporrhoë being copied underneath an Ison or Oligon, etc.). This sometimes creates some puzzles, as I already pointed out the necessity of interpreting all the signs in a peculiar neume-combination of the first piece in which the Petaste has to be read with its own value in addition to the other neumes superimposed above it. Of several similar places (which are not worth listing in full) one deserves some attention: in the beginning of the fourth line of text of the third piece there is an unusual combination of two Oligons atop one another separated by a Klasma. If both Oligons were to be counted the transcription would have taken the melody upward for the interval of a second and thus depart from the Mode in which it is written (Thibaut was then correct when he ignored it in his own transcription which we follow here too). Only a few steps further in that very same line there is the single appearance of the neume Kylisma in this manuscript. It seems to us that this neume is misplaced, as the character of the musical piece does not tolerate melismatic embellishment at that place.

The orthography of the text also contains some departures from the standard ways of spelling. Thus, for example, in the third piece the scribe used η instead of ι in the word: πίστης instead of πίστις. Strange also is the appearance of the nominative case in the fourth piece in the word βασιλεύς which, furthermore, has been written out without the 'sigma finalis'. Other instances of such variants are: πιστειούς instead of πιστούς; φύλαττε and φύλατε. The graphic form of the letter F = Φ is unusual in the fourth piece. According to Gardthausen[24] such a form of the letter is not normally to be found in the minuscule of the period, but in a rather archaic form of the fourth century.

These various points indicate that the copyist of this manuscript seems to have been well-versed in Byzantine hymnography, but that he committed some errors which, if even some more recent experience can be adduced, result from adherence to models while writing and not from free, direct, creative writing. In a number of instances where letters appear grossly stylized (ypsilon in the fourth piece) it can clearly be seen that the scribe is involved in a copying process. The orthographic

[24] Gardthausen, *op. cit.*, Plate 4b, 1.

mistakes lead us also to believe that the scribe was not necessarily a Greek though he may have known the language, that he was apparently writing phonetically, and that therefore he may easily have been a Bulgarian.

A paleographic analysis of the letters indicates that the shapes of letters belong to the more recent minuscule type and that they show great similarities to letters found in Byzantine manuscripts of the thirteenth and even the first quarter of the fourteenth centuries.[25] Due to the presence of some of the 'great hypostases' in the musical notation in the Synodikon, the manuscript cannot be dated earlier than the middle of the thirteenth century. We believe that the neumes show considerable similarity to the neumes with which the Akathistos Hymn is notated in the Codex Ashburnhamensis in Florence, dated in the second half of the thirteenth century.[26] On these grounds we feel impelled to reject the assumption of Mme Verdeil that the music found in the Synodikon of Tsar Boril was composed in A.D. 1211.[27] It seems rather that the neumatic notation is contemporary with the period in which this manuscript, the so-called 'Palauzov Copy', was written and that its immediate model must have been another Greek manuscript of the second half of the thirteenth or first half of the fourteenth centuries. As a consequence of this assumption, we have to presume the existence of another manuscript which must have been written in the period *after* the original writing of the older sections of the text in the Synodikon of Tsar Boril in the beginning of the thirteenth century and *before* the actual writing of the manuscript available to us. The latter, i.e. the 'Palauzov Copy', thus incorporated some features from that 'presumed' Greek model which is at present unknown to us. If we were to adopt the point of view of Mme Verdeil ('. . . le MS date du XIIIe siècle, mais les chants ont été composés en 1211')[28] we would face a mystery as to why the texts of the chanted pieces were not translated (and even notated!) into Bulgarian. This would have been required by the solemn circumstances which led to the writing of the manuscript, and would have been appropriate

---

[25] *Ibid.*, pp. 225-38, Plate 9, cols. 10, 14; Plate 10, col. 10.
[26] Wellesz, E., *The Akathistos Hymn* (*Monumenta Musicae Byzantinae*, series *Transcripta* ix, Copenhagen, 1957), pp. xxxix-xl. Cf. also Lazarov, *op. cit.*, pp. 58-9.
[27] Verdeil, *op. cit.*, pp. 214, 205.   [28] *Ibid.*, p. 205.

and in accord with the preparation of the whole Synodikon in its Bulgarian form. The fact that the pieces were copied in Greek seems to point unquestionably to the Greek origin of these musical pieces. Clearly they are of Byzantine origin and their texts could in no way be the product of a Bulgarian man of letters. They were simply copied into a Bulgarian document. There are no traces of Bulgarian influence in the musical versions of these pieces as there is not a trace of Bulgarian ductus in the writing of the letters in the texts of the musical pieces. As for the neume No. 30, as pointed out, one encounters a much greater degree of resemblance to signs in various stages of Byzantine musical notation than to that in the Zografou Trephologion. The creative element encountered in the bilingual manuscripts from Moldavia in the sixteenth and seventeenth centuries[29] is totally lacking. There is not even that tendency toward originality which one finds in the *Psalterium Bononiense* of the thirteenth century.[30] In other words, the musical notation in the 'Palauzov Copy' of the Synodikon represents the result of a dogmatic and liturgical tradition which was not easily subject to change.

In A.D. 1211, at the time of its appearance, the Synodikon of Tsar Boril was a document bearing witness to a deeply divided society. Until the Turks conquered Bulgaria in 1396, the Synodikon preserved its character as a document supporting the Church and the State against the popular unrest and anti-feudalistic strivings, in the first place of the doctrines of the Bogomils.[31] Tsar Boril needed it just as much as did his successors Ivan-Alexander (1331–71) and Ivan-Shishman (1371–93). This being the case, it is only natural that, the first document of that type in Bulgarian literature, everything that might have been found in its Byzantine model was translated and transmitted in the Bulgarian version, including the music as well. It remains unknown, however, whether in the oldest version of 1211 there were musical pieces. The absence of these in the later sixteenth century copy of the Synodikon ('Drinov Copy') is inexplicable.

29 *Ibid.*, pp. 215-19.   30 *Ibid.*, pp. 222-7.

31 *Istoriia na bŭlgarskata literatura, T. I: Starobŭlgarska literatura* [History of Bulgarian Literature, Vol. I: Old-Bulgarian Literature] (Sofia, Bulgarian Academy of Sciences, 1963), pp. 262-6.

Under these circumstances it seems that the thesis of Mme Verdeil, of a 'dépendence musicale complète' of Bulgaria on Byzantium may be too strongly stated. The existence of musical pieces in the fourteenth-century copy of the Synodikon, in this writer's view represents an important if not unique case in the ancient history of Bulgarian music. It shows a peculiar type of Byzantino-Bulgarian musical contact. The Bulgarian priests and writers were undoubtedly familiar with the Byzantine musical notation and could have used it freely, because they were well versed in Greek as well as in Latin and knew the proper forms for formulations of liturgical and of official statements. It would be a tremendous mistake not to take into account the extent of Byzantine influence on the culture of the Christian countries of the Balkan Peninsula, South Eastern Europe and even Eastern and Northern Europe. Yet it is just as much of a mistake to exaggerate the degrees of this influence. The word 'influence' presupposes the existence of bilateral contacts. Influence can stimulate the creative imagination of the 'receiving' nation and need not represent a submission and/ or cultural assimilation. The significance of the Synodikon of Tsar Boril is truly great, not least in the realm of Byzantino-Bulgarian musical relations which are still not yet sufficiently studied.

8

Maureen M. Morgan

ARDSLEY, NEW YORK

The 'Three Teachers' and their Place in the History of Greek Church Music

THE music currently in use in the modern Greek Church is based upon the musical theories and the notational principles devised by Chrysanthos of Madytos and his two collaborators, Gregory the Protopsalt and Chourmouzios the Archivist.[1] These music theories appeared in print for the first time in a treatise entitled *Introduction into the Theory and Practice of Church Music* published in Paris in 1821 and were later presented in the *Mega Theoretikon*, published in Trieste in 1832.[2] Chrysanthos claimed that the foundation of his musical system was rooted in that of Greek Classical Antiquity, and his countrymen, in succeeding generations, accepted this assertion of a historical connection with complete trust and assurance. By the end of the nineteenth century, however, European musicologists began to take issue with these claims and to lament the destruction of the Medieval Byzantine tradition.

Who are the 'Three Reformers' as they are called? In the Near East, where the anonymity of the artist is traditionally maintained, biographical details about these men are sparse. It is known that Chrysanthos lived from 1770 to 1846, that he was well-educated by ecclesiastical standards of the time, with

---

[1] The only extensive biographies of all three reformers are to be found in Georgeios Papadopoulos' book Συμβολαὶ εἰς τὴν ἱστορίαν τῆς παρ' ἡμῖν ἐκκλησιαστικῆς μουσικῆς (Athens, 1890), pp. 329-35. Madytos is a village in the area of the Gallipoli Peninsula.

[2] The first of these, Εἰσαγωγὴ εἰς τὸ θεωρετικὸν καὶ πρακτικὸν μέρος τῆς ἐκκλησιαστικῆς μουσικῆς was not accessible to me. The second has as its title: Θεωρετικὸν μέγα τῆς μουσικῆς. In accord with accepted practice I refer to it as *Mega Theoretikon*.

a good knowledge of Latin and French, and that he was familiar with European as well as with Arabic music, being proficient as well in playing the European flute and the Arabic 'nay'. He had learned the art of Church psalmody from Peter Byzantios, a protopsalt, who in turn had been a pupil of Peter Lampadarios of Peloponnesus, probably the most important figure in Greek Church Music between the Fall of Constantinople in 1453 and the time of Chrysanthos. As an archimandrite, a rank which in the ecclesiastical hierarchy is equivalent to an abbot of a monastery, Chrysanthos was somehow and somewhere responsible for the teaching of music.[3] In such a position he became acutely aware of the need for more clarity in the process of studying and understanding of music. To facilitate this and simplify the teaching of this difficult art he invented a set of monosyllabic sounds for the musical scale in a kind of *sol-fa* system.[4] In addition to that he also made a number of 'interpretations' of traditional melodies. It is difficult to render correctly the exact meaning of the word 'interpretation' as used in this context. The Greek verb used to describe his activity—ἑρμηνεύω—does not carry the implication of a personalized understanding but rather the implication of apprehending the meaning of a given work. It could also imply a translation; in this case the old and traditional music being translated from the old notation into the new one. Without a thorough study and comparison of earlier documents and of the later versions one can only guess at the degree of authenticity and accuracy of any music that has thus been 'interpreted.'

For this break with the traditional methods of teaching, Chrysanthos is said to have been exiled to Madytos by order of the Patriarch in Constantinople at an unspecified date. Yet, this did not apparently stop the archimandrite from pursuing his original approach to the teaching of ecclesiastical music. In Madytos he found that his pupils were able to learn in ten months what had formerly taken ten years. The crucial device speeding up the process of learning appears to have been his use of newly invented solmization syllables. According to

[3] Papadopoulos, *op. cit.*, p. 333.
[4] The equivalents of Chrysanthos' syllables in the Western European solmization system are:

$$\Pi\alpha \; — \; Bov \; — \; \Gamma\alpha \; — \; \varDelta\iota \; — \; K\varepsilon \; — \; Z\omega \; — \; N\eta$$
$$\text{Re} \; — \; \text{Mi} \; — \; \text{Fa} \; — \; \text{Sol} \; — \; \text{La} \; — \; \text{Ti} \; — \; \text{Do}$$

G

tradition, his success in imparting musical knowledge to others was discovered in an unusual way: Once, the story goes, Meletios, the Metropolitan of Heracleia,[4a] was supervising the building of his house in a locality referred to as Tzibalio when he heard the masons, who had come from Madytos, singing from the top story of his house. They were performing traditional melodies of Church Music, the so-called *Koinonika* (communion hymns) and the *kalophonic Heirmoi* with great ease. The Metropolitan asked for an explanation of this remarkable feat. The masons then explained that their countryman, Chrysanthos, had used the easiest method in teaching this holy art. The responsible members of the Church hierarchy soon realized that they had acted unwisely toward the archimandrite and he was recalled to Constantinople. The Holy Synod of the Greek Church then gave Chrysanthos a free hand to teach music as he saw fit.[5]

It was at this point that he joined forces with Chourmouzios and Gregory, both of whom apparently had less formal education than Chrysanthos, yet according to their biographies possessed a great natural ability for music.

Gregory was a son of a priest and was born in Constantinople in 1777, on the same day on which Peter Lampadarios died. In his youth Gregory was self-taught, gaining some musical experience in a nearby Armenian Church. This apparently displeased his father, who removed him from the Armenians and sent him to a monastery farm on the island of Crete. Later on, because of his natural ability for singing he became apprenticed to Jakovos the Protopsalt and afterwards to Peter Byzantios and a George of Crete.[6]

Jakovos and George of Crete are also listed as teachers of Chourmouzios, who was born on the island of Halke, sometime around 1780. He is said to have served as a protopsalt in Tetroulos before becoming a teacher in the Third Patriarchal Music School from 1815 to 1821.[7]

The sources presently available are very imprecise as to the exact role of each of the three reformers, but there are general statements of the area in which each one of them specialized.

[4a] There are many places of this name. The one referred to here appears to be near Constantinople.

[5] Papadopoulos, *op. cit.*, pp. 333-4.

[6] *Ibid.*, pp. 329-30.   [7] *Ibid.*, pp. 331-2.

Chrysanthos, who had already devised his solmization syllables, began working on the systematization of the Greek Modes
and on a definition of the exact tonal relationship of one Mode
to another. This the Greeks call 'parallage', using this term to
designate the basic knowledge of the relative position of each
Mode. The term that indicates the reckoning or counting of the
'size' of each interval is 'metrophonia'.[8]

Gregory also participated in the determination of the types
of intervals within a scale. His larger contribution, however,
was in the clarification of the rules of modulation from one
Mode into another. Signs used to designate a modulation,
known as 'phthorae', were then divided into three 'families',—
diatonic, enharmonic, and chromatic. Each of these families has
its own set of 'phthorae.' There were 'phthorae' in medieval
Byzantine music and their use had been much refined during
the intervening centuries.

According to Chourmouzios' biography he managed to fill
some seventy volumes with his own 'musical interpretations' of
the works of the great figures of Greek Church Music. In other
words Chourmouzios is credited with having 'reinterpreted' the
complete works of the following composers: John Koukouzeles,
John of Kladas, Germanos of Neon Patron, Manuel called the
'New Chrysaphes,' Peter Glykis called 'Bereketis', Daniel the
Protopsalt, Peter Lampadarios of Peloponnesus, Jakovos the
Protopsalt, Peter Byzantios, Theodore Phokaeus, and Manuel
the Protopsalt. This collection was presumably deposited in the
library of the Metochion of the Holy Sepulchre in the Phanar.[9]
Without access to this body of chants one can only respond to
this list with incredulity! Again, one must become concerned
about the exact meaning of the word 'interpret'. Chourmouzios
also established the rules of musical orthography, that is, of the
correct writing of the musical characters according to the revised
system of musical notation.

Gregory's contribution to the new method of musical notation was the elimination of certain signs which were not essential
to the direction of the melodic movement. In this condensed or

[8] Jørgen Raasted, *Intonation Formulas and Modal Signatures in Byzantine Musical Manuscripts*, Monumenta Musicae Byzantinae, Subsidia, vii (Copenhagen, 1966), p. 45.

[9] Papadopoulos, *op. cit.*, p. 331. For data about these composers see the respective entries in the same book.

reformed notation he devised all the possible combinations needed for the three families of modern Greek Church Music, diatonic, enharmonic, and chromatic, within the framework of the eight Modes. He was apparently as detailed in his explanations as was Chourmouzios in his work, since one is told that Gregory's contribution filled some 1281 pages in a 'Papadike' collection. Gregory composed many pieces of his own, among them Cherubic hymns, Koinonika, Polyelea (hymns using the text of Pss. 134 and 135), Doxologies and verses for 'stichologia.'[10]

These three musicians are said to have developed their new method of music theory and to have presented it in 1814 to their superiors. Patriarch Cyril VI and the Holy Synod, after being at first suspicious about the motives of these three men, finally became convinced of the worthiness of their efforts.[11] As a result of these deliberations, Gregory was promoted to the position of a lampadarios and he and Chourmouzios were then appointed as instructors in the practice of music, while Chrysanthos was appointed an instructor in theory of music.[12]

In a special school, founded in 1815 and later called the Third Patriarchal Music School, knowledge of the new method was disseminated.[13] Letters were sent from the Patriarchate to all the provinces urging promising students to come to Constantinople. Even those without financial resources were admitted for two years' free study of music. At the end of this period a certificate was issued to each student stating that he was now qualified to teach the necessary foundations of the new theory

---

10 *Ibid.*, p. 330.

11 The Introduction to the *Mega Theoretikon* and the account in Papadopoulos' book refer to Patriarch Cyril VII but since his dates are 1855-60 this is an obvious error. The dates for Cyril VI are March 1813 to December 1818. Cf. *Dictionnaire d'Histoire et de Géographie Ecclésiastique*, xiii (Paris, 1956), s.v. 'Constantinople', column 633.

12 *Mega Theoretikon*, Introduction, p. 6 (letter-numbered).

13 The numbering of the Patriarchal Music Schools apparently did not take place until the appearance of Papadopoulos' listing in his book, pp. 370-6. Following are the dates of each school:
> First Patriarchal Music School—1727-?
> Second Patriarchal Music School—1776-91
> Third Patriarchal Music School—1815-21
> Fourth Patriarchal Music School—1866-8
> Fifth Patriarchal Music School—1868-72
> Sixth Patriarchal Music School—1882-?

of music. In this way the new approach to ecclesiastical music reached a nearly maximum exposure in a minimum of time. The school survived until about 1821. By that time Chrysanthos had been appointed Bishop of Dyrrachion[13a] in 1819 and Gregory had risen to the position of a protopsalt in the 'Great Church' where he served for three years until his death in 1822.[14] Chourmouzios became 'archive-keeper' at about that time. He was later instrumental in establishing a print shop in the Phanar section of Constantinople and is reported to have lived until 1840.[15]

In Dyrrachion, according to tradition, Chrysanthos' pupils became skilled musicians under his teaching. Many decades after his tenure in Dyrrachion, the people in that province were able to compete successfully for participation in a special chorus for religious holidays. Chrysanthos went from Dyrrachion to Smyrna in 1833 and from there he went on to become Metropolitan of Proussis[15a] in 1836, where he remained until his death in 1846.[16]

For more than fifty years the musical theories and practices of Chrysanthos remained unchallenged. The changeover to his method of learning Church Music was complete. The obvious simplicity of the new method of musical notation, as opposed to the excessively complex old system, encouraged the success of Chrysanthos' teachings. However, in 1881 a Patriarchal Commission was formed by Patriarch Joakeim III to correct what were simply termed 'mathematical errors.'[17]

In determining the intervals in his scales, Chrysanthos had divided the octave into 68 parts, called 'moria,' and then used

[13a] Slavonic Drač, Albanian Durrës, Italian Durazzo. A port on the Adriatic, now in Albania.

[14] The term 'Great Church' refers to the Hagia Sophia cathedral in Constantinople. It is unknown at present to which church this term may have been applied during the Turkish rule. It may have been a simple title without practical meaning at the time.

[15] *Mega Theoretikon*, Introduction, p. 8 (letter-numbered); Papadopoulos, *op. cit.*, p. 332.

[15a] Bursa, near the sea of Marmara.

[16] The exact date of Chrysanthos' death appears to be disputed. Papadopoulos, p. 333, states that he died in 1843, yet the pertinent entries in the Θρησκευτική καὶ Ἠθικὴ Ἐγκυκλοπαιδεία, Vol. 10 (Athens, 1967), s.v. 'Prousa', col. 679, agree on the year 1846.

[17] Constantine Maltezos, 'Sur les gammes diatoniques de la musique ecclésiastique grècque,' Πρακτικὰ τῆς Ἀκαδημίας Ἀθηνῶν, iv (1929), pp. 331-2.

the ratio 12 : 9 : 7 as the basic pattern for successions of intervals. The origin of his scale will be discussed later. When the Patriarchal Commission convened it discovered that Chrysanthos' scale would not divide mathematically in those proportions. However, the Commission, even though it was aware of this fictitious division, chose to ignore its own findings and decided to take measurements of intervals from live chanting. The music that the Commission took as a base was said to have come from 'long ago'! Yet the singing in Greece had been influenced for at least sixty years by Chrysanthos' teaching methods. Therefore, the singing that was assumed to be 'ancient' and 'traditional' merely reflected the effect of the new music theories that Chrysanthos had so efficiently promulgated between 1814 and 1819. Though the committee was conscientious in its efforts, the ultimate effect of its findings on the real live music as practiced in the modern Greek Church remained nonexistent.[18]

The controversy over Chrysanthos was again revived in 1898 by Jean Baptiste Thibaut, a French Assumptionist monk and scholar with extensive travel experience in the Near East. He pointed out that the teacher of all three reformers, George of Crete, had conceived the idea of condensing the 'Great Hypostaseis' (meaning the 'great signs'), that had been evolving from the time of Koukouzeles in the fourteenth century.[19] As George of Crete was unable to execute his own plan he suggested that his students, Chrysanthos, Gregory, and Chourmouzios carry on the work of reform. They were unwilling at first to proceed without their master's counsel, but the lack of time and the subsequent sudden death of George of Crete in 1816 compelled them to proceed without him.[20]

Thibaut deplored the complete and total acceptance of the *Mega Theoretikon* by everyone in Greece. Even more incredible,

---

[18] *Ibid.*, p. 333.

[19] There is some confusion in the existence of both a Gregory and a George of Crete. Thibaut and Rebours in their writings mention both of these names, yet research has failed to trace any Gregory. However, George of Crete is well documented. One can only assume that a *lapsus calami* created two individuals where one existed and that the slip was then perpetuated. See the entry No. 24 in Θρησκευτικὴ καὶ ’Ηθικὴ ’Εγκυκλοπαιδεία, Vol. 4 (Athens, 1964), s.v. 'Georgios', col. 481.

[20] *Ibid.*; see also J.-B. Thibaut, 'La musique byzantine et le chant liturgique des Grecs modernes,' *La Tribune de St. Gervais*, iv (1898), p. 244.

according to Thibaut, was the supreme faith even among educated Greeks that Byzantine musical theory was still intact and nearly untouched by the passage of time.[21] He argued that this great teaching manual had neither regard nor respect for the ancient theory of music and that Chrysanthos' first and clear result was to change the true nature of Byzantine Chant: 'L'idée d'une réforme pour la musique byzantine était bonne en elle-même; il faudra toujours regretter sa mise à éxécution, car elle fut déplorable. Sans doute, l'oeuvre des trois réformateurs n'est pas toute à blâmer; plusieurs de leur innovations ont été très heureuses et avaient leur raison d'être. Tel fut, par example, le complément apporté aux signes rhythmiques; mais, à côté de quelque bonne modifications, combien d'autres sont à déplorer!'[22]

Thibaut assumed that Chourmouzios was the more knowledgeable in reading and understanding Byzantine manuscripts because of his extensive 'interpretations' mentioned earlier, and regretted that Chourmouzios seemed to have had the least amount of influence on the total reform.[23] He also pointed out that the simplification of the music notation was started by Gregory the Protopsalt as far back as 1805, and that it followed the abridged system of George of Crete.[24] This, however, was only a beginning and further simplification was in order. The new system reduced the number of ancient signs but complicated things by adding many new and strange signs. The so-called signs of cheironomy were a particular problem to Thibaut since 'only a dozen found grace with the reformer. It was a veritable extermination!'[25]

According to Thibaut the cheironomical characters were replaced by the hypostatic signs (ὑποστατικὰ σημεῖα). The illogical naming of some of the signs especially distressed him. For example, the hypostatic sign called 'heteron' (ἕτερον) was originally the second one of two similar signs, the first being 'parakalesma' (παρακάλεσμα) and the second 'heteron parakalesma' (meaning 'another parakalesma'—ἕτερον παρακάλεσμα). The decision to drop one of these signs and call the remaining one merely 'heteron' is indeed illogical.[26]

[21] Ibid., p. 245.
[23] Ibid., p. 246.
[25] Ibid., p. 247.
[22] Ibid.
[24] Ibid.; see also note 19, above.
[26] Ibid.

In addition, Thibaut complained that the Greeks had made the question of intervals the main point of their music. To him it appeared to be an indigestible compilation of principles and definitions, all borrowed from the ancient Greek theoreticians.[27]

The second part of the *Mega Theoretikon* is merely a list ('a very incomplete list,' says Thibaut) of Byzantine composers whose names, recognizable for the most part, are to be found in manuscripts of liturgical chant. Though Thibaut is severe in his opinion of Greek scholars in writing about their own music, he does give praise to Tzetzes, who is 'one of the rare if not the only one among the Greeks who has taken the trouble to consult the old documents before publishing studies on religious music. Although the true theory of Byzantine Modes eluded Dr. Tzetzes completely, it did so to many others as well. . . . (Though Tzetzes says much, little of it is clear) and this, we can say in all frankness, is the fault of most of the Greeks who have published studies on Oriental sacred music. One of the most famous protopsalts in Pera, M.E.P. sketched the situation by saying: 'Monsieur, nous avons trop de phraséologues!' 'Truly,' Thibaut continues, 'I have asked myself more than twenty times, when I read some articles on the Greek Chant, how could one write two long columns in a periodical on a specific subject and not say a thing about it; one must confess—c'est là un tour d'adresse qui requiert un subtil mais réel talent!'[28]

It is obvious that Thibaut's real interest was in restoring medieval Byzantine music, and his sympathy did not extend to the nineteenth-century Greeks and their 'interpretations' of ecclesiastical music.

Eight years after Thibaut wrote his three articles in the *Tribune de St. Gervais*,[29] another French musicologist, Jean Baptiste Rebours, published what may be the only exhaustive study of the Chrysanthine system in the West, *Traité de Psaltique* (Paris, 1906). In the introduction Rebours reminds one of Thibaut when he says in a true Gallic superlative, 'le fait est que nous ne sommes pas ici en présence d'une réforme pacifique mais d'un massacre!'[30] However, Rebours has gained a little

---

[27] *Ibid.*, p. 270.   [28] *Ibid.*, p. 273.
[29] The series of articles was also reprinted in *Échos d'Orient*, I (1897-8), pp. 353-68.
[30] J.-B. Rebours, *Traité de psaltique* (Paris, 1906), p. xiii.

perspective on the three reformers because he goes on to say 'cependant hâtons-nous de reconnaitre malgré le désastre, il reste encore de bien belles choses, et s'il nous est permis de regretter le passé, le plus pratique assurément est de nous appliquer à tirer tout le parti possible du peu qui reste.'[31] In contrast to Thibaut, Rebours accepted that there was a positive step in this reform. He also conceded that Westerners are very bad judges of Oriental music. 'We do not have enough background and do not know how to listen.' In spite of the state of ruination that Rebours sees in Greek music he believes that in principle at least it remains 'superior' to European music. In the Western European system one has only Major and Minor Modes, while in Greek music there are eight Modes each having a perfectly defined character, at least in theory.[32] 'Il est certain que tout n'est pas parfait et quelques auteurs out prétendu qu'il y a eu corruption de la gamme primitive. Nous sommes bien de leur avis, mais d'où est venue la corruption? La question, croyons-nous, n'est pas sur le point d'être résolue.'[33]

Rebours raises a particularly interesting point when he stresses that the realm of the Greek Church is not confined to the territory between the Adriatic Sea and the Islands of the Aegean Sea. To its domain belong Asia Minor, Syria and Egypt and in the last countries Turkish and Arabic are the indigenous languages. Rebours uses these points to prove that polyphony would have been rejected by those non-Greek congregations; furthermore, their influence on the musical scales of the Greeks cannot be ignored.[34] Before further consideration of these scales, however, the thoughts of a Greek music writer must be noted.

In 1917 Constantine Psachos published in Athens a volume entitled ʻΗ παρασημαντικὴ τῆς Βυζαντινῆς μουσικῆς in which he attempted to answer the European critics of the modern Greek music system. He stated that foreign musicologists had failed to recognize the development that had taken place in the centuries between the writing of the ancient and medieval Greek manuscripts and modern Greek Church Music. The intermediate period is totally ignored. Psachos also complained that 'they read without really reading,' subjectively and arbi-

[31] *Ibid.*
[33] *Ibid.*, p. 35.
[32] *Ibid.*, p. xiv.
[34] *Ibid.*, p. xiv.

trarily, paying attention only to the phonetic characters. The remaining characters they merely enumerate and attempt a certain interpretation assuming that all these characters are only for expression in music. Thus 'their judgement is limited by their ability to judge.'[35]

There is undoubtedly some justification for Psachos' complaint. Here however one can only mention his more familiar argument, known as the 'stenographic theory', which has been widely disputed by Western European musicologists. In brief, this theory holds that the medieval Byzantine neumes were merely a musical shorthand. It implies, in Velimirović's words, that 'regardless of what century is in question, the music of a given hymn was always the same, and if one looks at a manuscript and finds that it does not contain the melody as known from the present day practices, then it must have been written down with a 'stenographic system' which would only remind the singer of the proper turn of the melody which had been learned by heart and thus remained identical throughout the centuries.'[36] A critical discussion of the merits of this theory is contained in several articles of Tillyard's.[37]

In 1929, Constantine Maltezos, not a musician but a mathematician, made a thorough study of the Greek scales described by the Patriarchal Commission and by Chrysanthos. On the basis of an analytical approach, Maltezos stated his belief that there were two scales in use in Constantinople at the beginning of the nineteenth century. The first scale was essentially a Pythagorean scale found experimentally by the Patriarchal Commission of 1881 and expressed in rational-diatonic intervals. He calls this the 'diatonic Byzantine scale' and claims that there can be no doubt about the fidelity of the tradition in the exactness of the 'tonic intervals.'[38]

The second scale discussed by Chrysanthos was also derived from the Pythagorean scale yet with the introduction of

[35] Psachos, *op. cit.*, pp. 51-2.

[36] Miloš Velimirović, 'Study of Byzantine Music in the West,' *Balkan Studies*, Vol. 5 (Thessaloniki, 1964), p. 70.

[37] H. J. W. Tillyard, 'Byzantine Musical Notation—A Reply,' *Byzantinische Zeitschrift*, xxiv (1923-4), pp. 320-8; also 'The Stenographic Theory of Byzantine Music,' *Laudate*, ii (1924), pp. 216-25; iii (1925), pp. 28-32; *Byzantinische Zeitschrift*, xxv (1925), pp. 333-8.

[38] Maltezos, *op. cit.*, p. 337.

(chromatic) 'three-quarter tones'. Maltezos calls this scale 'Turko-Greek.' The three reformers, i.e. Chrysanthos and his companions, in determining the intervals of their scales used the 'pandourides'[39] (an instrument with three strings) which must have been suited to such intervals. Furthermore, Chrysanthos considered the aulos to be a proper wind instrument for Greek Church Music.[40] For practical purposes, however, the Arabic 'nay' as well as the European traverse flute were also considered as suitable instruments for demonstration, though Chrysanthos himself preferred the nay because 'it has the intervals our music needs.' Maltezos suspected that the particular nay that Chrysanthos had in mind was a type of flute more suited to Turkish music.[41] Any mention of Turkish influence on Greek music is met with extraordinary resistance by Greek musicologists, yet Maltezos goes one step further by asking whether it is possible that this Turko-Greek scale might have been used by Greeks, especially in Asia Minor, *before* the appearance of the Turks on the political scene.[42] Since the possibility of any chromaticism within the body of the medieval Chant has never been completely resolved to everyone's satisfaction, this theory may be worth some consideration.

After 1453, the Greeks could not avoid becoming familiar with Turkish music. The professional singers in the Greek Church had mastered Turkish music also because they were required to sing before the Turks. These same musicians were also composing liturgical hymns and chants in which they may have used a non-diatonic scale.[43] The most recent opinion on this subject is contained in one of the latest volumes of the *Monumenta Musicae Byzantinae* series. In studying intonation formulae, Jørgen Raasted compared contemporary melodic formulae with their Byzantine counterparts. In his opinion

---

[39] One of the Greek terms for 'tanbura', a lute-like instrument with a thin fretted neck, either pear-shaped or round, which could have from three to ten strings. Cf. Curt Sachs, *Reallexikon der Musikinstrumente* (Berlin, 1913 [also reprinted in New York, 1964]), pp. 288 and 376.

[40] For 'aulos' see Sachs, *op. cit.*, p. 23.

[41] Maltezos, *op. cit.*, p. 337; according to Sachs, *op. cit.*, p. 269, the term 'nay' means 'wind instrument' in both Persian and Arabic. More specifically it refers to a long pipe of reeds, rather difficult to play as it has no mouthpiece or openings as in a flute. It usually has seven or eight holes for change of pitch.

[42] Maltezos, *op. cit.*, p. 339.

[43] *Ibid.*, p. 338.

Chrysanthos was aware of the medieval intonation signs yet viewed them as merely graphic abbreviations of more elaborate melodic formulae; their true melodies, Chrysanthos believed, were preserved in an oral tradition which he then presented in his own notational system.[44]

In the *Mega Theoretikon* there are many references to the existence of two traditions: κατὰ τοὺς νεωτέρους and κατὰ τοὺς παλαιούς which serves to illustrate the awareness of the radical change that had occurred in modern Greek theory.[45] Raasted is very moderate in his assessment of the role of Chrysanthos in the history of Modern Greek Church Music for he says 'even though Chrysanthos' reform introduced a great many changes, not only in notation but also as regards signatures and intonations, the differences between the modern tradition and that of the preceding period must not be exaggerated. On the contrary, the stability of this late end of the tradition is really surprising.'[46]

In this last opinion on the work of Chrysanthos one can sense a more dispassionate approach to the reform in Greek Church Music as found formulated in the *Mega Theoretikon*. Chrysanthos' work presents a picture of church music in Greece in the early nineteenth century. His intent was not to suppress or alter the existing chant but to simplify it. It is impossible to assess completely his success or failure on these points without a thorough knowledge of the chant that immediately preceded his reform. Modern scholars have not yet felt compelled to study the four centuries of Turkish domination following the fall of Constantinople. To compare the chant discussed in the *Mega Theoretikon* with the medieval Byzantine Chant, as many scholars have done, is however quite illogical.

In embarking on his reform Chrysanthos did not feel compelled to 'purify' the Greek Chant because he did not recognize any impurities. In other words, he did not make a conscious attempt to return Greek Chant to its medieval tradition, being convinced that this tradition had never been lost. While defending Chrysanthos' motives, one cannot but wish that the Greek Church hierarchy had been more concerned with the historical aspects of their music reform, and not only with simplification.

[44] Raasted, *op. cit.*, p. 148.   [45] *Ibid.*
[46] *Ibid.*, p. 150.

The *Mega Theoretikon* could well contribute to the under-standing of the medieval Byzantine Chant if the emotional response to the efforts of these men could be removed. The chant of the immediately preceding centuries must be compared with medieval melodies, and these results should be critically ana-lyzed before a real understanding can be achieved of the three reformers and their contribution. These four centuries of Turk-ish domination represent a historical fact, and must be consid-ered in any analysis of nineteenth-century Greek Church Music.

9

Jørgen Raasted

ROSKILDE, DENMARK

A Newly Discovered Fragment of a Fourteenth-Century Heirmologion

In October 1966, Mr. J. S. Dearden, the curator of the Ruskin Galleries, Bembridge School, Isle of Wight, called my attention to a Heirmologion fragment which he had acquired for his private collection of manuscripts a few years earlier. At my request, Mr. Dearden sent the fragment to Copenhagen and later gave me permission to publish the leaf in a suitable way. I am greatly obliged to Mr. Dearden whose liberality has made this new source for the medieval Heirmologion accessible for students of Byzantine music.

The recent history of the leaf is described in a letter which Mr. Dearden addressed to me on 7 November 1966: 'In 1964 the bookseller Alan Thomas of Bournemouth catalogued eight leaves in a modern red morocco binding in his catalogue No. 14. By the time I ordered it, it had been sold to the Folio Society of London. They split the 8 leaves up and sold them separately in their catalogue 35. Alan Thomas said that it had various loose notes on the manuscript with it, but these had been lost by the time I asked the Folio Society for them! However, the Folio Society, rather than Alan Thomas's catalogue, describe the MS as being written in Rhodes. This statement was possibly based on the now-lost notes.' I have not yet tried to investigate the fate of the seven folios and the 'now-lost notes', nor have I made any inquiries through the bookseller of Bournemouth in view of the earlier history of the manuscript.

There is no need to describe the leaf (for which I suggest the designation '*Dd*'), since reproductions of its two sides can be seen in Plates 7 and 8. The reproductions are slightly reduced, *Dd* actually measuring 168 × 125 mm. The red ink can hardly be seen on the original, and even less on the reproductions. From the faint traces it is possible, however, to reconstruct most of the rubrication. On top of the *recto* page the two lines of rubrication contain the end of the verses which introduced the Plagios Protos section of the manuscript.[1] The preserved verse runs ἔχειν σε καὶ λέγειν σε, πρῶτον πλαγίων:— Apart from these lines the rubrication comprised only the Ode numbers and modal signatures which accompany each Heirmos. The marginal addition on the *recto* is illegible, except for its beginning which seems to read τὰσ ἐ. . . . On the same page there is a big erasure in the margin; there are no traces of any letters under the erasure.

In *Monumenta Musicae Byzantinae Transcripta VI* the Heirmoi of the first Akolouthia of Plagios Protos are transcribed from a number of sources, together with drawings of their musical notation. Due to this happy coincidence we have no difficulty in assigning the version of the Dearden leaf to its proper place within the melodic tradition of the Heirmologion: Dd belongs to the same tradition as Saba 599 (*Sa*). Now, since Høeg opened the discussion about '*Sa* and kindred MSS',[2] a number of scholars have sought to define the connection between this small group of manuscripts and the 'classical' Heirmologion (Høeg's *H* group).[3] Whether we follow Strunk's line of thought and see in these manuscripts a late tradition, associated somehow with Joannes Koukouzeles, or prefer to consider Saba 599 and its

[1] Printed in the current editions of the *Parakletike*. For a medieval example see the Grottaferrata Heirmologion E.γ. II (facsimile edition in *Monumenta Musicae Byzantinae*, iii, 1950), fol. 129r. The poems about the Modes will be discussed in a forthcoming study by M. Velimirović.

[2] *The Hymns of the Hirmologium*, Part I. The First Mode. The First Plagal Mode, transcribed by Aglaïa Ayoutanti and Maria Stöhr, revised and annotated by Carsten Høeg with the assistance of Jørgen Raasted. *Monumenta Musicae Byzantinae*, Series *Transcripta*, vi (Copenhagen, 1952), Introduction, pp. xxxiv-vii.

[3] *Ibid.*, pp. xxxvii-viii; Cf. Oliver Strunk's contributions to the 12th and 13th International Congresses for Byzantine Studies—*Actes du XIIe Congrès international d'études byzantines, Ochride 1961*, Tome I (Belgrade, 1963), pp. 368-73; *Proceedings of the XIIIth International Congress of Byzantine Studies, Oxford 1966* (London, 1967), pp. 245-54; also M. Velimirović, *Byzantine Elements in Early Slavic Chant: The Hirmologion, MMB, Subsidia*, iv (Copenhagen, 1960), pp. 68-9; Egon Wellesz, 'Melody Construction in Byzantine Chant,' in *Actes du XIIe Congrès international . . .*, Tome I (1963), pp. 146-51.

relatives to be late descendants of an early (Palestinian?) tradition, it is obvious, however, that substantially new evidence in support of either of these views cannot be expected from one single leaf of the Dearden Heirmologion.

The interest of the new manuscript lies primarily in its information about the internal relationship of the members of the '*Sa* group'. If we compare, in detail, the version of *Dd* with its nearest relatives—Saba 599 (*Sa*), Sinai 1256 (*Ku*), and Vatican Palat. Gr. 243 (*Rp*)—we notice a clear subdivision of the group, with *Ku* and *Rp* against *Sa* and *Dd*. The collations printed below offer full evidence for this statement. In order to show the grouping as clearly as possible, readings common to *Sa* and *Dd* have been given in a separate line (called '*Sa* + *Dd*'); the other group (*Ku* + *Rp*) is seen in the many places where no reading from *Rp* is recorded, since this implies identity of *Rp* with the *text-base* (*Ku*).

At the end of his long article on '*The Byzantine Heirmos and Heirmologion*'[4] Velimirović transcribes a Heirmos (Τεμνομένην θάλασσαν, Mode III) from six sources to demonstrate 'the inter-dependence of a variety of melodic traditions'. Two of these sources (*H* and *G*) belong to the 'classical' *H* group, whereas the *Sa* group is represented by *Ku*, *Sa*, and *Rp*; the last manuscript quoted is *Sb* (Saba 617). In commenting on this example Velimirović describes the manuscripts *Sa* and *Rp* as belonging to the same tradition as *Ku*, but points out that each of them displays some idiosyncrasies of its own. As long as only three witnesses to a manuscript tradition are known, variation between them can be described only in terms of 'idiosyncrasies'. The addition of a fourth member to the group—however fragmentary that manuscript may be—makes it possible for us to form a more distinct picture of the tradition.

---

[4] Submitted for publication in *Gattungen der Musik in Einzeldarstellungen-Gedenk-schrift Leo Schrade*, now in preparation by the Department of Music of the University of Basel, Switzerland.

Collations: Ode I

Ku: Ιπ πον και α να βα την   εισ θα λασ σαν
    a G   G   G G   G   F   E   F   G · a b

Sa: βα την   εισ θα λασ
               a   G   F   F   G

Dd: Ιπ πον και α να   σαν
    ab   a   G   a G   a b

Ku: ε ρυ θραν ο συν τρι βων   πο λε μουσ   εν
    a G   a   a   a   ab   a   G   a   G   F

Sa+Dd: συν τρι βων
            b   c   a

Sa: ε   πο λε μουσ   εν
   a   G   a   a   a

Dd: εν
                                     F

Ku: υ ψη λω βρα χι ο νι χρι στοσ   εξ ε τι να ξεν
    E F   a   a   a G   a   a   ab   a   G   ab   a   G

Rp: τι   ξεν
                              b   G

Sa+Dd: τι να ξεν
                             a   G   G

Sa: υ ψη λω βρα χι ο νι χρι στοσ
    a a   a   a   G   a G   F   F   ab

Dd: λω βρα   χρι
      ab   a   a   a

H

Ku: ισ ρα ηλ δε ε σω σεν ε πι νι κι ον υμ νον
a F G FG a G G G G a G a F G

Rp: ισ ρα ηλ δε
E F a G

Sa: ισ ρα ηλ δε ε
G G a FGa a

Dd: ισ ρα ηλ δε   ον υμ νον
a G ab G   G F G

Ku: α δον τα
a GaF G

Sa+Dd: α
a

Dd: α δον τα
a G G

Collations: Ode III

Ku: O πη ξασ επ ου δε νοσ την γην τη προσ τα
G a G G G G a a b a G a

Rp: πη ξασ επ
a F G

Sa+Dd: νοσ την
a G

Sa: την γην τη προσ τα
G G F E F

Dd: την γην τη προσ τα
G a F G a

Ku: ξει σου   και μετ ε ω ρη σας   α σχε τως
    a   a   ab   a   a G Ga   F   E   F   G

Rp: και μετ ε ω ρη σας
         a   a   a G Ga   F

Sa: ξει σου   και μετ ε ω ρη σας
    G   G   G   G GF G   F

Dd: ξει σου   και μετ ε ω ρη σας
    G   G   G   G GFG a   F

Ku: βρι θου σαν   ε πι την α σα λευ τον   χρι στε
    a   a   a   a a a G c   b   a   G   a

Rp: την α σα λευ τον
         a   a c   b   a

Sa+Dd: την α σα λευ τον (Dd: α σα)
         a   a bc a   a   b c

Ku: πε τραν των εν το λων σου   την εκ κλη σι αν σου
   ab   a   G   a G a   a   G F   G   ab' a   a

Rp: σου

Sa+Dd: πε τραν (Sa: πε) λων σου
      bc   a   bc   a   G

Sa: την εκ κλη σι αν
             F   F   G   ab a

Dd: την εκ κλη σι αν
             F   F   F   ab a

Ku: στε ρε ω σον μο νε α γα θε και φιλ αν θρω πε
G a a aFG a G G G a F G a GaF G

Rp:
θρω
GaGF

Sa: στε ρε ω σον μο
G a G F a

Dd: στε ρε ω σον   φιλ αν θρω πε
G a F G   G a G G

Collations: Ode IV

Ku: Την θει αν εν νο η σας σου κε νω σιν
G a G G G a F G b a G

Rp: εν νο η σας σου κε νω σιν
G G a a a b a G

Sa:
σιν
G

Dd:
κε νω σιν
a G G

Ku: προ βλεπ τι κως ο αβ βα κουμ χρι στε εν τρο μω
G G G G F E D D a c a ab a

Sa+Dd:
κως ο
a F

Sa:
κουμ χρι στε εν τρο μω
D EF a G a b a

Dd: προ βλε πτι   χρι στε
G G G G G G   a bc

Ku: ε βο α σοι   εισ σω τη ρι αν λα ου σου
     G a G F   G E F ab a G a F

Rp: εισ σω τη ρι αν
     F F F ab a

Sa+Dd: εισ σω
     F E

Ku: του σω σαι τουσ χρι στουσ σου ε λη λυ θασ
     G a G G   G   a   F G a GaF G

Sa+Dd: λη
     a

Dd: χρι   ε λη λυ θασ
     GG   G a G G

Collations: Ode V

Ku: Ο α να βαλ λο με νοσ φωσ ωσ ι μα τι ον
     a a a a a G F   E F G a a a

Rp: ον
          ab

Sa: Ο α να βαλ·λο με νοσ
     a a a G a G F

Dd: Ο α να βαλ λο με νοσ   ι μα τι ον.
     G a G G a G F   G ab aG a

Ku: προσ σε ορ θρι ζω   και σοι κραυ γα ζω
     a   a   G   a   a   a   b   G   a   a

Rp: προσ σε
     G   a

Sa: ορ θρι ζω   κραυ γα ζω
         G   ab   a   G   ab   a

Dd: προσ σε ορ θρι ζω   και σοι κραυ γα ζω
     G   a   FG   a   G   G   G   E   FE   D

Ku: την ψυ χην μου φω τι σον   την ε σκο τισ
     a   a   a   G   c   b   a   a   a   a   G

Sa: φω τι σον
             a   G   F   a

Dd: την ψυ χην μου φω τι σον   την ε σκο τισ
     a   a   bc   a   a   F   G   ab   a   G   G

Ku: με νην χρι στε   ωσ μο νοσ ευ σπλαγ χνοσ
     a   G   a   F   E   F   G   a   G   a   F   G

Sa+Dd: ευ
                        a

Sa: με νην χρι στε
     Ga   G   G   F

Dd: με νην χρι στε   ευ σπλαγ χνοσ
     a   G   a   F   a   G   G

Collations: Ode VI

Ku: Μαι νο με νην κλυ δω νι ψυ χο φθο ρω δε
    a a c a   c b a   b G a a   a

Sa+Dd: ψυ χο φθο ρω δε
                                 a G ab a   a

Sa: Μαι νο με νην κλυ δω νι
    C D EF G   a a a

Dd: Μαι
    a

Ku: σπο τα χρι στε   των πα θων την
    G F E F   a a a G

Sa+Dd: σπο τα χρι στε (Sa: χρι)   των
        G F E FGa   F E   a

Dd: των πα θων την
                                 a a c a

Ku: θα λασ σαν κατ ευ να σον   και εκ φθο
    ab a a   G a G F   F F G

Sa+Dd: και εκ φθο
                               F E F

Dd: θα λασ σαν
    ab a a

Ku: ρασ αν α γα γε με ωσ ευ σπλαγ χνοσ
    a G a G a F G a G a F G

Rp: σπλαγ
                                    G aGF

Sa+Dd: ρασ   (Dd: και εκ)   ευ
        a   G E   a

Collations: Ode VII

Ku: 0 υ περ υ ψου με νοσ   τῶν πα τε ρων
    a a a a c b a   a a a G

Rp: 0
    a

Sa+Dd: υ περ υ ψου με νοσ (νοσ Sa)
        a a G a G FGa   FGE

Sa: τῶν πα τε ρων
                        F   G a G

Dd: πα τε ρων
                          a b G

Ku: κυ ρι οσ   την φλο γα κατ ε σβε σε τουσ
    c b a   a ab a G a G FGa a

Sa: κυ ρι οσ   την φλο γα   σε τουσ
    a a a   F ab a   F   F

Dd: σε
                                    FGa

Ku:	παι	δασ	ε	δρο	σι	σε			
	ab	a	G	a	G	F			

Ku:	συμ	φω	νωσ	με	λω
	G	ab	a	a	G

Sa:	παι	δασ				
	ab	a				

Sa:	συμ	φω	νωσ	με	λω
	F	ab	a	G	FG

Dd:	συμ	φω	νωσ	με	λω
	G	a	G	G	F

Ku:	δουν	τασ		ο	θε	οσ	ευ	λο	γη	τοσ	ει.
	a	G		G	a	F	E	F	G	baGF	G

Rp:	τασ
	G

Sa:	δουν	τασ		ο	θε	οσ	ευ	λο	γη	τοσ	ει
	a	G		G	G	EF	G	a	FE	D	D

Dd:	δουν	τασ		ο	θε	οσ	ευ	λο	γη	τοσ	ει
	a	G		G	F	EF	G	F	E	D	D

Collations: Ode VIII

Ku:	Σοι	τω	παντ	ουρ	γω	εν	τη	κα	μι		νω	παι	δεσ
	G	F	E	D	D	E	C	D	E	FG	FG	a	a

Rp:	εν	τη	κα	μι		νω	παι	δεσ
	E	C	D	E	FGa	FG	ab	a

Sa+Dd:	εν	τη	κα	μι	νω
	D	C	D	E	FG	G

Sa:	παι	δεσ
	ab	a

Dd:
///////

IO

Dr. Lukas Richter

BERLIN, GERMANY

'Psellus' Treatise on Music' in Mizler's 'Bibliothek'*

UNDER the influence of the ideas of the Enlightenment there was a complete change in the traditional understanding of music as a science, a conception on which its educational value had rested since the days of Ancient Greece.[1] From the beginning of the eighteenth century the view prevailed that music is an Imitative Art rather than an expression of the laws of numbers.[2] The *Musica theoretica* had already been neglected for a long time in the curricula of the Universities, partly in favour of the study of natural science. Now, the teaching of music and musical practice disappeared also from the gymnasia.[3]

Lorenz Christoph Mizler (1711–78), whose views were strongly shaped by the rationalistic philosophy of Christian Wolff (1679–1754), tried, as in his dissertation 'Quod musica ars sit pars eruditionis philosophiae' (1736), to demonstrate that music was the mathematical element of Philosophy—the highest science of all. In other words, Mizler advocated an up-to-date renewal of music's former status as a component of the

---

[1] L. Richter, *Zür Wissenschaftslehre von der Musik bei Platon und Aristoteles* (Berlin, 1961), pp. 2ff.

[2] Cf. H. Hüschen, article 'Musik' in *Musik in Geschichte und Gegenwart*, 9 (1961), especially cols. 988ff. and the bibliography cited there.

[3] P. Wagner, 'Zur Musikgeschichte der Universität,' *Archiv für Musikwissenschaft*, 3 (1921), pp. 8ff.; G. Schünemann, *Geschichte der deutschen Schulmusik* (Leipzig, 1931), pp. 224ff.

* This article represents a translation and edited version of the author's study published in *Beiträge zur Musikwissenschaft* Vol. 9 (1967), pp. 45-54. Warm thanks are due to Professor Heinrich Hock of the University of Illinois for his kind assistance in preparing this translation.

Quadrivium.[4] All of Mizler's numerous activities[5] were subordinated to his rationalistic 'main intention . . . to give to music the full stature of a science, to study its history, and set it in order.'[6] This undertaking did not, however, remain unchallenged. The sensuous approach of the most influential contemporary music theorist, Johann Mattheson, for instance, diverged greatly from Mizler's view of music as a 'sounding mathematics.' Thus Mattheson's encyclopedic *Der vollkommene Cappellmeister* (1739) directed some polemical blows at Mizler, and in the title of the pamphlet *Aristoxenis junioris Phtongologia systematica* (1748), Mattheson unfurled 'the name of Aristoxenos as a banner' against the Pythagoreanism of Mizler (and Leonhard Euler as well).[7]

Mizler expressed his views on the theory of music in the journal, which became the organ of the society he had founded, *Neueröffnete Musikalische Bibliothek oder gründliche Nachricht nebst unpartheyischem Urteil von musicalischen Schriften und Büchern*, which he published himself from 1736 until 1754. At first it appeared twice yearly, but later, when his difficulties in making a livelihood forced him to move to Poland, at ever longer intervals.[8] Obsessed with missionary zeal and increasingly isolated, Mizler, as the propagator of a musical view 'more geometrico', was not much interested in reporting on actual musical life or in reviewing new publications. He rather concentrated on the presentation of his own theories, but in independent articles, in general reviews of the literature, and even in notes on individual publications. At first he gave preferential treatment to German

[4] F. Wöhlke, *L. Chr. Mizler, Ein Beitrag zur musikalischen Gelehrtengeschichte des 18. Jahrhunderts* [Diss.] (Berlin, 1940), pp. 8ff. and pp. 38ff.; for bibliography cf. H. G. Hoke, 'Mizler,' *MGG*, 9 (1961), cols. 388f.

[5] They included, among others: teaching at the University of Leipzig, theoretical publications (mostly in his own periodicals), and finally the organization of the first genuine musicological society in Germany—the 'correspondierende Societät der musicalischen Wissenschaften' (which counted as its members Handel and Bach). Cf. Wöhlke, *op. cit.*, pp. 96ff.; also A. Schering, *J. S. Bach und das Musikleben Leipzigs*, iii (1941), pp. 193ff.; W. C. de Jong, 'Händel, Bach en de Mizlerse Societeit in Leipzig,' *Mens en Melodie*, vii (1952), 2.

[6] Cited from his autobiography published in Joh. Mattheson's *Grundlage einer Ehrenpforte* (Hamburg, 1740, new ed. by M. Schneider, Berlin, 1910), p. 230.

[7] J. Handschin, *Der Toncharakter, eine Einführung in die Tonpsychologie* (Zürich, 1948), 177; cf. W. Braun, *J. Mattheson und die Aufklärung* [Diss.] (Halle, 1951), pp. 8ff.; R. Schäfke, *Geschichte der Musikästhetik* (Berlin, 1937), pp. 300ff.

[8] Wöhlke, *op. cit.*, pp. 18ff. and 86ff. (with citations of contemporary views).

writers on music from the period 1650–1750 and, as Johann
Adolf Scheibe said in a review, the personal 'views [of Mizler,
the publisher] too strongly penetrate the [original] text'.[9]
Later Mizler increasingly reproduced the original Classical
sources, with annotations. Already in his preface he had stated
his aim 'to examine the works of the Greek writers on music . . .,
[but] it would be even more useful to translate them verbatim
and henceforth to give to our readers one such writer with our
annotations as an appendix to each volume.'[10]

Mizler had recourse to the ancient Greek writers in order to
strengthen his own position. For, according to him, they 'were
much more concerned with the origins, relationships, and concordances of notes than our present-day *Musici*, who cannot
really be blamed for not understanding anything about Ancient
Greek music, since for such an understanding knowledge of
both the Greek language and the mathematical sciences is
needed . . .'[11] Mizler realized that for an understanding of
Greek music theory a combination of both mathematical and
philological knowledge is necessary, the latter being normally
inaccessible to a professional musician of his time. Nevertheless,
Mizler undoubtedly overestimated his own powers when he
considered himself equipped for this task.

Mizler apparently intended to append complete German
translations to the existing editions of Greek writers on music,
instead of the customary Latin translations. Thus, Mizler
hoped, he could exercise some influence on the larger audience
of professional musicians and interested laymen.[12] He had
already furnished a summary translation of the treatises in the
collections of Marcus Meibom (*Antiquae musicae auctores*, Amster-
dam, 1652) and of John Wallis (*Opera mathematica*, III, Oxford,
1699),[13] together with notes on Aristoxenos (partly from Mei-

[9] J. A. Scheibe, in *Hamburgische Berichte von gelehrten Sachen* of June 14, 1737 (No. 42,
p. 394); see also Wöhlke, *op. cit.*, pp. 20 and 88ff.
[10] L. Chr. Mizler, *Musikalische Bibliothek*, I, Preface.
[11] *Ibid.*, I/1, p. 2.
[12] *Ibid.*, III/2, p. 200, n. 24.
[13] For references to the editorial activities of Meibom and Wallis (beside those
contained in the new editions of the nineteenth century), cf. above all R. Schäfke
Aristides Quintilianus (Berlin, 1937), p. 25f.; I. Düring, 'Die Harmonielehre des
Klaudios Ptolemaios,' *Göteborgs Högskolas Årsskrift*, XXXVI (1930), fasc. 1,
p. xciii. See also G. Fellerer, 'Zur Erforschung der antiken Musik im 16.—18. Jh.',
Jahrbuch Peters, 42 (1936), pp. 84ff.

bom's preface and partly from Suida's lexicon).[14] According to his plan each volume of his journal was to end with a scholarly supplement containing an annotated translation of an ancient treatise. The only publication which he completed, however, was that of a Byzantine treatise.

Michael Psellus (1018–78), a Platonist philosopher and productive writer of excellent mastery of form and abundant encyclopedic knowledge, enjoyed a reputation which spread from Byzantium into Western Europe.[15] It is, therefore, no accident that sixteenth-century editions of his writings may include a compendium of the four mathematical disciplines (Σύνταγμα εὐσύνοπτον εἰς τὰς τεσσάρας μαθηματικὰς ἐπιστήμας) which is not correctly attributed to him.[16] The first publisher of the treatise, Arsenius, in his Praefatio of 1532 only tentatively ascribed the Syntagma to Psellus. The attribution to Psellus was however adopted in the Paris edition by Bogardus (1545). From that time on Psellus's name is found in all editions, among which that by Wilhelm Xylander (Basel, 1556) stands out on account of its valuable critical and exegetical notes to the Latin translation. 'Psellus' treatise on music' was also published separately in Paris (ed. Vinet, 1557) and in Wittenberg (1560). It started gaining importance from a musicological point of view after its appearance in the appendix to Lampertus Alardus' work De veterum musica (Schleusingen, 1636, pp. 177–203), in spite of the fact that he used a corrupt text derived from the Paris edition of 1545.[17]

---

[14] 'Meiboms Vorrede über die Scribenten von der alten Griechischen Musik' Musikalische Bibliothek, I/1, pp. 1ff.; 'Wallisi . . . Vergleichung der alten Musik mit der zu seiner Zeit,' Ibid., I/2, pp. 1ff.; 'Nachricht von Aristoxeni Harmonik und dessen Leben,' Ibid., I/3, pp. 1ff.

[15] See especially K. Krumbacher, Geschichte der byzantinischen Literatur² (München, 1897), pp. 433ff.; the monographs by Chr. Zervos and E. Renaud (both published in 1920) and by B. Tatakis (publ. in 1949); also the pertinent passages in G. Moravcsik, Byzantinoturcica, I (1958), pp. 437ff.; G. Ostrogorsky, Geschichte des byzantinischen Staates² (München, 1952), pp. 261ff.; H. G. Beck, Kirche und theologische Literatur im byzantinischen Reich (München, 1959), pp. 538ff.

[16] A critical new edition edited by J. L. Heiberg, Anonymi Logica et Quadrivium, cum scholiis antiquis [Det Kgl. Danske Videns kabernes Selskab. Hist.-filol. Meddelelser, XV/1] (Copenhagen, 1929). Cf. review by K. Praechter in Byzantinische Zeitschrift, 31 (1939),pp. 82-90.

[17] For a demonstration that Psellus is not the author, see L. Richter, 'Antike Überlieferungen in der byzantinischen Musiktheorie,' Deutsches Jahrbuch der Musikwissenschaft für 1961, 6. Jg. (Leipzig, 1962), pp. 95 and 112 (bibliography,

The treatise on harmony, written in the beginning of the eleventh century and in some manuscripts attributed to a monk named Gregorios Solitarios, deserves attention as the earliest known musical treatise from Byzantium, though eclectic in content.[18] It would be too much to expect the rationalist Mizler to comprehend all the special problems involving this treatise, when he included in the third volume of his *Musikalische Bibliothek* a study entitled 'Des Psellus vollständiger kurzer Inbegriff der Musik.'[19] The personality of the alleged author was no doubt thought likely to exert a greater attraction on the potential reader than the little-known names of the authors of the truly ancient treatises. The description of the eventful life of Psellus,[20] appeared to Mizler an additional inducement for the interested reader to study the didactic treatise that followed. The compendium-like, didactic design of that treatise probably appeared to serve Mizler's intention of popularizing his views, while its largely arithmetical aspect must have seemed to him an authoritative support for his own philosophical and mathematical tendencies. In a procedure which for his time undoubtedly was very modern, Mizler provided a German translation which was generally fluent and clear and which was printed parallel to the Greek text, and commentary in the form of footnotes. Shunning the corrupt text and often absurd translation of Alardus, Mizler used Xylander's version (although it too was not a definitive edition by any means), and completed Xylander's annotations by his own notes.

---

especially C. v. Jan, *Musici Scriptores Graeci* (Leipzig, 1895), pp. xxxiv ff., lx ff., lxx ff).

[18] Richter, *op. cit.*, pp. 95ff. (survey of concordances).

[19] The title of this treatise, which is listed after the table of contents, is the following: 'Psellus kurzer Inbegriff der Musik, aus dem Griechischen ins Deutsche übersetzt, mit Xylanders u. L. Mizlers Anmerkungen,' in *Musikalische Bibliothek*, III/2 (1746), pp. 171-200.

[20] 'Michael Psellus lived at the time of Romanus Diogenes, Emperor of Constantinople, and was well known in the year 1070 A.D. He was a Greek theologian and historian, and beside many other writings, he also compiled this short treatise on music. Psellus was born in Constantinople, of noble parents. He was a teacher of Emperor Michael VII Ducas, as is reported in the chronicle of the monk John Zonaras. But when this emperor was deposed and sent into a monastery, Psellus, his favourite, also had to resign his high positions and become a monk, and as such he lived for about another thirty years ...' *Musikalische Bibliothek*, III/2, p. 171, n. 1. (Even the rumour formerly current about an 'older' Psellus is found in this note.)

The very first mention of the alleged author, Psellus, is connected with an *argumentum e consensu gentium* for Mizler's basic thesis that music is a mathematical discipline. This contention is accompanied by an attack on Mattheson.[21] It is also significant how Mizler, while interpreting music in a strictly rationalistic sense, retraces the argument raised in the *prooimion* of the treatise, namely that the harmony of the world manifests itself in music.[22] Though Mizler is far from providing a critical examination of sources or a historical interpretation of the text, he nevertheless clearly understands that, contrary to modern usage, 'harmony' in this context is to be interpreted as a horizontal sequence of notes.[23] Yet elsewhere in the text he interprets the intervals in a harmonic (in the modern sense) fashion.[24] While pursuing his secondary aim of advertising his own ideas by using an ancient writer as an authority for those views, he by no means forgets his basic aim of providing easily understandable information about ancient music theory. Besides the interpretation of technical terms which is implied by the choice of words in the translation, he achieves this aim by discussing specific topics. In the case of some matters of importance, such as the catalogue of names of notes (p. 176f.), the composition of intervals (p. 184f.), the sections on modes and tetrachords (p. 197), and on scales (p. 198), Mizler does not give any deeper explanations but refers to earlier systematic descriptions, above all to the article based on John Wallis's 'Comparison of the Ancient Music and that of the present day' (*Musikalische Bibliothek*, I/2). Mizler undoubtedly considered Xylander's mathematical account of the divisibility of the whole tone (p. 178ff.) to be sufficiently exhaustive not to warrant any additional comments. But he personally concerns himself with

[21] 'In his days no one thought of denying that music is a mathematical science or, what amounts to the same, is a part of mathematics. In these our own days, however, Herr Mattheson desires to reverse the matter by stating that mathematics in a way is a part of music. Such a view, however, so far has not found any acceptance by any of our contemporary scholars.' *Ibid.*, p. 173, n. 1.

[22] 'Now, since music depicts in miniature the very best order which the human mind can envisage, the Ancients were correct in saying that music represents the harmony of the whole structure of the world.' *Ibid.*, p. 174, n. 2.

[23] 'Psellus here uses the word "harmony" in a meaning different from that in which we understand it today. In his text, the word means "a combination of different tones in accordance with a certain order", i.e., a "mode", a musical scale, a system.' *Ibid.*, p. 194, n. 18.

[24] See below, p. 125f.

the interpretation of textual passages which were especially
attractive to him as a music theorist, namely those dealing with
consonant intervals and the numerical ratios contained therein
(p. 188ff.). The fact that Mizler also possessed some philological
and antiquarian knowledge is demonstrated in the last note
(referring to Exodius), which happens to be the only note in
which he corrected and supplemented Xylander and the only
note which is not essentially theoretical in character. In Mizler's
treatment of the central questions of the theory of consonant
intervals, only the conclusiveness of given doctrines is open to
debate, while their development is not. In spite of the fact that
Mizler is aware of the essential difference between the ancient
and the contemporary musical systems, his deductive and
theoretical disposition prevents him from grasping the importance of any questions about the historical conditioning which
may have limited certain parts of the theory, let alone about
the existence of different layers of tradition in the transmission
of the text.

While the line of investigation of harmony pursued in
Pseudo-Psellus basically follows that of the Aristoxenian
School,[25] the actual core of the text, the theory of intervals,
progresses from an Aristoxenian determination, in terms of
additive distances in space, to the Pythagorean-Platonic interpretation of the consonances as numerical ratios, mostly in the
version expounded by Theon of Smyrna.[26] The classification of
intervals according to their degree of consonance presented by
Pseudo-Psellus (p. 187ff. Mizler = p. 68. 19ff Heiberg) creates
certain problems because of its odd terminology. These problems
vexed Mizler, just as they had bothered Xylander, but neither
of them attempted to undertake an analytical investigation
of the original sources.[27] Meibom, however, alread *had* cited

---

[25] Cf. G. Seydel, *Symbolae ad doctrinam Graecorum harmoniae historiam* [Diss.] (Leipzig,
1907), pp. 5-7, 56ff.; see also C. v. Jan, *Scriptores* . . ., pp. 167ff.; *Gymnasium
Program* (Landsberg, 1870); *Gymnasium Program* (Strassburg, 1890 and 1891);
R. Schäfke, *Aristides* . . ., pp. 9ff.

[26] The basic work is C. Stumpf, *Geschichte des Consonanzbegriffes*, I, publ. in
Abhandlungen d. Münchner Akad., Philos.-Philol. u. Hist. Kl., 21 (1901); see
also especially J. Handschin, *Der Toncharakter*, pp. 133ff. and 205ff.

[27] The passage which is especially in need of interpretation, in Pseudo-Psellus
(p. 187, 1-8 Mizler = p. 68, 19-21 Heiberg), together with Mizler's translation (which partly paraphrases it and partly corrects it) is the following:
Σύμφωνεῖ δὲ ἡ μὲν διὰ τεσσάρων διάστασις καὶ ἡ διὰ πέντε κατὰ παράφωνον,

parallel passages elsewhere and had considered it necessary to make a conjectural emendation (at p. 187, 3 M = p. 68, 21 H). In connection with Gaudentius' classification of the melodic tones (c. 9, p. 338, 37 Jan)[28] he attempted to give further instances of the rare technical term *paraphonia* (which here designates the intermediate value between the sym-phonous and dia-phonous intervals), as it occurs in Thrasyllos, an author quoted by Theon, together with the more usual term *antiphonia* (i.e. opposition of voices, or repetition of a melos on a different pitch).[29]

The expression *antiphonia*, which was probably first used by Plato (Laws 812 D) as a technical term referring to musical phenomena,[30] serves in the pseudo-Aristotelian *Problemata* above all to characterize similarities of the octave-species (esp. *Probl.* XIX 7, 13, 17, 39b). Since the first century A.D. it was considered a special case of the *symphonia* (i.e. 'simultaneous sounding', or tonal relationship, or consonance).[31] In Thrasyllos' article in Theon of Smyrna's work (p. 48, 17ff. Hiller) we find for the first time consonances divided into the two categories of antiphony and paraphony, i.e. in terms of two degrees of relationship which are manifested by their greater or lesser fusion. Consonances in the sense of antiphony (σύμφωνα κατ' ἀντίφωνον) were the intervals of octave and the double octave, consonances in the sense of paraphony (σύμφωνα κατὰ παράφωνον) are the intervals of the fourth and fifth. Thereafter consonances

---

ἡ δὲ διὰ πασῶν καὶ ἡ δὶς διὰ τεσσάρων καὶ ἡ δὶς διὰ πέντε καὶ ἡ δὶς διὰ πασῶν* κατὰ ἀντίφωνον. = 'But the intervals of the fourth and the fifth agree according to the genus which the Greeks call "paraphonum", whereas the octave, the superimposed fourth and fifth, and the double octave agree according to the genus of consonances which the Greeks call "antiphonum".'

[28] M. Meibom, *Antiquae musicae auctores*, Nota ad Gaudentium, p. 35; cf. C. v. Jan, *Scriptores* . . . , p. 338. Meibom conjectures that before the last two words of the text (indicated by an asterisk *) the following words are to be added: καὶ ἡ δὶς διὰ τεσσάρων καὶ ἡ διὰ πασῶν καὶ διὰ πέντε.

[29] On the term 'paraphonia' see J. Handschin, 'Musikalische Miszellen,' *Philologus*, 86 (1930), pp. 52ff., especially p. 54 listing the derivation of the term from a passage in Ps. Longinus' Περὶ ὕψους ('On the sublime'), 21.1.

[30] On this much discussed passage see especially C. Stumpf, *Geschichte des Consonanzbegriffes*, pp. 13ff. and in *Sammelbände für vergleichende Musikwissenschaft*, I (1922), 167; also Handschin, *Der Toncharakter*, p. 23 and *Musikgeschichte*, p. 61; C. Sachs, *The Rise of Music in the Ancient World* (New York, 1943), 257f.

[31] C. Stumpf, 'Die Pseudo-Aristotelischen Probleme, über Musik,' *Abhandlungeu d. Berliner Akad.*, Phil. Hist. Klasse, 3 (1896), pp. 25ff., especially 32; cf. Handschin, *Toncharakter*, pp. 227 and 353.

I

'according to relation' (κατὰ συνέχειαν) are listed, such as the whole tone and the quarter tone (diesis). These latter then are melodically useful intermediate steps which are only indirectly related to the immediately related basic tones of the tonal system (cf. Aristoxenos, p. 27 M 35, 9ff. Da Rios). According to this treatise, the intervals of antiphony are 'sym-phonous' insofar as the low-pitched tones 'symphonize' with the juxta-posed high-pitched tones (cf. Theon, 51, 4ff). The intervals of paraphony are 'sym-phonous' insofar as one tone in relation to the other tone sounds neither 'mono-tonous' nor 'dia-phonous', but sounds similar, though it is at a clear distance (παρὰ τι γνώριμον διάστημα ὅμοιον). Those small intervals which pre-viously, in terms of melodic sequence, were called symphon-ous, are now considered dia-phonous ('sounding apart from each other'). For though they represent a 'principle of sym-phonia, yet they are not the symphonia itself.'[32]

sym-phonous ⟨ antiphona: Octave, Double Octave
             paraphona: Fifth, Fourth

symphonous 'according to relation'
= diaphonous (principle of symphonia): Whole tone, Diesis

From this particular section derive syncretistic paraphrases in the writings of the Byzantine music theoreticians. They transfer into Thrasyllos' system, with its distinction of different degrees of consonance, the added-octave intervals which had been classified as consonances by Claudios Ptolemaios. Ptolemaios disagreed with the Pythagoreans who excluded from the con-sonances the interval of 'octave plus fourth', or the eleventh (3.8, as one not belonging either to the numerical ratios ob-tained by a clear division, such as n : 1, or by a division with a rest, such as $(n + 1) : 1$. He equated the 'upper fourth' (i.e. the eleventh) with the simple fourth as a corollary of the (assumed) identity of the octave (Harm 1.5.6). As far as the intervals of uneven tensions (anisotones) are concerned, Ptolemaios grouped them in terms of the degree of approximation toward identity and established the following ranking:

(a) homophonic intervals, such as the octave and double octave with the ratios 2 : 1 and 4 : 1;

---

[32] C. Stumpf, *Geschichte* . . ., 48ff.; Handschin, *Ibid.*, 229; see also C. Dahlhaus' article 'Konsonanz-Dissonanz' in *MGG*, 7 (1958), cols. 1504-5.

(b) symphonous intervals, such as the fifth and the fourth, both being the first ratios of a division with rests, $3:2$ and $4:3$. To these he added those intervals consisting of these two and the homophonic octave-expansion, i.e. the twelfth $(2:1 \times 3:2 = 3:1)$ and the eleventh $(2:1 \times 3:4 = 3:8)$.

(c) emmelic intervals (melodically usable ones), such as the whole tone $(8:9)$ and the series of the micro-intervals, i.e. those ratios which exceed the ratio $4:3$ (Harm. i.7).

Thus the same degree of fusion was ascribed to the expansion of an interval by means of an octave as was ascribed to the simple intervals within the range of the octave; in other words, the intervals of the type N-plus-octave were considered equivalent to the primary consonances (N).[33]

Anisotones
- homophonous: Octave, Double Octave
- symphonous: Fifth, Fourth, Twelfth, Eleventh
- emmelic: Whole tone and micro-intervals

The Ptolemaic teachings on harmony strongly influenced the archaizing tendencies in Byzantine writings on music theory.[34] Since no intermediate stages can be found between Ptolemy and Pseudo-Psellus, let us first, in order to reconstruct the historical development, quote parallels to this passage from the far better investigated treatises of late Byzantine music theory.[35] Georgios Pachymeres (1242–1310) refers (c.10) specifically to the argument by which Ptolemy counts the eleventh as a consonance (at the same time adding the arithmological argument of the *tetraktys*). But his analysis of the main consonances (c. 13, 14) which is an addition to Ptolemy's refutation of the Aristoxenians (I.10, 11) does not go beyond the realm of the octave. Manuel Bryennios (early fourteenth century) who systematized the Byzantine musical writings sanctioned by Ptolemy, grafts the Ptolemaic 'octave-expansion' (I.5) into the hierarchy of consonances found in Theon's writings in such a way that Theon's trichotomy was expanded into a four-fold

---

[33] Stumpf, *Ibid.*, pp. 56ff.; Handschin, *Ibid.*, pp. 88, 115, 151-2, 208-9, 222-3' 226-7; cf. L. van der Waerden, 'Die Harmonielehre der Pythagoreer,' *Hermes,* 78 (1943), pp. 166ff.; also I. Düring, 'Ptolemaios und Porphyrios über die Musik,' *Göteborgs Högskolas Årsskrift*, xl (1934), pp. 173ff.

[34] L. Richter, 'Antike Überlieferungen ...', pp. 84ff. and 93ff.

[35] *Ibid.*, pp. 98ff. and 101ff.

hierarchy (but cf. II.2). Bryennios divided the symphonous intervals into antiphonous intervals, such as octave and double octave, paraphonous intervals, which include only the fifth and the twelfth, while he uses the general term *symphonia* for the interval of the fourth and the eleventh, that is, he considers the latter intervals to be unqualified consonances. Following the Aristoxenian model, he interprets as diaphonous those intervals which are smaller than the fourth, such as the diesis and its combinations up to the di-tonus, as well as the intermediary intervals betwen the symphonies, which comprise three, four, and five tones (cf. Aristoxenus, p. 20 M 25, 11 Da Rios, and esp. Cleonides, c.5, p. 187, 15ff., as the direct model).[36]

	antiphonous: Octave, Double Octave
Symphonous ←	paraphonous: Fifth, Twelfth
	generally symphonous: Fourth, Eleventh
Diaphonous:	Diesis, Half-tone, Whole tone, Tone-and-a-half, Ditonus

Acoustical properties serve as an *argumentum a posteriori* for the differentiation of the individual groups of intervals. Some notes about intervals as relationships of rhythmical impulses (frequencies) lead on to a paraphrase of the theory of consonances as mixtures of tone, the psychological consequence of physical relationships. It is stated that paraphonous intervals symphonize, but not simultaneously, by virtue of the fact that the sounds follow each other in a well-regulated and rhythmically well-ordered fashion. In antiphonous intervals the higher pitch is said to symphonize with the lower one simultaneously and in an identical manner, as for instance the octave with the prime (i.e. unison), the ninth with the second (cf. the more detailed presentation by Heracleides in Porphyrios in Ptol., p. 32, Düring; Euclid, *Sectio canonis*, p. 148f. Jan, Ps. Aristotelische *Problemata*, XIX 39b; Adrast. in Theon 50, 4ff.).[37] As far as the

---

[36] For the diesis, as the smallest unit of measurement in Aristoxenos, cf. L. Laloy *Aristoxène du Tarente* (Paris, 1904), pp. 113ff., 185ff. and *passim*. See also R. P. Winnington-Ingram's study in *Classical Quarterly*, 26 (1932), p. 195 and Handschin, *op. cit.*, pp. 146 and 149.

[37] Cf. Jan, *Scriptores . . .*, pp. 134ff.; E. Graf, 'Die Theorie der Akustik im griechischen Altertum,' *Gymnasium Program* (Gumbinnen, 1894), p. 6; L. Schönberger, 'Studien zum 1. Buch der Harmonie des Cl. Ptolemäus,' *Gymnasium Program* (Augsburg, 1914), pp. 26ff.; and especially, van der Waerden, *op. cit.*, pp. 192ff.

symphonia is concerned, it is said to represent a coincidence and blending of two tones which differ in weight and pitch, with the sense perception of a total fusion, so that it is no longer possible to perceive the individuality of each of the two components one of the two sounded notes is said to dominate (for textual concordances cf. Cleon., p. 187, 19ff. with some added manuscripts; Gaudentius, p. 337, 8ff.; Aelian in Porph. in Ptol. 33, 13ff.).[38]

These disquisitions are embedded as the second section in a comprehensive chapter on the intervals, which are characterized in terms of the following five criteria: range, degree of consonance, composition, tonal gender, and rationality. The disposition of these criteria is based on the Aristoxenian tradition, as it was first mapped out in Aristoxenos' own writings (Aristox. Harm. p. 16 M. 21, 17ff.) and developed further and more elaborately by Cleon. c. 5, p. 187, 3ff. (cf. Aristides I.2, Anon. Bellermann, § 58). The first three of these distinctive characteristics recur in the synopsis of the Pseudo-Psellus, although only in a rudimentary form. Various agreements between that treatise and Bryennius seem to indicate a relationship of dependency. Certain abbreviations, deviations, and obvious misunderstandings in the Pseudo-Psellus, however, would rather suggest the use of a common source. In the treatment of distances between tones, for instance, Pseudo-Psellus arranges them in the Aristoxenian way, starting with the quarter-tone as the smallest unit,[39] and hence proceeding all the way to the octave which is said to have been named diapason ('through-all'), since all others find their completion in the *octa-chord*, and if one were to go beyond the octave, such intervals then become 'doubled': the intervals which follow the octave are said to be the 'double fourth' (*disdiatessaron*) and the 'double fifth' (*disdiapente*), etc. (cf. p. 185f. M = 68, 14–18 H; for the terminology of the consonances, cf. Theon, p. 51, 4ff.). The over-schematic interpretation of the concept of duplication as covering *all* intervals in the octave leads Pseudo-Psellus astray. He not only speaks about the double octave, but also erroneously about a δὶς διὰτεσσάρων and a δὶς διαπέντε instead of the correct διὰ πασῶν καὶ τεσσάρων and διὰ πασῶν καὶ διαπέντε

[38] Jan, pp. 322ff.; Stumpf, pp. 41f. and 47f.; Düring, pp. 158, Handschin, p. 144f.
[39] See note 36, above.

respectively. That this formulation is not used as an abbreviation for the correct version (excepting, of course, attestations in certain Greek theoretical writings where, to be sure, the terms *disdiatessaron* and *disdiapente* are used, but merely in their only acceptable meaning, namely in reference to the dissonant [dia-phonous] intervals of the seventh and the ninth [as, for instance, in the pseudo-Aristotelian *Problemata*]),[40] is shown in Pseudo-Psellus where immediately alter the passage in question the multiplicative prefix 'dis-' is substituted for the noun 'diapason'. Later on, *dis* not only superfluously, but indeed absurdly, precedes the compounds beginning in *diapason*.

The preceding considerations now permit us to submit an interpretation of our starting point. In distinguishing the intervals by their degree of consonance (p. 187f. M = 68, 19ff. H), Pseudo-Psellus treats the intervals of the fourth and fifth as symphonizing paraphonically, but the intervals of the octave, the 'double fourth', and the 'double fifth' as symphonizing antiphonically. Ptolemaios' view of the equivalence of the octave extensions is injected into Theon's structural scheme, but with a mistaken use of terminology. The subsequent acoustic derivation of this difference in quality of intervals corresponds to what is later on transmitted by Bryennius, though without the latter's discussion of the phenomenon of fusion, while the definition of diaphony agrees with the final sentence in Thrasyllos.[41] Both Pseudo-Psellus and Bryennius accept the paired concepts of antiphony and paraphony, a pair of concepts which emerged in Late Antiquity. The earlier of these two Byzantine theorists, however, does not yet go beyond the model itself.

symphonizing
/ paraphonically: Fourth, Fifth
\ antiphonically: Octave, 'Double Fourth,' 'Double Fifth'

Principles of symphonia: Whole tone, Half tone, Diesis.

In the subsequent description of the consonances according to their composition (p. 188f. M = 69, 9ff. H) we find the same basic mistake in the nomenclature of the octave-expansions, a

[40] For this point see especially Stumpf's 'Die pseudoaristotelischen Probleme,' pp. 5ff.
[41] See p. 119.

mistake which recurs throughout the manuscript tradition of this text. The Byzantine author apparently found in his model the correct designation for the interval of an octave plus a fourth, or of an octave plus a fifth, yet no longer did he want to part with the intrusive spurious prefix. Thus one reads that an octave plus a 'double' fourth equals eight and a half tones, and the octave plus a 'double' fifth equals nine and a half tones. The error now becomes manifest, for if we were to believe the author, there would be eleven tones in the first octave-expansion, thirteen in the second, while the double octave comprises only twelve! The same applies for the explanation of the fractional-number ratios of the intervals by means of composite numbers.

Meibom, in his conjecture about the division of the consonances in Pseudo-Psellus (p. 187.3 M = 68, 21 H),[42] proposes to add the upper fourth and the upper fifth to the traditional set of paraphonies, namely to the fourth and fifth. In so doing he undoubtedly based himself on Ptolemy's second rubric, but this is not the meaning of the text. For given the fact that these octave-expansions (i.e., the octave + fourth and octave + fifth) have already been mentioned, the following antiphonous intervals ('double fourth' and 'double fifth') would, if one were to believe Meibom, have to be interpreted in a literal sense as doublings without any reference to the octave (from which they were derived) and outside the realm of consonances. Mizler, following Xylander, noticed the textual corruption at the very first appearance of the terms 'double' fourth and 'double' fifth. He pointed out that the correct reading should be 'superimposed fourth' and 'superimposed fifth' (= eleventh and twelfth) (annotation 9). Similarly he criticized the spurious use of the terms διὰ πασῶν καὶ δὶς διὰ τεσσάρων and διὰ πασῶν καὶ δὶς διὰ πέντε (at p. 189 M = 69, 9ff H; Mizler's annotations 11 and 12). At the mention of the intervals of the fourth and eleventh, he could not resist pointing out that their consonant character is only relative and dependent upon the harmonic function of that interval.[43] Thus the views of Mizler's age con-

---

[42] See note 28, above.

[43] '. . . But in the same way as the interval of the fourth is never a consonance by *nature*, but only under certain *circumstances*, thus also the composite fourth or eleventh can only under certain conditions be counted among the consonances, from which elsewhere it is excluded.' *Musikalische Bibliothek*, III/2, p. 186, n. 9.

cerning a harmonically regulated counterpoint were, in an entirely unhistoric manner, brought to bear upon the interpretation of this interval. In the basically monophonic music of Antiquity, it was the framework of the tetrachord and, as such, represented a structural consonance. Only with the highly developed polyphony of the High Middle Ages, was it subjected to the degraded to a 'dissonantia per accidens'.[44]

As far as the ordering of consonances in Pseudo-Psellus is concerned, Mizler is inclined to understand the opposing terms paraphony and antiphony, not as different degrees of relationship, but rather as mutually exclusive aspects of tonal relationship. Thus he considered the former of these terms to indicate 'consonance in melody' and the latter to designate 'consonance in harmony' (p. 188, annotation 10),[45] since the only examples given for this term are octaves.[46] As a rationalistic theorist, Mizler apparently imagined the octave consonance of Antiquity to have been a real 'di-chord' (Zweiklang), used for the purpose of singing in parallel motion, partly in lieu of the consonances of the third and sixth (which at that time had not yet been legitimized), partly because of an aversion to motion in parallel fourths or fifths (which would have run counter to the rules of euphony). The probable reason for this view was a belief in historical progress: Antiquity, to be sure, was far removed from the ideal state (of the eighteenth century) where the third was recognized as a consonance; on the other hand, it had not yet reached the transitional stage of early medieval organum with its motion in parallel fifths and fourths.[47]

---

[44] Cf. H. Riemann, *Geschichte der Musiktheorie*[2] (Berlin, 1920), pp. 110ff. and 186ff.; Dahlhaus' article in *MGG*, 7, col. 1506. See also the distinction of the fourth as a dissonance (with the lower tone in the Bass part) and a perfect consonance (based on an arithmetical division of this interval) in J. J. Fux, *Gradus ad Parnassum* (Wien, 1725), I.17, pp. 25f.

[45] The same misinterpretation of paraphony as a 'consonant progression in the melody' is found later on in the relatively thorough representation of the concept of consonance among the Ancient Greeks in Fr. W. Marpurg's *Kritische Einleitung in die Geschichte und Lehrsätze der alten und neuen Musik* (Leipzig, 1759), p. 142.

[46] 'But the reason that he cited only examples of octaves is that the Ancients did not consider the third to be a consonance, and even less so the sixth; and their sense of hearing prevented them from moving upward or downward in [parallel] fourths and fifths.' *Musikalische Bibliothek*, III/2, p. 188, n. 10.

[47] For further discussion as well as a list of more specialized literature on the concept of consonance in the Middle Ages, see Dahlhaus, *loc. cit.*

It would be unfair to expect of the eighteenth century the store of musicological knowledge and expertise which is available today. Nevertheless, the misinterpretations might have been avoided by a closer investigation of the text and by proper reference to parallel passages which had already been assembled by Meibom. Where Pseudo-Psellus offers only a quasi-abbreviated and hardly explicit text, his predecessors would have permitted Mizler to realize that not only the octave, but also the fourth and the fifth were considered true consonances and, as such were contrasted with less consonant intervals. It would have become evident that those intervals (the octave, as well as the fourth and fifth) were 'framework' intervals, between which lay the micro-intervals which were useful for melodic movement. These micro-intervals had been pregnantly called 'emmelic' by Ptolemy, while, following Aristoxenos, Thrasyllos (as quoted by Theon) called them 'symphonous depending on the context' or considered them defined in terms of the criterion of observable distance, with the addition 'principle of symphonia, but not the symphonia itself', an addition which in the Pseudo-Psellus survived alone and out of context.[48] Yet Mizler in no way discusses the surprising fact that the Byzantine author of the treatise suddenly departs from this Aristoxenian additive view of the intervals (according to which the diesis serves as the brick, as it were, of which the intervals are built) and (p. 189 M = 69, 16 H) moves on to the Pythagorean computational principle of defining intervals according to their numerical ratios.

Mizler does not seem to have harboured any misgivings about the legitimacy of using such an incomplete account as the source of information about ancient music in general, or as a vehicle for demonstrating his own theories. Yet, at the end of his commentary, there is a certain feeling of sadness about the fact that his ambitious plans to translate a comprehensive body of Greek writings on musical theory had so far yielded such diminutive results. He no longer announces the translation of complete works, as he had originally done in the foreword to the *Musikalische Bibliothek*, but only excerpts or brief summaries of the ancient writings on music contained in the collections of Meibom and Wallis, to which he refers for a more detailed and

[48] See note 32, above.

comprehensive orientation. In the meantime, the Byzantine treatise is offered as a 'foretaste' of things to come. For those who are truly interested in the subject-matter, the text is given in its original language, while a German version is provided for the amateur.[49]

Mizler is thus the first to have translated into German a Byzantine treatise on music and to have commented upon it. In this way he contributed to the popularization of Greek teachings on music. The merits of this pioneering work cannot be denied, in spite of its great deficiencies in interpretation. Although Mizler did his best to act as an interpreter of methodology he could not bring himself to cease advocating his own cause. Nor could he as an editor achieve what eluded even the most learned philologists of his time, namely a solid and diplomatically well-founded edition of the text. It was only in the nineteenth century that critical editions were provided, above all for the texts of *Ancient* Greek musical theorists. And even today, the editorial and exegetical study of *Byzantine* sources has hardly progressed beyond the first tentative steps.

[49] 'Moreover, one can well see that these pages will offer no satisfaction to those who wish to obtain detailed information about the music of Antiquity (although they may perhaps contribute a little to their knowledge). He who wishes to be fully informed must consult the writings of the Ancient Greek writers of music and try to understand them. In due time, I shall endeavour to go over those writings and present their most useful aspects in writing. Meanwhile it has become necessary to present a foretaste of things to come to those who are interested in this matter; and in order to please them I have appended Psellus' treatise in the original language, while for the benefit of Germans who know something about music, I have furnished a translation.' *Musikalische Bibliothek*, p. 200, n. 24.

II

Nanna Schiødt

COPENHAGEN, DENMARK

A Computer-Aided Analysis of Thirty-five Byzantine Hymns*

ONE of the main characteristics of the musical style of Byzantine Chant is its formulaic structure and one of the main paths toward an understanding of this structure lies in an examination of the *melodic formulae*.[1] When one sings a Byzantine hymn, after an initial impression of a lilting flow upward and downward, one soon encounters melodic configurations which appear familiar, giving to the listener that 'Schein des Bekannten' which is an essential element of any artistic structure. In relatively short hymns one recognizes such melodic turns rather quickly, almost every time a cadence is sung. In longer hymns it is more difficult to distinguish the structure. But little by little one can discern a firm and solid framework which serves to underpin the whole composition which, at first, gives the impression of being a casually composed, perhaps even a through-composed melody. The eyes begin to observe similarities be-

---

* This article represents a summary as well as a considerable expansion and elaboration of some of the ideas formulated in my already published study 'Application of Computer Techniques to the Analysis of Byzantine Sticherarion Melodies,' published in *Elektronische Datenverarbeitung in der Musikwissenschaft*, edited by Harald Heckmann (Regensburg, 1967), pp. 187-201.

[1] The principle of structural organization of a chant by using melodic formulae was discovered by Egon Wellesz and discussed in his article 'Die Struktur des serbischen Oktoechos,' *Zeitschrift für Musikwissenschaft*, II (1919-20), pp. 140-8. See also Wellesz' *A History of Byzantine Music and Hymnography*, 2nd ed. (Oxford, 1961), pp. 325-62, especially ch. XIII—'The Structure of Byzantine Melodies.' More recently, Christian Thodberg has analyzed melodic formulae in fifty-nine melodies in his *Der byzantinische Alleluiarionzyklus. Studien im kurzen Psaltikonstil* ('Monumenta Musicae Byzantinae,' *Subsidia*, VIII. Copenhagen, 1966).

tween sequences of neumes and the ears simultaneously recognize certain recurring motifs. One wonders whether it is possible to rediscover the basic principles upon which these hymns were composed several centuries earlier. One wonders whether the same basic principles are applicable to any type of hymns sung in the Greek Orthodox religious services. Finally, being aware that the whole body of the Byzantine Chant is preserved in a 'system' of eight Modes, one wonders whether a melodic formula may be characteristic for a single Mode and, in turn, whether a Mode may be defined as a 'formula-complex.' In order to provide satisfactory answers to these questions one would, ideally, have to examine as large a number of Byzantine melodies as possible.

I have embarked on a study of the melodies in the *Sticherarion*, a type of service book which may, at times, contain as many as two thousand hymns. A conventional—'manual'—analysis of this repertory would be a difficult and time-consuming undertaking. Among the tools which modern technology places at the disposal of researchers the computer seemed a logical possibility. This view was strongly supported in consultations with Professor Barry Brook, of Queens College of the City University of New York, and Assistant Professor Bjarner Svejgaard, of the Institute of Mathematics at the University of Copenhagen. Professor Svejgaard was convinced that the problem at hand, a study of hymns of the Sticherarion, was a suitable, although rather complex, subject for computer-aided research.[2] For the present project we have used a computer GIER II at the Institute of Mathematics at the University of Copenhagen.[3]

The nature of the subject matter—hymns of uneven length—suggested the use of paper tapes rather than punch cards, which would require carry-overs onto the next card. Paper tape also has the advantage that no interruption would occur in the coding of longer or shorter rows of symbols needed. One of the first points was to decide what was going to be coded on the tape. While it is entirely possible to encode a complete hymn as

[2] I want to thank publicly Mr. Bjarner Svejgaard for his interest and for writing the complicated program. I also wish to express my admiration for his ability—though a mathematician—to solve many difficult problems concerning the coding of Byzantine neumatic notation.

[3] Full details about this computer may be found in *IEEE Transactions on Electronic Computers*, Vol. EC-12 (December, 1963), No. 5, pp. 629-49.

it appears in a manuscript with its text and neumes, intonations and medial signatures, for the present purpose it was decided to encode only the starting pitch and the neumatic notation. It is important to realize, however, that the omitted data can be added onto the tape whenever required.

Table I. Code Symbols for Intervallic Neumes

Neume	Name of Neume	Code Symbol
⌐	*I*son	I
–	*O*ligon	O
╱	*O*xeia	X
‿	*P*etaste	P
⌒⅄	*K*ouphisma	U
•	*K*entema	K
∟	*H*ypsele	H
>	*A*postrophos	A
∩	*E*laphron	E
S	Hypo*rr*hoë	R
×	*C*hamele	C
••	*D*yo Kentemata	D

Table II. Code Symbols for Neumes designating Accent and Rhythm

Neume	Name of Neume	Code Symbol
╲	Bareia	1
╲╲	Piasma	2
∼	Xeron Klasma	3
≈╱	Kylisma	4
⌒	Apoderma	5
//	Diple	6
⅄	Kratema	7
∪	Tzakisma	8
⌐	Gorgon	9

Table III. Additional Symbols

:	End of hymn
—	Used in combination with D
,	Separates neumes and groups of neumes
space	Separates neumes and groups of neumes

Table IV. Dogmatic Hymn of the IV Plagal Mode
Χαίροις τὸ ἐργαστήριον

Intonation

νε-α-γι-ε

Ordinary
transcription

Neumes

Computercode   AAE, KX, I, I, I, I, P, E ɪ A, A,

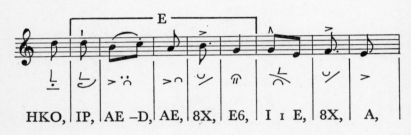

HKO, IP, AE –D, AE, 8X, E6, I ɪ E, 8X, A,

AA, KX, I, I, P, E ɪ A, A,

OH, I8X, EA –D, OK, K ɪ A, O6, A, A A, I6,

The next step was to devise a code to be 'read' by the computer, a code in which the Byzantine neumatic notation could be represented by symbols found on a standard typewriter keyboard. Formidable as this problem seemed at first, its solution turned out to be relatively simple. For the twelve basic neumes indicating musical intervals a set of twelve letters proved to be sufficient (Table I); for the neumes indicating accents and rhythmical values the numerals from 1 to 9 were used (Table II) with a few additional signs for punctuation (Table III).

This code can easily be augmented or altered should additional symbols be needed. The code was conceived in this particular way so that it would approximate the original notation as closely as possible. Thus it should be possible to encode a hymn and then use the reverse procedure from symbols converting them into neumes and obtain exactly the same patterns. A specific example may demonstrate this procedure. Table IV shows side by side the neumatic notation of a Dogmatic Hymn to the Virgin, Χαίροις τὸ ἐργαστήριον. Above the neumatic notation is the transcription into modern notation, while beneath the neumes is the computer code for these same neumes.

Since the computer can only accept symbols written horizontally, while the neumes in some of their combinations are sometimes superimposed one atop another, a rule had to be devised for complexes of neumes: *read the neumes in a manuscript from left to right and from top to bottom.* The only symbol which presented problems in applying this rule was the one for the neumatic sign *Dyo Kentemata* which is *written* either above or to the side of the neume (or group of neumes) with which it is associated. However, in a performance, it is *sung* invariably as one step upwards at the end of the melodic figure. While the appearance of the *Dyo Kentemata* to the side of a neume did not present a problem for the coding process, it was decided that for those instances in which *Dyo Kentemata* appears above the neume a hyphen be used immediately preceding the symbol D and thus a precise representation of the neumatic notation in a codex was obtained. Table IV also demonstrates the separation of letters and numbers by means of a comma and spacing. The reasons for this procedure will become apparent from the ensuing discussion.

One of the points which has to be indicated for the computer is what tonal pitches are used in the hymns. Since Byzantine music is purely vocal and does not rely on absolute pitch, it has been necessary to decide what notes in the Western staff notation may be used in order to provide a plausible equivalent of Byzantine melodies. Thus the sequence of notes shown in Table V has been established.[4]

Table V. Sequence of Notes Used

Step   0   1   2   3   4   5   6   7   8   9   10   11   12   13

Since in an analysis of any given hymn the computer must be able to identify for the researcher exactly where, within the sequence of pitches, the melodies are moving, the computer must also be provided with a 'dictionary of intervals,' as demonstrated in the following Tables VI and VII. The numbers in these Tables indicate how many steps (semitones or whole tones) a neume or a group of neumes moves upward or downward.

Table VI. Upward Intervals

0	+1	+2	+3	+4	+5	+6	+7
I	O	K	KO	OH	HP	HOX	HKO
IP	P	OP	KP	PH	HX		
IX	X	OX	KX	XH			
IU	U	OK		KOP			
T⁵	D	XK					
		PK					

Table VII. Downward Intervals

I	—2	—3	—4
A	E	EA	AC
AA	R	EAA	AAC
AP	EP		
	AE		
	AAE		

An example will illustrate the workings of this system: If we inform the computer that the starting pitch for the musical example in Table IV is the note 'F' and let it start 'reading' the coded set of symbols, the first such symbol will be AAE. From

---

[4] Oliver Strunk, 'The Tonal System of Byzantine Music,' *Musical Quarterly*, xxviii (1942), pp. 190-204.

[5] When Hyporrhoë (R) stands besides Piasma (2) it loses its interval value and we call the group 2R for T with the interval value of zero.

K

the 'dictionary of intervals' the computer will recognize that this symbol means —2. Should we thereupon request from the computer to write out the pitch on which we are at that point in the melody, it would 'answer' by writing '3' which is the symbol for note 'D'. In this way the melodies of the hymns can be checked whenever desired.

The following example will illustrate the use of a comma and of spacing.

Table VIII. Coding of large groups of neumes

a)   = I6, X X A 4 E O,

b)   = I 3 A 8X,

c)   = 8OK 2 7 A A8 AA,
                                      I6,O6,XK,A AA,

By using a comma and the appropriate spacing the computer can differentiate between a single symbol and a group of symbols that have to be counted according to the 'dictionary of intervals.' The computer can be so programmed that for an analysis of the melodic formulae it may ignore symbols for accents and rhythm. For example, the last line in Table VIII, the one designated as (c) contains the symbol 8 which the computer can ignore because it refers to rhythm. The symbol O is not counted as an interval because there is neither a comma nor spacing after it, but OK will be counted as two steps upward because it is followed by a spacing and because the symbol OK appears in the 'dictionary of intervals' in which it is listed in the category which signifies +2. The single numerals, 2 and 7, are not counted being rhythmical signs. The symbol A, since it is followed by a space, results in the melodic movement of one step downward. In 'reading' the symbol A8 the computer ignores 8. Since the comma provides the computer with the same impulse as spacing, it will count AA as one step downward and then 'read' the symbol following the comma.

The use of a space (or spacing) is especially convenient for the reverse procedure from an encoded notation into neumatic

notation. A convenient example appears in the first line—(a)—
of Table VIII. By now a simple glance suffices to show that
between the commas there is a group of neumes surrounding a
Kylisma for which the computer-symbol is '4'. Preceding it are
the symbols XXA which result in //> . After these three letters, when converting the computer-symbols into neumatic
notation, one may proceed horizontally or vertically, yet from
an acquaintance with the Byzantine notation one knows that a
Kylisma (⁓) cannot stand alone without any neume above it.
Therefore the neumatic sign for the *Kylisma* must be written
underneath the already identified neumes. Coming to the next
symbol—E—its neumatic equivalent could be written either to
the right of or underneath the *Kylisma*. From practical experience it is known that a *Kylisma* must have a neume underneath
as well so the reconstructed form appears as //> . Furthermore, both musically and graphically there must be still another
neume to round-up the *Kylisma* group and since O appears
before the comma the whole group is then fully reconstructed as
//> —. It would thus appear that the process of transcribing the Byzantine neumatic notation into computer symbols can
be mastered relatively easily. The movement in the opposite
direction, from computer symbols back into neumes requires the
knowledge of the rules of the notation.

With a basic code, a 'dictionary of intervals', and symbols
for fourteen different pitches one can begin the process of
'translation' of neumes into a 'machine-language', and the
codex (which the computer cannot read) is transformed into a
punched paper tape. Simultaneously with the typing on paper,
a corresponding combination of holes is punched on the paper
tape. The typewritten sheet of paper is for the researcher's own
control whereas the punched paper tape is for the computer.

One of the frequently asked questions in connection with this
type of work has been: 'Is it worthwhile to use a computer when
it is necessary to write out every single neume for it?' There are
several answers and all are pertinent. In the first place, the code
of letters and numerals as symbols for the neumatic notation is
relatively simple so that with a little practice (in less than one
hour) one can master it to the extent that it can be written down

faster than copying each neume by hand. Secondly, if one wishes to study the hymns 'manually' their notation has to be written out anyhow. Working with the aid of a computer one needs to write the hymns only once. Afterwards, with the paper tape in the machine one can ask any question concerning the encoded material. And last but not least, if one wishes to study the frequency of a melodic formula or all the melodic formulae in a specific repertory 'manually' one has to examine the available material, one formula at a time, yet still facing the possibility of missing an occurrence of a formula at some place. The computer can be asked to seek out more than a dozen formulae at the same time, and it will locate all of them much faster than a 'hand-count' ever could. Our computer took only three minutes to find the exact location of some fifteen formulae in thirty-five rather lengthy hymns. The preparatory work does take a certain time, but even this process can become faster as time goes on. It was possible, for instance, to encode some twenty-eight pages from a musical manuscript, each with seventeen lines of text with neumes, in about fourteen hours of work.

The programmer now writes a processing program which in detail tells the computer how to examine the hymns. This program can be altered and augmented whenever needed.

A very reliable manuscript from the Bibliothèque Nationale in Paris, a Sticherarion *Coislin* 42, from the late thirteenth century, was chosen as target. On folios 356r to 368v this manuscript contains the *Stichera Dogmatika* which were selected as the first pieces to be encoded and studied by means of a computer. These hymns are to be found in each of the eight Modes of the Byzantine Chant, and their distribution is:

Echos Protos	(IA)	5	hymns
„ Deuteros	(IIA)	5	„
„ Tritos	(IIIA)	4	„
„ Tetartos	(IVA)	4	„
„ Plagios Protos	(IP)	4	„
„ Plagios Deuteros	(IIP)	5	„
„ Barys	(IIIP)	3	„
„ Plagios Tetartos	(IVP)	6	„

With the exception of one hymn in the Fourth Plagal Mode, these thirty-five hymns in all eight Modes constitute a significant body of musical material that is manageable for handling and for attempting to find characteristics which would be common for all eight Modes. As each of these hymns is of considerable length, they also contain a representative selection of melodic formulae which could be located in shorter hymns as well.

How does one find and define a melodic formula? This problem has been studied and discussed by more than one writer,[6] yet in the final analysis one is still often forced to make one's own decisions. Some of the ways of handling this problem are:

(a) A hymn may be divided into sections which frequently coincide with punctuation signs, commas and full stops, in the text. The corresponding musical phrases contain almost invariably some kind of cadence at that point. These phrases, in turn, can be classified into several groups determined by the concluding pitches, e.g., phrases ending on G or on D, etc.

Table IX. First Hymn in Mode I (fol. 356r)

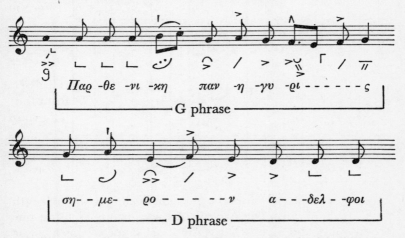

Each of the musical phrases is then compared with the other phrases in order to determine the frequency and the extent of a formula. One looks, in other words, for some 'familiar melodic outlines,' especially those in which the same sequence of neumes appears, particularly if it also happens to be on the very same pitch. This is not an easy process as one has to keep

---

[6] See, for instance, Miloš Velimirović, *Byzantine Elements in Early Slavic Chant*, MMB, *Subsidia*, iv (Copenhagen, 1960), chapter V.

an eye open for possible variants of the basic formula. The following table demonstrates the relationship of a basic melodic outline—a melodic formula—found in fourteen different locations and involving five different concluding pitches.

Table X. Determination of a Formula

This body of material raises the question dealing with the length of the melodic formula. Are all of these examples using one formula only and if so, what is the basic shape of this melodic formula?

Phrase No. 1 has some peculiarities in its notation and length which are not found in any other instance and therefore cannot be viewed as the 'prototype' of the formula being investigated. By eliminating the first and the last neumes from this phrase one encounters a sequence located in phrases Nos. 2 and 3. This brief melodic phrase, common to phrases 1, 2 and 3, may be found in some other phrases as well, in fact in those numbered

5, 6, and 7, even though the neumes differ and the length of the latter phrases is shortened by dropping off the last neume of the earlier phrases. Thus, for the first seven phrases in this Table one may surmise the existence of a basic melodic formula which has two additional variants in notation:

Table XI. First Provisional Formula

The remainder of Table X reveals, however, that if the last neume of the formula represented in Table XI is eliminated, the notation of phrases numbered 8 to 13 shows an added body of similar melodic materials. It thus appears that all these thirteen phrases are in fact based on one essential formula which appears in six notational variants:

Table XII. The Notational Variants of Formula B

One more glance at Table X might tempt one to reduce this formula even further in order to fit the phrase numbered 14, yet in such an instance one runs the risk of dealing with a formula which is much too short to be either significant or characteristic. Thus, in the light of the stability encountered in the thirteen previous instances it is possible to view No. 14 as a variant of the formula already determined.

When the computer is asked to find formula B1 with its variants, the order for search of this formula can be done in two different ways: the computer may be requested to locate the formulae in which the neumatic notation is identical, or we can ask to have a frequency count of the formulae in which the melodic movement is alike. The latter method is the pre-

ferred one because what *is* essential for a formula is its melodic
movement, i.e. what one hears. This aspect must have been
the important feature at the time when these hymns were transmitted only orally. The rhythmic vacilations and the accen-
tuation are variables which could differ and be dependent on
texts rather than on an inherent musical content of the formula.
By requesting the computer to locate the melodic movement
by intervals rather than the identity of neumes, it will also be
possible to detect the presence of a formula at some point in
which the neumatic picture has beclouded the melodic movement to the human eye, though not to the ear. If this 'interval-
question-method' is applied, the B formula will, in its encoded
form, be transformed in the following fashion:

Table XIII. Formula transformed for Computer Question

$$B_1 = IP,A8 \ A, \ A \ D,O6 \quad = 0,-1,-1,-1,1,1.$$
$$B_2 = E6,A8 \ A,A \ D, \ O6 \quad = -2,-1,-1,-1,1,1.$$
$$B_3 = P,A8 \ A,A \ D,O. \quad = 1,-1,-1,-1,1,1.$$
$$B_4 = AE,A8 \ A,A \ D,o6 \quad = -2,-1,-1,-1,1,1.i$$
$$B_5 = OK_7,A8 \ A,A \ D,O. = 2,-1,-1m-1m1m1,$$
$$B_6 = OK_7,A8 \ A,A \ D,O6 = 2,-1,-1,-1,1,1.$$
$$B_7 = O,A8 \ A,A \ D,o6 \quad = 1,-1,-1,-1,1,1.$$

Although the listing given in Table XIII is clear to the eye
as far as its 'descriptive' quality is concerned, the computer's
quest will follow the path of numerical values listed to the right.
These seven formulae could, in fact, be reduced to only four
patterns, as seen in the following table:

Table XIV.   Final Form of Computer Question

$$B_1 \qquad = 0, \ -1, \ -1, \ -1, \ 1, \ 1,$$
$$B_2 + B_4 = -2, \ -1, \ -1, \ -1, \ 1, \ 1. \quad \text{(Henceforth called } B_2)$$
$$B_3 + B_7 = 1, \ -1, \ -1, \ -1, \ 1, \ 1. \quad \text{(Henceforth call } B_3)$$
$$B_5 + B_6 = 2, \ -1, \ -1, \ -1, \ 1, \ 1. \quad \text{(Henceforth called } B_4)$$

Thereupon the computer will be asked to 'look' for the patterns
B_1, B_2, B_3 and B_4 as well as for some other formulae found in
this way. The paper tape with the thirty-five hymns is fed into
the machine and the answer comes out moments later. An
example of the answers for one hymn appears in Table XV.
The numbers in the first column indicate from which step the

Table XV. Computer Output with Formula Answers

STICH. DOGM. I AUTH. COISLIN 42..F.356 V. TILLYARD NR.3.

```
7   16    F1
5   19    P1
5   19    B4
6   25    C1
4   41    S.
6   47    F2
4   77    S.
6   87    D..
7  100    P1
6  106    Q.
9  115    B3
5  135    P1
5  135    B4
6  156    D.
6  167    C2
6  175    F2
6  191    N2
5  199    Y.
4  206    S.
6  213    B3
6  219    C1
9  237    B3
7  246    Y.
7  254    H.
7  261    B1
7  283    H.
7  291    H.
8  296    D.
9  297    B2
7
```

first neume in a formula is counted. The numbers in the middle column indicate on which neume number in the hymn the formula begins, and the letters in the last column give the designated 'names' of the formulae. The number standing alone at the bottom represents the last note in the hymn. From a glance at Table XV it is possible to see dimly the rough musical structure of the hymn, a point which is suggested by dotted lines. When the computer is requested to seek out more formulae, it will be possible to obtain a more detailed picture of the uses and combinations of formulae. Eventually it might be possible to locate those periods in the hymns which are not based on formulaic principles but are freely composed by a composer. Such musical periods may again help in a future project in tracing the individualistic stylistic traits of a certain composer, at a time when a more detailed scanning of medieval manuscripts and service books could be undertaken.

The hymn analyzed in Table XV consists of five sections. The first section cadences by using the formula C1-step 6 (this formula has been found in separate investigation to belong to Mode IA). The next musical period moves to a cadence on D-step 6 (which has been traced in IA and IP). The third part, while using the transitional formula B (which is analyzed further, see below), also cadences using formula D-step 6. The

Table XVI. Computer Output of One Hymn

[STICH. DOGM. I AUTH. COISLIN 42. F.356 V. TILLYARD NR.3.]

A.

I,I,P-D,EA,06,P,A8,EA D,0,0,OK 3 A8,AA,I5,

EA-D,OK7,A8 A,A D,0,P,EAA,X,A AA,0-D 2 EA,
       ——B4——

OK-D,0,80 2 AC,0,0,XK-D,

A,A,I,80 2 EA,06,06,X,I,I,I6,OK7 R X,98X,A AA,

I,I,0-D,P,AC,06,P,A8,A,0 3 A 8X,

EA,0,XK-D,A,A,A8,A,0,OK7,A,P,EP,A8,AA,I6,

I,X D,AE,OH,I,I,I,80K 2 7 A A8 AA,I6,06,XK,A AA,

I,I,OK6,I6,P,A8 A,A,06,8X,AE,I,I,
            B3

I,I,0,X,A,A,A8,A,IP,A,0,OK7,A8 A,A-D,06,
                  B4

I,I,PK-D,AE,IP,A,P,A8 A,

A,0,OK7,A,I,X,AE,A,A,I,

I,0-D,0,I,I,P,EA,9P,8AE,

A,OK,0,X D,EA D,06,X,I,I,I,0,X,A,A,

I,I,8X,AE,K 1 E,06,A A,I6,9 X X A 4 E 0,

A,0,XK-D,A,A,P,A,

P,A8 A,A D,0,P,EAA,X,A AA,0-D 2 EA,
  ——B3——

OK6,06,06,07,OK,I,I6,A,P-D,A8 A,A,06,8X,E6,I6,9 X X A 4 E 0,
                            B3

A,0,0-D,P,AE,8X,E6,I,IP,A8 A,A-D,06,X,I6,I,

IP,AAC,XH,I,I,I6,OK7 R X,98X,A AA,I,0-D,P,AE-D,AE,I,I,

0-D,0 1 E,P,E6,A8 A,A D,06,X,I6,I:
        B2

fourth section returns to C1-step 6. A peculiarity of the last segment is its use—three times!—of the very rare melodic phrase here designated as H. Comparisons with the text would probably reveal that the composer at this point in the melody has been tempted to transgress the laws of formulaic structure.

By using the formula output these melodic formulae will now easily be located in the coded hymn output. (Table XVI.)

The appearances of B1, B2, B3 and B4 in all the thirty-five hymns are tabulated in Table XVII (see over), which sums up the findings in which Mode, with what neumatic notation and on which step the B formulae have been traced.

Conclusions to be drawn from Table XVII are: B is a transitional melodic formula used in all eight Modes. It is most fre-

Table XVIII. Starting Tone in B1, B2, B3, B4 in all Modes

Mode	Formula								
I A	B1			X					
	B2			X		X	X		
	B3			X					
	B4			X					
II A	B3			X		X	X		
III A	B1			X					
	B3						X		
IV A	B1								X
	B3						X		
	B4							X	
I P	B1		X						
	B3	X	X	X					
	B4			X					
II P	B3		X	X					
	B4		X						
III P	B1			X					
	B3		X	X					
	B4			X					
IV P	B1					X	X		
	B3				X	X	X	X	
	B4					X		X	

TABLE XVII

Formula	Step	First note	I A	II A	III A
B1	6				
	7		IP,A8A,A—D,O6 (7 times)		IP,A8A,A—D,O5
	9				
	10				
	12				
B2	9		E6,A8A,A D,O6 (2 times) AE,A8A,AD,O6 (2 times)		
B3	4				
	5		(P—)D,AP,A AA,O—D ('false')		
	6		P,A8A,A D,O	(OP—)D,A 8A,A—D,O	
	8		P,A8A,A,O,O	(X—)D,A,A,A,O6,P(—D)	
	9		P,A8A,A,O6,8X (P—)D,A8A,A,O6,8X	P,A8A,A6,XD	P,A8A,A,O,O (2 times) X,A,A8,A,O—D
	10				
B4	4				
	5		OK7,A8A,A D,O6 (3 times) OP,A1A,AA,X D		
	7				
	9				

IV A	I P	II P	III P	IV P
	IP,A8A,A,O—D IX,A,A,A,O6,8X			
			IP,A8A,A—D, O6 (2 times)	
				IP,A8A,A—D,O6 (2 times)
				IP,A8A,A,O—D (2 times)
IP,A8A,A,O,O (2 times)				
	X,A,A,A,O,P(—D)			
	X,A,A,A,O6,8X (2 times) P,A8A,A,O—D	X,A,A8,A,O—D	P,A8A,A,O—D	
	P,A8A,A,O,O (2 times) O6,A,A1A,O6,O ('false')	(OP—)D,A8A,A—D,O6 (2 times)	X,A,A,AA,X,O6	O7,A8A,A—D,O6
				(IP—)D,A8A,A—D,O6
P,A8A,A,O,O				O5,A8A,A,O—D (IP—)D,A8A,A—D,O6 (2 times)
				X,A,A,A,O6,X
		OP,A8A,A,O—D		
	OK7,A,A8,A,O,P OK7,A,A8,AD,O		OK7,A8A,A—D,O6 (3 times)	
			XK,A,A82A,O—D	OP,A3,A8,AD,P(—D)
OK7,A8A,A—D,P·				OP,A8A,A—D,O5

quently found in IA (in which it had been located originally). B1 is not used in IIA and IIP. B2 is found only in IA. B3, being the 'most transitional' of the variants beginning with a step upwards, is used in all the Modes. B4 is not used in IIA and IIIA.—The Neumation of the formula is stable. Only a few 'false' answers appear, that is, answers in which the neumes differ so much from the normal usage that the formula must have been composed of two other formulae or melodic phrases. The *Petaste* or *Oxeia* are used on the first note in B1, B2 and B4 in almost all instances. When *Petaste* is involved then A8 A = ⋝ᴗ always follows immediately. When *Oxeia* is found at the beginning of the formula then the softening effect of the *Tzakisma* is not necessary.

In order to clarify the uses of varying starting notes for formula B the scheme shown in Table XVIII (p. 145) can be extracted from the preceding Table. Table XVIII shows that the melodic formula B can have as its first note any pitch from F to f except b. That is to say that a formula beginning on b:

is never sung in any of the thirty-five hymns. If a B flat could have been used or if that little melody could easily be sung from b, the melodic formula B on step 8 would not have been missing completely. This hypothesis, however, has to be checked in further investigations. Finally, the most common starting notes are a, c, and d as those which lie most conveniently in the scale.

(b) Another way of finding melodic formulae is to analyze one hymn, translate all the phrases to interval-questions, and request the computer to find out whether some of them are in fact formulae. If the computer does not provide enough answers, the phrases must be reduced in size by eliminating Isons (tone-repetitions) as well as special endings until several of the basic formulae appear. This experiment was conducted with the hymn already cited in Table IV. The following configurations were asked for:

Table XIX

$$D = 1,-2,-1,-1$$
$$E = 0,-2,1,-2,1,-2$$
$$F_1 = 0,-3,1,2$$
$$F_2 = 1,-3,1,1,1$$
$$G = 1,-1,-1,-1,0$$

Variants of a formula have to be sought out separately because the computer cannot locate formulae that are not exactly spelled out. For instance, F_1 will not include instances in which the last third is broken down into two successive seconds, therefore we have to ask for F_2 also. And if E happens to contain in its middle one or two Isons, we have to indicate that as well, because seen through a computer's 'eye' this would represent quite a different question. This particular problem cannot be solved at this time even if using the method discussed further on p. 152 under (d).

Table XX

Formula D. Main Results

I A	II A	III A	IV A	I P	II P	III P	IV P
	D-step 6						
8	1			8	6		3
	D-step 10		7				
	D-step 3			1			
	D-step 8						
5		6		1		1	

The answers obtained about the configurations represented in Table XIX, with respect to all thirty-five hymns, can be schematically arranged in analogy to Table XVII. From these schemes several conclusions may then be drawn. An example of a diagram that can be made is given in Table XX (on the previous page) in which the numbers indicate the frequency of formula D.

Thus, the formula D-step 6 is more frequently found in IA, IP and IIP rather than in IVP in which it was first located. D is also used in a major form on step 8 where it is found in IIIA (the neumation in four of the five instances in Mode IA being uncharacteristic).

As for formula E it is found in only one other hymn (in IVP). If the first Ison is eliminated from the count, it is found four times in IIP also, once in each hymn. On the basis of this it appears that formula E might be a 'special effect' rather than a formula.

The distribution of F₁ and F₂ in the Modes can be seen in the following table:

Table XXI

Formula F

I A	II A	III A	IV A	I P	II P	III P	IV P
		F 1-step 7					
3				I			3
		F 2-step 6					
5	I			I		I	2
		F 2-step 8					
		2					

The material is rather limited in number, yet it seems that as a formula F belongs to IA and IVP. In this case, also, a major form of the formula is used in IIIA.

The distribution of the melodic formula G, the last question asked, can be demonstrated in Table XXII.

Table XXII.

Formula G

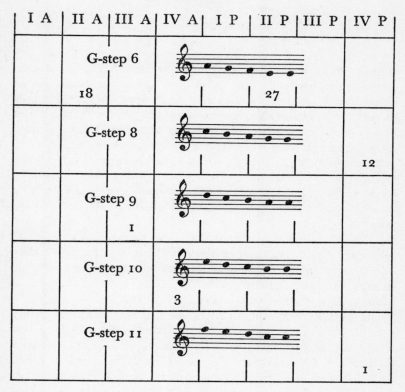

I A	II A	III A	IV A	I P	II P	III P	IV P
	G-step 6						
	18				27		
	G-step 8						
							12
	G-step 9						
		1					
	G-step 10						
			3				
	G-step 11						
							1

The minor form of G belongs to IIA and IIP whereas the major form is used only in IVP. The answers for steps 9, 10 and 11 are 'false,' but they show what Table XVIII has already demonstrated, that this brief melody can be sung beginning on all pitches (6–11) except from pitch 7 = b.

(c) Formulae already located in some different musical material may also be asked for from the computer. In his *A History of Byzantine Music and Hymnography*, pp. 418–27, Wellesz listed some formulae from the First Mode in the Heir-

mologion. These could be used exactly as they stand in the
volume: A with 20 variants, B with 21 variants, etc., but in
translating the 20 variants of A into questions for a computer,
they can be reduced to only three questions, namely:

$$A = -1, -2, 1, 1, 1$$
$$A1 = -1, -1, -1, 1, 1, 1$$
$$A2 = -3, 1, 1, 1, 2, -1, -1$$

If these three formulations were to be 'asked' from Wellesz'
material then the computer would find all the locations cited in
in the book, all twenty variants. One may wonder whether
these formulae from the Heirmologion can also be traced in the
Stichera Dogmatica. So, the computer was asked to locate some
fifteen formulae, namely Wellesz' formulae A, B, C, D, E, F
and G with variants (H was not included because it is the same
as F). Answers came out in great quantity. Preliminary results,
based only on the formula output (like the one in Table XV)
indicate that eleven out of fifteen formulae have their correspondences. Formulae D and G with one variant each are not
used at all. Either they are peculiar and used only in the Heirmologion repertory, or they may be 'special effects', or they
may be proper for a group of manuscripts to which our basic
source, Coislin 42, does not belong. The greatest number of
answers came from IA and IP, IIIa and IIIP.

(d) Finally, a method can be mentioned which is purely
mechanical. The computer may be asked to discover formulae
by taking the first three melodic intervals in a hymn and look
for them in all the encoded hymns. Thereafter, it can be asked
to follow up with the interval combinations of neumes 2, 3,
4, and so on. The same process could then be repeated taking
the first 4 intervals, then the first 5 etc., until at last no further
answers can be obtained.

The disadvantage of such a method is that the output will be
overwhelming and the effort invested into sorting and arranging the answers will be far greater than by preparing the
questions in advance by methods (a), (b) or (c). The only
advantage would consist in the fact that nothing has been left
overlooked except, as has already been mentioned, those instances in which a formula is either enlarged or contracted.

Conclusions

In the present work only problems concerning the melodies have been taken into consideration. Many other questions still remain to be studied. Among these are the question of how the text affects the rhythm, the accents, and the combination of melodic formulae; how the medial signatures are used,[7] etc. These investigations will be easier if one has *a clear and exact copy of the codex* like the one in a neume-code output (see Table XVI), instead of a microfilm of a manuscript or an ordinary transcription. The intonations and medial signatures can be coded and inserted in the already encoded material.

The *rapidity of the computer* has such an effect on the researcher that one is never forced to abandon an idea only because it would be much too time-consuming. Questions posed to a computer would receive answers in minutes.

The *precision of the computer* has been demonstrated in the investigations of the melodic formula B. A 'manual' study of the material had revealed thirteen instances of that formula (Table X). The computer located fifteen such instances and in addition to that three instances of the same formula used on different melodic steps (Table XVII). With this result one can be certain that no more such instances will ever be found in the body of materials that were examined.

The computer's *ability to handle and to store considerable quantities of data* can be used, among other things, to produce all sorts of indices and concordances. The more material one stores into a computer the more help one will obtain from it. When the two thousand hymns from a whole Sticherarion as well as manuscripts from other periods and genres are stored in a computer, the possibilities of research transcend one's imagination.

[7] This could be combined with the studies already conducted by Jørgen Raasted in his *Intonation Formulas and Modal Signatures in Byzantine Musical Manuscripts*, *MMB*, *Subsidia*, vii (Copenhagen, 1966).

With reference to the use of computers, the editors have received a communication from Dr. Hanoch Avenary of the Tel-Aviv University which may be of some interest to readers:

The whole body of Byzantine hymns found in the nine volumes of 'Monumenta Musicae Byzantinae' — series 'Transcripta' — has been computer-recorded by the Department of Musicology of the Tel-Aviv University. In addition to its own research work, the Department is prepared to accept external commissions for processing the stored musical data (including the programming of planned research schemes). For information please apply to Dr. Hanoch Avenary, Department of Musicology, Tel-Aviv University, Ramat Aviv, Israel.

12

Miloš Velimirović

MADISON, WISCONSIN

The Musical Works of Theoleptos, Metropolitan of Philadelphia

THE life and literary works of Theoleptos, Metropolitan of Philadelphia in Asia Minor, are fairly well known in Byzantine studies. He was a prominent figure in the religious life of the late thirteenth and the first quarter of the fourteenth centuries.[1] In some of the listings of his writings there are references to his poetic works which still remain to be published. Yet nowhere in all the available literature is it indicated that Theoleptos was also a composer of religious music. This may be due to the fact that scholars studying literary figures seldom analyse and explore the wealth of data about poets in the extant Byzantine musical manuscripts.

It is quite possible to argue about the authenticity of the works preserved in musical manuscripts: the texts may well have been written by well-known literary figures, while the music itself may have been composed by a musician whose name is lost to posterity, or vice versa. Yet for the musical documents of the late Byzantine Empire, especially after A.D. 1200, it would seem that the degree of attention paid to the execution of the musical manuscripts warrants the assumption that *in most instances* the references to authors are quite trustworthy. In such sources one frequently encounters only a

---

[1] The most recent encyclopedic article on Theoleptos is that by the Reverend V. Laurent in Θρησκευτικὴ καὶ ἠθικὴ ἐγκυκλοπαιδεία, vol. VI (Athens, 1965), cols. 249-50. Cf. also Hans-Georg Beck, *Kirche und theologische Literatur im byzantinischen Reich* (München, 1959), pp. 693-4 and the extensive study by J. Gouillard in *Dictionnaire de théologie catholique*, vol. 15[1] (Paris, 1946), 339-41.

single name listed as author (presumably of both text and music). The custom of practicing both arts—hymnography and music—is known for more than one period of the history of Byzantine literature. Thus it would seem that the evidence offered by musical manuscripts may be accepted at face-value until other data require its modification.

Probably the document closest to the period of Theoleptos' lifetime, recording his name as the author (of both text and music!) is a fragment at present in the Parliament Library in Athens, No. 58, which contains a hymn in honour of John of Damascus.[2] The fact that this hymn is preceded by a monody attributed to Nicephor Gregoras, another contemporary of Theoleptos, supports the assumption of an early dating of this fragment, in addition to the purely paleographic evidence which suggests an early fourteenth-century date. The neumatic musical notation is rather archaic, a quite clear sample of Middle Byzantine Notation, and certainly could not be dated later than the middle of the fourteenth century. A detailed examination of the fragment also reveals that the original notation was written in a now faded brownish ink and that almost all neumes were at a later date retraced with a black ink. This can be proved by a glance at the second word on folio 8r where above the last syllable there is an *elaphron* with *dyo kentemata*. The elaphron was retraced, but the *dyo kentemata* were not and still can be clearly seen to have been written in a different and earlier ink. An additional point of interest is the shape of the *petaste*, which appears throughout this fragment in a peculiar shape encountered relatively seldom in obtainable musical manuscripts. The closest parallel to the shape of the *petaste* in this fragment is that found in an early fourteenth-century Heirmologion, MS Saba 617, now in Jerusalem.[3]

The hymn is preceded by an inscription beginning close to the middle of folio 7v, and the hymn ends before the end of

[2] This manuscript was described briefly by Sp. Lambros in his catalogue published in *Νέος 'Ελληνομνήμων*, vol. III (1906), pp. 243-4. My measurements of this fragment are 21.8 × 14 cm. It appears that this quire of eight folios may have been torn out of a larger gathering since there is an original quire-numbering at the bottom right corner of the first folio recto indicating it to be the first quire.

[3] For an easily accessible facsimile see this writer's *Byzantine Elements in Early Slavic Chant*, Volume of Appendices, *Monumenta Musicae Byzantinae, Subsidia*, IVb (Copenhagen, 1960), Plate 12*.

folio 8r. The inscription reads: Μηνί δεκεμβρίου δ΄. Στιχηρόν εἰς τὸν ἅγιον Ἰω(αννην) τ(ὸν) Δαμασκηνόν. Ποίημα τοῦ πανϊερωτάτου Μητροπολίτου Φϊλαδελφείας καὶ πανϋπερτίμου Κῦρου Θεολήπτου. The memory of St. John of Damascus is celebrated in the Greek Orthodox Church on 4 December, and thus this piece, which is missing in the present-day Menaia, is liturgically correct. The question may be raised as to why Theoleptos would compose such a sticheron in honour of John of Damascus. It would seem that in the light of one of his activities a plausible suggestion may be made: a unique reference to the relics of John of Damascus in a Constantinopolitan repository appears rather late, in the early fifteenth century, in the writings of the Russian Zosima.[4] According to him these relics were in the church of the Virgin 'Kekharitoméni' which was next door to a nunnery dedicated to Christ 'Philanthropos.' If one were to follow Reverend V. Laurent's identification this would present almost no problem at all.[5] It is known that Theoleptos was the confessor and spiritual father of Princess Irene, who as nun received the name Eulogia and became the abbess of the nunnery of Christ 'Philanthropos.' There is only a difficulty if there were two monasteries of the same name in Constantinople.[6] If Laurent's identification is correct, Theoleptos, who was deeply involved in preaching in Irene-Eulogia's monastery, might have known of the existence of these relics and have quite appropriately composed this sticheron. This is, however, a hypothesis which will have to be verified at a later date, when the problem of 'one versus two churches of the same name' can satisfactorily be solved.

This attribution will undoubtedly find additional support in some of the Sticheraria written in the fourteenth and fifteenth centuries, when the full indexing of these manuscripts and collation of titles is accomplished. We have been able, however,

---

[4] Deacon Zosima's trip took place in 1419-21 and is usually cited in a French translation by B. de Khitrowo, *Itinéraires Russes en Orient* (Genève, 1889), pp. 199-201, especially p. 204. The best Russian edition of the original text is that by Chr. M. Loparev in the series *Pravoslavnyĭ Palestinskiĭ Sbornik*, fasc. 24 (St. Peterburg, 1889), where the pertinent passage may be found on p. 7.

[5] 'Une princesse byzantine au cloître,' in *Échos d'Orient*, 29 (1930), pp. 29-60, especially pp. 45-8.

[6] This problem is raised in R. Janin's *La géographie ecclésiastique de l'empire byzantin*, Part I: *Le siège de Constantinople et le patriarcat œcuménique*, Tome III—Les églises et les monastères (Paris, 1953), pp. 539-44.

to locate the same hymn in a late fifteenth (or early sixteenth) century manuscript in the National Library in Athens, MS No. 917, which appears to be an anthology compiled by a certain Akakios Chalkeopoulos, who deemed it necessary to 'embellish' nearly every musical composition included in this manuscript. Curiously enough, the text of this sticheron seems to be somewhat better preserved in Akakios' version (fols. 159r–160r), although the music is completely different. Akakios' authorship of the music is supported by his monogram preceding the music. The inscription in MS No. 917 preceding this piece reads: *Τοῦ πανϊερωτάτου Μ(ητ)ροπολίτου Φιλαδελφίας Κύρου Θεολύπτου, ἐγγόμιον ἰδιόμελον εἰς τὸν ἅγ(ιον) 'Ιωάννην τὸν Δαμασκηνὸν, καὶ ἐπακόλουθον πρὸς τὸν ἅγιον 'Ιωάννην τὸν Πρόδρομον.* Appended to this study are the full version of this hymn from the fourteenth-century fragment in the Parliament Library in Athens as well as a few of the opening lines of Akakios' version of the same hymn.

The only other known musical setting by Theoleptos has been traced in appendices to two Sticheraria, both from the fourteenth century. The hymn begins with what seems at first glance to be a well-known text: *Οὐράνιε βασιλεῦ.* This incipit is recorded only in Euchologia.[7] The two manuscripts in which this hymn was located are both in the National Library in Athens, MS 884, fols. 221r and 221v; and MS 895, fols. 246r and 246v.[8] The version in MS 884 omits a few words in two places so that for the text itself the version in MS 895 is preferable and fuller than in the other manuscript. Musically, the two versions contain some variants, yet the main body of the musical structure is of the same melodic substance. As for the liturgical indications, MS 884 has none, simply preceding the hymn with the inscription: *ποίημα μητροπολίτου Φιλαδελφίας.* The other manuscript, No. 895, contains this inscription: *Θεολήπτου Φιλαδελφίας εἰς παράκλισιν.* According to Goar's edition of the Euchologion[9] this text is listed as a Troparion to

[7] According to the pertinent entry in Enrica Follieri's *Initia Hymnorum Ecclesiae Graecae*, III ('Studi e Testi,' 213, Città del Vaticano, 1962), p. 228.

[8] The listings in I. and A. I. Sakkelion, *Κατάλογος τῶν χειρογράφων τῆς ἐθνικῆς βιβλιοθήκης τῆς Ελλάδος* (Athens, 1892), pp. 159-60 and 163 are very brief and do not mention the name of Theoleptos.

[9] Jacobus Goar, *Euchologion sive Rituale Graecorum* (2nd ed., Venice, 1730), p. 623.

be sung after the kanon 'εἰς φόβον σεισμοῦ.' The possible reason and inducement for this composition of Theoleptos has yet to be determined.[10]

The compositional procedure followed by Theoleptos in these two hymns agrees with the basic tenets of musical composition of the period in question, and the hymns are good examples of reliance on melodic formulae to structure the pieces, with careful observances of melodic and textual stresses. Stylistically neither of the pieces displays 'individualistic' elements. In fact, the melodic lines of both hymns resemble those to be found in numerous similar hymns. Yet the fact that these were written by Theoleptos is significant, in that with these works another name of a composer of liturgical music is added to the roster of names of Byzantine musicians, from which it has hitherto been missing.

---

[10] During the lifetime of Theoleptos there was at least one quite serious earthquake in Constantinople, in 1296. Cf. Glanville Downey, 'Earthquakes at Constantinople and Vicinity, A.D. 342-1454,' *Speculum*, 30 (1955), pp. 596-600. If it were possible to prove that Theoleptos composed his poem shortly after this calamity, this could easily become one of the few Byzantine musical compositions for which immediate circumstances which led to their creation may be known.

Γ″ Ἡμὸν χεῖρ τοῦ βαπτιστοῦ δεσποτικῆς κορυφῆς ἁ-ψαμένη

τρόμῳ συν-ή-χε-το. ἡ δὲ σὴ _____ χεῖρ πάτερ

᾿Ι--ω-άν-νη. τὰ εὐσεβῆ τῆς ἐκκλησίας γρά-φου-σα δόγ-μα-τα

τὸ μὴν ὑπέστη παρὰ τῶν μὴ τὰ θεῖα τρέμων τῶν ἀ-νο-σί-ων.

καὶ ὁ μέν δακτίλῳ _____ τοῖς λαοῖς καθυπέδειξε τὸν αἴροντα

τὴν ἁμαρτίαν τοῦ κόσμου. σὺ _____ δὲ τὴν χεῖρα πάλιν

σὺ ἀν-α-πολα-βῶν, καὶ πρὸς τὸ γράφειν ταύ-την ἀτρόμως κινῶν.

τοῖς μὲν πιστοῖς ἐσαφήνι-σας τὰ ἀπόρ-ρη-τα. τῶν δὲ ἀπίστων

ἐστηλί-τευσας τὰ φρονή-μα-τα. οὔτε _____ γὰρ ἐκεῖ _____

ὁ ἐκ τῆς ἀφῆς τρόμος τῷ ἀψαμένῳ βλάβην προσέφε- ρεν. _____

οὔτε πάλιν ἐνταῦθα ἡ τῆς σῆς χειρὸς ὑ-πέρ-χη ἐκ-το-μὴ

κολό - βω-σιν ἢ — νεγκεν. ἐπ᾽ εἶδε τῶν ἀμφοτέρων αἱ χεῖρες

Χριστῷ δὴ οἰκο νο μει το τῇ χειρὶ δι - ακρατουν-σι τα σύμπαντα.

δι - ὸ _____ καὶ ὡς ἐκεῖνος τὸ πνεῦμα τε-θέ-α-ται, καὶ

σὺ _____ τὴν τοῦ πνεύματος ἔλ λαμ-ψιν ὑπε-δέ-ξω μακάριος καὶ

θεωρός. τῶν μυ-στη-ρίων γε - γενή - σαν, καὶ τῶν εὐσεβῶν τὰς

δι-α-νοί-ας ἐφώ-τι-σας σέβειν τὴν τρι-ά-δα τὴν ἄ-κτισ-τον.

Since this hymn appears in a so far unique manuscript, it was necessary to emend certain sections in order to maintain the steady appearance of the typical cadential formulae of Mode III. All emendations are marked with an asterisk above the respective note for which a change in pitch appears to have offered the most plausible solution. The emendations are:

1) Line 5, second note: the manuscript has a second upward.
2) Line 8, ninth note: after this the manuscript has a second downward.
3) Line 13, third word: the text appears to be garbled and (including the preceding syllable) reads: δι οἰκονομυντο. An additional note has been added to fill in the melodic progression from d^l to a.

For the sake of comparison, the opening of the version embellished by Akakios Chalkeopoulos is here quoted:

Ἡμον χεὶρ τοῦ βαπτιστοῦ   δεσποτικῆς   κορυφῆς

ἀ-ψαμέ-νη,   τρο - - - - - - - - τρο-μῳ   συνή-χε-το. ἡ δὲ σὴ

χεὶρ πάτερ Ἰ-ω-αν-νη. τὰ εὐσεβῆ   τῆς ἐκκλη--σί--ας γράφουσα

δόγ-μα-τα. τὸ μὴν ὑ--πεσ-τη παρὰ τῶν τὰ θεῖα μὴ τιμων

τῶν ἀν-ο--σί-ων.   καὶ ὁ μέν   δακτίλῳ τοῖς λαοῖς . . . .

Athens, MS 895, fol. 246r.

Οὐράνιε βασιλεῦ,   φιλάνθρωπε Κύ-ρι-ε, μακρόθυμε καὶ πολυ--έλε--ε,

ἔ-πι-   δε ἐξ ἁ-γί-ου κατοι-κη-τη-ρι--ου σου

ἴ-   δε τὴν ταπείνωσιν ἡμῶν, ἴ-   δε καὶ τὴν κάκωσιν ἡμῶν,

μὴ τῷ θυμῷ   σου ἐλέξῃς ἡ-   μας,   μηδὲ τῇ ὀργῇ   σου

The most significant variants in MS Athens 884 are:

1) The two opening words:

Οὐράνιε   βασιλεῦ

2) After the first Medial Signature (line 2 above):

ἔ - πι   δὲ ἐξ   ἁγίου   κατοικητηρί-   ου

3) After the Medial Signature in line 5 above:

μὴ παραδώῃς ἡμᾶς   εἰς   χεῖρας   τῶν ἀνόμων.

4) After the Medial Signature in line 8 above:

ἔ-χεις   ἔμφυτον   τὴν ἀ - γα-θό- -τητα

π ϡ   σκέ -   πε τὴν πόλιν ταύτην.

5) The text and music for μετὰ τοῦ ἀρχαγγέλου (line 10 above) are missing; the following word χορόν appears in the following setting:

6) The second half of line 12 (above) and the whole of line 13
contain the most extended set of differences between the two
manuscripts. The segment following the Medial Signature
in line 12 above, appears in this setting in MS 884:

The text and music for τῶν σε παρακαλούντων (beginning of
line 13 above) are completely missing in MS 884 and the
preceding segment is immediately followed by the text which
is to be found after the Medial Signature in line 13 with
this melody:

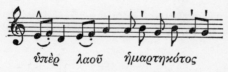

7) Finally, the endings of this piece differ in the two manuscripts. These have already been written out in line 15
above with the accompanying variant.

13

Miloš Velimirović

MADISON, WISCONSIN

An Unusual Russian 'Spiritual Verse'

LATE in 1967, the distinguished Russian musicologist Maksim Viktorovich Brazhnikov published an interesting volume of transcriptions of melodies from Russian musical manuscripts of the seventeenth century.[1] Among the thirteen pieces contained in this volume, one is attracting special attention as it represents a unique composition for which a purely liturgical attribution appears extremely unlikely due to its text. Brazhnikov supplied a brief commentary on this piece giving some interesting data about the origin of this 'verse'. This, it appears, must have been composed in the 1620s and in its text refers to the statuary on one of the main towers over a gate leading into the Kremlin in Moscow.[2] The text of this 'verse' in a free English translation reads:

> 'O come, let us enter into the ruling city of Moscow and see how the diabolic charms appeared from the evil enemies, Greek magicians. With their witchcraft and evil intentions they threw charms over the ruling and very wise leaders of the Russian state, abusing our orthodox faith. They elevated their idols and placed them above the gates of the city, above the representation [painting] of Our Lord Jesus Christ, which is not made by human hands, but sent by God to Avgar, the prince of Edessa, for his own healing and to all the faithful for their salvation. So then, brothers, let us all weep, let us exclaim calling upon the all-powerful God so that he may save us from bowing to the idols. Through the intercessions and prayers of the Mother of God and of all of your saints, have mercy upon us.'

The source for this 'spiritual verse' is Manuscript No. 637 in

---

[1] *Novye pamiatniki znamennogo raspeva* (Leningrad, 1967), 82 pages.
[2] *Ibid.*, pp. 37-41 (transcription) and 81-2 (commentary).

the collection of A. A. Titov, folios 62v–64r where it appears without any special heading.[3]

The episode to which this text refers is quite well documented even though the statuary which seems to have led to the composition of the 'verse' no longer occupies a prominent place. Brazhnikov refers only to the extensive study of the Moscow Kremlin by Bartenev, which contains very detailed architectural plans as well as a few photographs of some of the surviving statuary; these however represent only animals.[4]

The gate in question is a well-known one, on the northeastern walls of the Kremlin, and to this day can be seen in its 'reconstructed' form, the first gate to the south-east of Lenin's mausoleum. While in earlier times it was known as 'Frolov's gate' (*Frolovskiya vorota*) since 1658 it has been called the 'Saviour's gate' (*Spasskiya vorota*) after a wall-painting of Jesus over the passage-way inside the gate, above which the tower with its clock and bells were clearly visible.[5] Even in earlier periods, a structure with a bell-tower did exist there, which may be discerned in one of the drawings with a map of the Kremlin of 1610.[6] Although Russian historians believe that a clock may have been installed as early as the construction of the first gate (*c.* 1491), the first documented reference to a special person in charge of the clock dates only from 1585. It is also recorded that in 1614, when stability returned to Russia after the 'time of troubles,' the clock on Frolov's gate was repaired.[7]

[3] *Ibid.*; for basic information about Titov see *Entsiklopedicheskiĭ slovar* [Brokgauz–Efron], Vol. XXXIII (St. Peterburg, 1901), p. 256; This manuscript has not yet been described in available literature. A rather detailed description of some 140 (of more than 4,000) manuscripts in this collection is available in *Opisanie slaviano-russkikh rukopiseĭ* ('Obshchestvo liubiteleĭ drevneĭ pismennosti,' vol. 106, St. Peterburg, 1893).

[4] S. P. Bartenev, *Moskovskiĭ Kreml' v' starinu i teper'* (Moskva, 1912), pp. 123-50, especially p. 139. See also pictures No. 151 (p. 135), Nos. 156-9 (pp. 139-41) and No. 161 (p. 143). If there had been representations of human beings these do not seem to have survived; and the reference implying that human figures were also carved and exhibited may be found in *Istoriia Moskvy*, Vol. I (Moskva, Akademiia Nauk SSSR, 1952), p. 494.

[5] Bartenev, *op. cit.*, p. 126; see also *Po Kremliu, kratkiĭ putevoditel'* (Moskva, 1964), pp. 30-4.

[6] Bartenev, *op. cit.*, p. 138, picture No. 155.

[7] *Ibid.*, p. 139; see also Ivan Zabielin, *Istoriia goroda Moskvy*, 2nd ed., Vol. I (Moskva, 1905), pp. 186-7.

M

The interesting part of the subsequent developments begins with the arrival in Russia, in 1621, of a certain Christopher Halloway—'clockmaster from England'[8]. Halloway is said to have suggested the building of a brick-and-stone tower, of larger proportions than the previous one and with a new clock of his own manufacture. This suggestion was accepted and the tower materialized in the course of 1624–5. In describing this well-known tower, basically the same today in spite of a number of reconstructions, Russian historians of architecture stress the harmonious blending of Western European Gothic elements with the native Russian use of successive layers of bricks and white stones.[9] Halloway is believed to have planned and supervised the execution of the work, in which a number of Russian builders participated.[10] In September 1624 the old machinery was sold by weight for forty-eight roubles,[11] and by the end of 1625 the new machinery with a carillon was installed, as may be inferred from a reference to a bell-maker, Kyril Samoïlov, who in that year made some thirteen bells especially for the new tower.[12] On 29 January 1626 Halloway was richly re-

---

[8] The available Russian literature is unanimous that Halloway was an Englishman even though some references occasionally call him a 'German'. The spelling 'Halloway,' which Russian sources imply to have been the original one, is seldom found in British biographical dictionaries. More often one encounters names like 'Galloway' or 'Holloway' (either of which would have made little difference to the Russian pronunciation!). Cf. G. H. Baillie, *Watchmakers and Clockmakers of the World* (London, 1929), p. 182 where the earliest related reference appears to be to a John Holloway in 1611. In the *Bolshaia Sovetskaia Entsiklopediia* 2nd ed., Vol. 10 (1952), p. 151, Halloway is said to have been of Scottish origin, yet he is not listed in John Smith's *Old Scottish Clockmakers from 1453 to 1850* (Edinburgh, 1921). At any rate Halloway can be traced in Russian documents until *c.* 1645, as either 'clockmaster' or builder of waterworks. Cf. N. I. Falkovskiï, *Moskva v istorii tekhniki* (Moskva, 1959), pp. 115 (waterworks), 232 and 417-19 (the latter referring to his work on the tower-clock). The absence of any contemporary reference in England is understandable since the 'Clockmakers' Company' of London was incorporated only in 1631. Cf. Herbert Cescinsky, *The Old English Clockmakers* (London, 1938), p. 17. For a discussion of this step as an attempt to stem the tide of foreign clockmakers on the English market, see Carlo M. Cipolla, *Clock and Culture* (London, 1967), pp. 65-8 and 143-4.

[9] N. I. Brunov and others, *Istoriia russkoi arkhitektury*, 2nd ed. (Moskva, 1956), p. 180.

[10] *Istoriia Moskvy* (see note 4 above), *loc. cit.*

[11] Zabielin, *op. cit.*, p. 187; Bartenev, *op. cit.*, p. 139 gives the date as 1625! The total weight did not exceed 'sixty puds' or approximately 2160 lbs., counting one 'pud' as 36 lbs. Cf. N. V. Ustiugov, 'Ocherk drevnerusskoï metrologii,' *Istoricheskie zapiski*, xix (1946), pp. 344ff.

[12] Zabielin and Bartenev, in the same places.

warded for his work by both the Emperor Michael Romanov and the Patriarch Filaret.[13]

No sooner had the work been completed than a fire, in May of the same year, destroyed the tower. Everything had to be rebuilt. This time the work was brought to completion in 1628 and in August of that year Halloway as well as other persons were again rewarded amply for their endeavours.[14] Halloway's further stay in Russia does not appear to have been connected with this clock and its carillon. It is not known to what extent Halloway's masterpiece was damaged in the great fire of the Kremlin on 5 October 1654, but it is generally assumed that after that calamity a completely different mechanism was in use.

While Halloway's original work was still in progress, the appearance of the statues seems to have created sufficient stir among the populace for the Emperor to issue a special decree on 6 October 1624, authorizing the purchase of English cloth in various colours to cover up the 'heathen statues' on the tower being built above Frolov's gate.[15] This suggests that the musical composition under discussion must have come into existence as soon as the statuary became visible, since it lost its topicality once the statues were covered. The decree, in other words, seems to represent a direct reply to the plea enunciated in the 'spiritual verse' set to music of which a transcription follows.[16]

The formulaic structure of this musical composition is easily apparent, yet even though the melodic formulae permeate this work there is no strict musical form observable. The profuse use of formulae as one of the structural elements provides an additional insight into the process by which new pieces can be composed relying on a melodic repertory which has, for centuries, been more or less common property in the vast body of the Russian Chant.

---

[13] Halloway received a silver cup and a number of different items valued at more than 10,000 roubles (at the 1912 exchange rate!). Cf. Bartenev, *loc. cit.*, for a full list. The expense book from which this is quoted is described briefly in A. Viktorov's *Opisanie zapisnykh knig i bumag starinnykh dvortsovykh prikazov 1584-1725 g.*, Fasc. I (Moskva, 1877), p. 129, item No. 281(923), fol. 715.

[14] Bartenev, *loc. cit.*   [15] *Ibid.*

[16] Compared to Brazhnikov's transcription, the note-values have been reduced by half. The Mode—'Glas 5'—corresponds to the First Plagal Mode in the Byzantine Chant. This writer is indebted to Mr. Brazhnikov for his permission to reproduce his transcription in a Western European publication.

fol. 62v.

Pri- i- di- te, vni- dem v tsa- rstvu- iu- ščii grad

Mo- skvu i vi- dim vsi ra- zu- mno,

ka- ko ia- vi- sia pre- lest vra- ži- ia ot zlyh

vra- gov e- llin-skih vol- hvov, i -že svo- im

f. 63r

ča-ro- va- ni- -em i zlym u- my- šle- ni- em

pre- l'sti- ša vla- do- myh i mno-go- ra- zum- nyh

na- čal-ni-kov rus- ski- ia der-ža- vy, ru- ga-

iu-šče-sia na- šeĭ pra- vo- slavneĭ ve- re;

ia-ko vo-zne- so- ša ku- mi- ry svo-ia i po- sta- vi- li

ih nad vra-ty grad- ny- mi, pre-vi-še o-

i-dol-sko-go po-kla-nia- ni- ia. Mo- litva-mi bo-go- ro-

di-

cy

i vseh sviatyh tvoih, po-mi- luĭ nas.

14

Edward V. Williams

LAWRENCE, KANSAS

The Treatment of Text in the Kalophonic Chanting of Psalm 2

By the beginning of the fourteenth century a new type of music manuscript was being used in the services of the Byzantine Church. Entitled 'Akolouthiai', this manuscript contained within one volume a collection of chants in the order of the morning and evening offices as well as music for the three Liturgies.[1] Two of the fifteen Akolouthiai manuscripts which survive from the fourteenth century are preserved in the National Library in Athens: MS. 2458 (A.D. 1336) and MS. 2622 (A.D. 1341– *c.* 1360). These have served as the basis of this study.[2]

---

[1] Professor Kenneth Levy gives a concise description of the contents of this type of music manuscript in his study 'A Hymn for Thursday in Holy Week,' *Journal of the American Musicological Society* xvi (1963), pp. 155, 157. The initial compilation of chants for the Akolouthiai manuscripts is believed to have been the work of John Koukouzeles, a fourteenth century Athonite monk and composer, who lived near the Great Laura.

[2] The oldest dated manuscript of this type is MS. 2458 (A.D. 1336). There are 31 quires remaining of which all but three are complete (i.e. eight folios each). The first quire is represented by only two folios while the last two quires are incomplete and contain only four and two folios respectively. The manuscript measures 22.3 × 14.6 cm. and now contains 232 folios.

Athens MS. 2622 measures 22.3 × 14.5 cm. and contains 423 folios. From the manuscript remain forty-nine complete quires of eight folios each and seven quires which are defective. Ten folios precede the first complete quire (δ); these are the only remaining folios from the first three quires (α, β, γ). If the last quire be the final one, there is a total of twenty-five folios missing from this manuscript. Professor Strunk dates MS. 2622 in the middle of the fourteenth century on the basis of its imperial acclamations, which include the name of the Empress-regent, Anne of Savoy (regnal years 1341-7). Oliver Strunk, 'The Antiphons of the Oktoechos,' *Journal of the American Musicological Society*, xiii (1960), pp. 53-4.

Great Vespers (*Μεγάλος ἑσπερινός*), which are preserved at
the beginning of the two Athens manuscripts, reveal two basic
types of musical setting for some of the Psalm texts prescribed
in the evening office: (1) a simple setting[3] of selected verses
from Psalm 103 (the Prooemiac Psalm) and also for the 'first
Antiphon', consisting of the texts of Psalms 1, 2, and 3, which
follow; (2) a more elaborate and extended treatment of selected
lines from Psalm 2 called 'kalophonic' verses. The latter are set
apart from the simple versions and are usually found immediately after the simple Doxology of Psalm 3.

The terse simple verses for Psalm 103 and the first antiphon[4]
(Psalms 1, 2, and 3) represent relatively straightforward settings
of not more than one line of Psalm text; frequently only a
portion of one line is set.[5] This text is followed by the refrains

[3] The term 'simple' actually embraces two kinds of settings which should be
distinguished. There are compositions designated by one of three words: ἀρχαῖον,
παλαιὸν, or ἄλλαγμα. This category of simple setting can be called 'quasi-
traditional', but the precise distinctions intended among the terms ἀρχαῖον,
παλαιὸν, and ἄλλαγμα are not entirely clear. 'Ἀρχαῖον and παλαιὸν are two
terms apparently used to indicate an anonymous chant melody which was 'old',
or 'traditional' as we would say. Levy has pointed out that the attribution
παλαιὸν, which some of the simple settings bear, indicates at least relative age.
Levy, *op. cit.*, p. 156. Ἄλλαγμα, on the other hand, denotes some kind of
'change' or 'exchange' that took place in singing. In MS. 2622 ἄλλαγμα occurs
in the margin beside verse 1 of Psalm 2 and Psalm 3 and may signal the change
of Psalm which took place at these two points. The use of ἄλλαγμα is much
more common for Psalm verses of Vespers in MS. 2458; roughly one verse in
four carries this designation. While the term usually stands alone, it can also be
found linked with other words and phrases such as: ἄλλαγμα παλαιὸν, ἄλλαγμα
τοῦ μαΐστορου κυρίου Ἰωάννη τοῦ Κουκουζέλη, or ἀπό χ[ο]ρ[οῦ] ἄλλαγμα.
The third example may be an indication that originally designated the shift
in chanting from the right-hand choir to the left-hand choir. But MS. 2458
certainly implies that ἄλλαγμα stood as a performance rubric and did not
necessarily designate an anonymous composition.
  The second kind of simple verse setting, which carries a specific attribution to
a given composer, can be called 'newly composed'. Concerning the Alleluiarion
cycle, Thodberg has used the term 'classical' to distinguish the shorter and more
conservative settings from the longer kalophonic versions. Cf. Christian Thodberg,
Der byzantinische Alleluiarionzyklus: Studien im kurzen Psaltikonstil, Monumenta
Musicae Byzantinae, Subsidia viii (Copenhagen, 1966), pp. 27-9.
[4] For a definition of the term 'antiphon' in Byzantine liturgical usage, see Strunk,
op. cit., p. 50.
[5] The two systems of verse division in the Greek Psalter are directly connected
with the difference in the system of verse numeration in the Constantinopolitan
and Palestinian Psalters. For an explanation of this difference as it affects
Psalmody in the Byzantine offices, see Oliver Strunk, 'The Byzantine Offices at
Hagia Sophia,' *Dumbarton Oaks Papers* 9-10 (1956), p. 192.
  Each Psalm verse contains one or more lines. When there is more than one

EXAMPLE 1

Simple verse setting
Athens MS. 2622, Psalm 2, v. 1, f. 13ʳ ἄλλαγμα

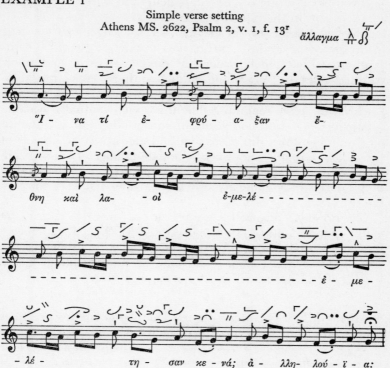

Δόξα σοι ὁ Θεός (for Psalm 103 in its simple form and with 'tropes'[6] and Ἀλληλούια (for Psalms 1, 2, and 3). The vocal style

---

line, each will be designated by a letter; hence verse 4a and verse 4b in Psalm 2. Sometimes a line is further subdivided into two parts; when this is the case each part will carry an additional numerical designation: verse 4a¹ and verse 4a². A diagram will clarify this procedure of text designation:

$$1 \qquad\qquad 2$$

Psalm 2, v. 4a: ὁ κατοικῶν ἐν οὐρανοῖς   ἐκγελάσεται αὐτούς
          v. 4b: καὶ ὁ κύριος ἐκμυκτηριεῖ αὐτούς

The Psalter used for this study is the edition of the Septuagint by A. Rahlfs: *Septuaginta X: Psalmi cum Odis* (Göttingen, 1931). Minor variants in the text orthography in MSS. 2458 and 2622 have been made to conform to this edition.

[6] In the West a trope was 'a relatively free but appropriate musical text interpolated in the authorized liturgy of the Roman rite during the period between the ninth and twelfth centuries. The interpolation . . . functions as an amplification, embellishment, or intercalation in the official text but in no way changes the identity of the text itself.' E. Leahy, 'Tropes,' *New Catholic Encyclopedia*, xiv (1967), p. 315. 'Trope' was also the term Oliver Strunk applied to the textual expansions of Δόξα σοι ὁ Θεός in a recent informal discussion with this

of this type of setting is syllabic or neumatic, very rarely melismatic except in the refrains.

The kalophonic or 'beautified' verses (στίχοι καλοφωνικοί) from the second Psalm,[7] as the name implies, are musical compositions which are considerably more expansive and unrestrained than the preceding simple settings. Since the kalophonic style evidently gave vent to a composer's own creative preferences, Levy maintains that this style eventually became a medium for free composition, independent of traditional models.[8] The most distinguishing and characteristic feature of the kalophonic style, however, is the abundance of chant using such syllables as τε ρε ρε, τι ρι ρι, το ρο ρο, etc. From these syllables is derived the name given to this particular style of chant—teretism.

The present study will examine the treatment of text in the kalophonic settings of Psalm 2 in Athens MSS. 2458 and 2622.[9] Upon this preliminary investigation of the treatment of the text of the second Psalm, a study of the musical idiom in the kalophonic tradition will be projected at a future date.

* * * * *

Athens MS. 2458 preserves ten kalophonic settings of lines from Psalm 2. All of these are by Koukouzeles[10] except for

---

[7] writer in Grottaferrata, Italy. In Athens MS. 2622, for example, at verse 20a of Psalm 103 (f. 7) the following 'trope' appears: Δόξα σοι ὁ Θεὸς δόξα σοι παντοκράτορ βασιλεῦ ἅγιε δόξα σοι τριὰς ἁγία δό-δόξα σοι δόξα σοι ὁ Θεός.

[7] In the Akolouthiai of the fourteenth and fifteenth centuries which I have studied, kalophonic settings in Great Vespers exist for the text of Psalm 2 only.

[8] Levy, op. cit., pp. 155-6.

[9] Great Vespers in Athens MS. 2458, preserved without lacunae, occupy ff. 11ʳ-56ʳ. Immediately after the simple verse-settings from Psalms 103, 1, 2, and 3 begin the kalophonic compositions which draw upon the text of Psalm 2 (ff. 22ᵛ-36ʳ). Athens MS. 2622, however, lacks the very beginning of Great Vespers but starts on f. 5ʳ with verse 33a of the Prooemiac Psalm 103. The music for the evening office extends to f. 90ᵛ and includes thirty-one kalophonic settings from Psalm 2 plus settings for the two halves of the Doxology. This section of kalophonic settings extends from ff. 25ʳ-72ᵛ.

[10] John Koukouzeles, the most renowned church music composer after John of Damascus, is often designated in manuscripts simply ὁ Μαΐστορος ('the Master') and is regarded historically as the second source of Greek music. The precise period of his activity is much disputed by scholars. Two Hirmologia manuscripts associated with the name of Koukouzeles, Leningrad 121 (A.D. 1302) and Sinai 1256 (A.D. 1309), indicate that he was active at least by the very beginning of the fourteenth century. Jean-Baptiste Thibaut, *Monuments de la notation*

setting number 10 (verse 12a) which is attributed to Tzaknopoulos. A cursory glance at the texts of the nine Koukouzeles
items will reveal that the sequence of lines differs from the
order found in the Septuagint.[11] In short, Koukouzeles has
edited and manipulated the lines of the Psalm to suit his own
aesthetic predilections.

The most rudimentary method of manipulating a Psalm
text was through the repetition of a syllable or syllables from
a word in the text:

Setting 3, verse 2a (Koukouzeles): Παρέ- παρέστησαν . . .
Setting 9, verse 11a (Koukouzeles): Δουλε- δουλεύσατε . . .
Setting 10, verse 12a (Tzaknopoulos): Δρά- δράξασθε . . .

A second and related kind of expansion which Koukouzeles
used was the repetition of a single word or a group of words
within a given line.

Setting 2, verse 1 (Koukouzeles): ἵνα τί ἐφρύαξαν ἔθνη ἔθνη
καὶ λαοὶ κενὰ ἐμελέτησαν ἐμελέτησαν κενά[12]

---

ekphonétique et hagiopolite de l'Église grecque (Saint Petersburg, 1913), pp. 126-7;
also Lorenzo Tardo, L'Antica melurgia bizantina (Grottaferrata, 1938), p. 70.
Although Gedeon states that the time of Koukouzeles' creative activity is
unknown to him, he also cites a statement from a manuscript in the library
of the Great Laura by one Cyril Lauriotes who relates that when Patriarch
Philotheos (1353?-4?; 1364-76) gave up his throne, he departed for Mount
Athos in 1355 and there found Koukouzeles. M[anuel] I. G[edeon],
'Προσθήκη εἰς τὰς περὶ Κουκουζέλη παραδόσεις,' Ἐκκλησιαστικὴ ἀλήθεια
33 (1913), p. 36. Since the kalophonic repertory in MS. 2458 stresses the
compositions of Koukouzeles, it is possible that this manuscript was intended
primarily as a special anthology of Koukouzeles' compositions.

[11] The history of the transmission of the Greek Old Testament is highly complex,
and the text used in Byzantium in the fourteenth century was by no means the
pure Septuagint. The pristine Septuagint had already passed through many
early Christian recensions—Aquila, Symmachus, Theodotion and others—
before Origen (d. A.D. 254) compiled his massive Hexapla. The Lucian recen-
sion, which was effected in Antioch probably in the last quarter of the third
century, had spread from Antioch to Constantinople by A.D. 400 and had
become the established text throughout Asia Minor. Cf. L. F. Hartman, 'Greek
Versions' and P. W. Skehan, 'Septuagint,' under 'Bible IV,' New Catholic
Encyclopedia, ii (1967), pp. 425, 427, and A. Rahlfs, op. cit., pp. 60-1.

[12] The following English translations of verses from Psalm 2 are those which
appear in the Revised Standard Version of the Bible, The Holy Bible (New
York, 1953). The English text has not been expanded to conform to the
reworked kalophonic text of the Greek.
Verse 1: 'Why do the nations conspire and the peoples plot in vain?'

Setting 8, verse 8a (Koukouzeles): *αἴτησαι αἴτησαι παρ' ἐμοῦ καὶ δώσω σοι καὶ δώσω σοι ἔθνη τὴν κληρονομίαν σου*[13]

A third type of kalophonic text treatment was word inversion. Here the composer has altered the word order in the text to suit his own purposes.

Psalter text, verse 2b: *καὶ οἱ ἄρχοντες συνήχθησαν ἐπὶ τὸ αὐτό*[14]
Setting 5, verse 2b (Koukouzeles): *συνήχθησαν οἱ ἄρχοντες ἐπὶ τὸ αὐτὸ συνήχθησαν*

In the above example not only has Koukouzeles reversed the order of verb and subject and repeated the verb at the end, but the word *καὶ* he has omitted altogether. This alteration was evidently made to facilitate the joining of verse 2c with verse 2b.

Still a fourth method of reworking the text consisted of the juxtaposition of lines from the Psalm. Setting 5 with inverted word order again illustrates this technique in its combination of verse 2c and verse 2b. The adjustment here in word order serves to effect a smooth juxtaposition between verse 2c and verse 2b.

Setting 5 (Koukouzeles):
  verse 2c: *κατὰ τοῦ κυρίου καὶ κατὰ τοῦ χριστοῦ αὐτοῦ*[15]
  verse 2b: *συνήχθησαν οἱ ἄρχοντες ἐπὶ τὸ αὐτὸ συνήχθησαν*[16]

In settings 7 and 8 Koukouzeles has juxtaposed verses 5a and 5b and verses 7b and 7c respectively.

Setting 7 (Koukouzeles):
  verse 5a: *τότε λαλήσει πρὸς αὐτοὺς λαλήσει τότε πρὸς αὐτοὺς ἐν ὀργῇ αὐτοῦ*[17]
  verse 5b: *ἐν τῷ θυμῷ αὐτοῦ ταράξει ταράξει αὐτοὺς ταράξει*[18]

Setting 8 (Koukouzeles):
  verse 7b: *εἶπεν Κύριος πρὸς μέ Υἱός μου εἶ σύ*[19]
  verse 7c: *ἐγὼ σήμερον γεγέννηκά σε σήμερον γεγέννηκά σε*[20]

The fifth technique, the most imaginative way of rearranging

[13] Verse 8a: 'Ask of me, and I will make the nations your heritage,'
[14] Verse 2b: 'and the rulers take counsel together,'
[15] Verse 2c: 'against the Lord and his anointed, . . .'
[16] Verse 2b: 'and the rulers take counsel together,'
[17] Verse 5a: 'Then he will speak to them in his wrath,'
[18] Verse 5b: 'and terrify them in his fury, . . .'
[19] Verse 7b: 'He said to me, "You are my son",'
[20] Verse 7c: 'today I have begotten you.'

the Psalter text, was through the interpolation of fragments from other lines of a verse (or even from other verses) into a given line of the Psalm. This technique dominates the text adaptations of Koukouzeles in MSS. 2458 and 2622 and assumes elaborate proportions in his settings. A representative and particularly striking example of this practice occurs in setting 6. Here the words ἵνα τί from verse 1 serve as the joint through which lines 2a, 2b, and 2c are converted into a series of terse rogations.

Setting 6 (Koukouzeles):

Verse 1	Verse 2	Line
ἵνα τί............................	παρέστησαν οἱ βασιλεῖς	a
ἵνα τί............................	συνήχθησαν οἱ ἄρχοντες	b
ἵνα τί............................	συνήχθησαν οἱ ἄρχοντες	b
	κατὰ τοῦ κυρίου	c
	συνήχθησαν οἱ ἄρχοντες	
	ἐπὶ τὸ αὐτό	b
ἵνα τί ⟨ Teretism ⟩ ἐφρύαξαν		
ἔθνη ἔθνη καὶ λαοὶ...........	παρέστησαν	a
	οἱ ἄρχοντες	b
ἵνα τί ἐφρύαξαν...............	κατὰ τοῦ κυρίου	c
ἵνα τί λαοὶ κενὰ ἐμελέτησαν		

The preceding examples illustrate the five principal techniques which Koukouzeles and Tzaknopoulos employed to rework a Psalm text for a kalophonic setting.[21] These five

---

[21] I am indebted to Markos Dragoumis of Athens College, Greece, for bringing to my attention the use of four of these five procedures in Greek folk music. The numbers correspond to the labels of phonograph records from the Merlier collection made in 1930-1 (Archives musicales de folklore, Athènes):

1. Expansion of verse by repetition of syllables.
   Read: Τὰ μαλλιά σου ῥίξ 'τα πίσω
   Sung: Τὰ μαλλιά σου ῥίξ 'τα πί(πί)σω (215β)
2. Expansion of verse by repetition of words and phrases
   Read: Νΐσια κάτω στὸ βουνάκι, καὶ στὸ χαμπελὸ τ 'ἀνάκι
   Sung: Νΐσια κά(νΐσια κα νΐσια κά)τω στὸ βουνάκι, (νΐσια κάτω στὸ βουνάκι) καὶ στὸ χαμπελὸ τ' ἀνάκι (43β)
3. Expansion of verse by inversion of words
   Read: Ἡ Παναγιώτα κίνησε
   Sung: Ἡ Παναγιώτα κίνησε, ἡ Παναγιώτα (200α)
4. Expansion of verse by interpolation
   Read: Νὰ βάλω τ 'ὄνομά μου
   Sung: Νὰ βάλω (Παναγιά μου) (νὰ βάλω) τ 'ὄνομά μου
   (Dragoumis gave no collection reference for this example.)

techniques I have labelled for the sake of convenient reference:

(1) Repetition of syllables
(2) Repetition of words and phrases
(3) Inversion of words
(4) Juxtaposition of successive lines (in their regular or inverted order)
(5) Interpolation of fragments from different lines

By applying these techniques to the text of Psalm 2, Byzantine composers developed the larger structure of a kalophonic text. In the ten verse settings from MS. 2458 two basic textual structures can be distinguished:

(1) 'Tripartite' structure—a rigid three-part scheme which consists of three clearly defined sections:
> I. Psalm text
> II. Teretism
> III. Alleluia   (Settings 4, 5, 8, 10)
> As an example, Athens MS. 2458 (Setting 4 by Koukouzeles), ff. 26ʳ–27ʳ has the following structure:

verse 2b: I. καὶ οἱ ἄρχοντες συνήχθησαν ἐπὶ τὸ αὐτό
> verse 2c
>
> οἱ ἄρχοντες ⌈κατὰ τοῦ κυρίου⌉ συνήχθησαν
> οἱ ἄρχοντες ἐπὶ τὸ αὐτό
> II. Teretism
> III. Ἀλληλούια

(2) 'Complex' structure—a procedure whose teretismatic sequences appear in the Psalm text, the Alleluia or both and whose multi-line texts are blended through the techniques of linear juxtaposition (7, 9) and fragment interpolation (1, 2, 3, 6)
For an example of this structure, Athens MS. 2458 (Setting 1, Koukouzeles), ff. 22ᵛ–24ʳ shows the following scheme:

verse 1:   ἱ ⟨ Teretism ⟩ να τί ἐφρύαξαν ἐφρύαξαν ἔθνη
> ἵνα τί λαοὶ κενὰ ἐμελέτησαν ἵνα τί
> ἵνα τί λαοὶ κενὰ ἐμελέτησαν ἐμελέτησαν κενὰ
> ἵνα τί ἐφρύαξαν ἔθνη καὶ λαοί
> ἵνα τί ἐφρύαξαν

verse 2a

ἵνα τί ‾παρέστησαν‾

verse 2b

ἵνα τί ‾συνήχθησαν οἱ ἄρχοντες ἐπὶ τὸ αὐτὸ‾ ἐμελέτησαν ἵνα τί
ἵνα τί 〈 Teretism 〉 ἐφρύαξαν ἐφρύαξαν ἔθνη ἔθνη καὶ λαοὶ
    ἐμελέτησαν ἐμελέτησαν κενὰ ἵνα τί
ἵνα τί κενὰ ἐμελέτησαν

ΠΑΛΙΝ

verse 2c

ἵνα τί κενὰ ἐμελέτησαν ‾κατὰ τοῦ κυρίου‾
ἵνα τί λαοὶ κενὰ λαοὶ κενὰ ἐμελέτησαν ἐμελέτησαν ἐμελέ-
    τησαν κενά
ἵνα τί 〈 Teretism 〉
ἵνα τί ἐμελέτησαν οἱ λαοὶ κενὰ
Ἄλλη 〈 Teretism 〉
ἀλληλούια ἀλλη-ἀλλη-ἀλληλούια

Not only is the treatment of the text much more sophisticated
in settings 1, 2, 3, 6, 7, and 9, but the harsh seams which separated Psalm text, teretism, and Alleluia in the 'tripartite'
structure (Type 1) have been considerably mollified. Koukouzeles apparently has seized the opportunity to make
abundant use of the words ἵνα τί as a pivotal phrase between the
Psalm text and the teretism because of the vowel sound contained in the two iotas. The first setting contains a short teretism
on the initial iota as well as teretisms on the second iota (τί).
A teretism also emerges from the '-λλη-' sound of ἀ-λλη-λού-ι-α
in setting 6. In setting 9 the composer has even developed a
teretism (ε ρε ρε τε ρε ρε) from the final syllable of δουλεύσατε.
Through his sensitivity to phonetic joints, Koukouzeles was
able to introduce teretisms at internal points in the Psalm text.

A close examination of the ten kalophonic verse settings
from the second Psalm in MS. 2458 will reveal one particularly
striking stylistic feature. While the 'tripartite' setting of Tzaknopoulos (10) is built upon only one line of Psalm 2 (verse 12a),
each of the nine settings of Koukouzeles incorporates at least
one phrase from another line of the Psalm. Frequently, Koukouzeles borrows fragments from another verse (or even other
verses) and weaves these into the texture of the principal line
of text.

EXAMPLE 2

a) Athens MS. 2622 (Koukouzeles, setting 24) f. 59ᵛ

b) Athens MS. 2622 (Koukouzeles, setting 3) f. 28ᵛ

In the slightly later Akolouthia MS. 2662 there is a much larger kalophonic repertory for Psalm 2 with attributions to nine different Byzantine composers. In addition to nine of the ten kalophonic settings already found in MS. 2458 (Koukouzeles and Tzaknopoulos), MS. 2622 also contains works by Glykys, Xenos Koronis, Kontopetris, Ethikos, Dokeianos, Thivaios, and Panaretos.[22] Altogether there are thirty-one kalo-

[22] In a catalogue of the names of composers and authors of texts in Athens MS. 2406 (A.D. 1453) by Miloš Velimirović, the names most frequently cited are those of Xenos Koronis, John Koukouzeles, John Lampadarios (of Klada), and John Glykys. See his 'Byzantine Composers in MS. Athens 2406,' *Essays Presented to Egon Wellesz* (Oxford, 1966), pp. 15-17. Velimirović also points out on page 8 that in addition to its different contents and repertory, the many attributions and names of composers were common to the Akolouthiai but appear to be an exception for other types of manuscripts.

phonic settings of selected lines from Psalm 2 plus a setting for
Δόξα πατρὶ . . . and one for Καὶ νῦν . . . .

The two basic structural types contained in MS. 2458 have
already been pointed out. In MS. 2622 there are four settings
(16, 19, 28, 31) of a structural procedure which seems to stand
midway between the simple 'tripartite' type and the 'complex'
structural examples found in MS. 2458. This scheme (which I
shall label 'intermediate') contains a restatement of the opening line or a portion thereof immediately after the teretism
and just before the Alleluia.

'Intermediate' structure. Athens MS. 2622 (Setting 28,
Ethikos), f. 64ᵛ. (For a transcription of this chant see Ex. 4).

verse 12a: Δρά- δράξασθε δράξασθε παιδεί- παιδείας
     δράξασθε δράξασθε παιδείας μήποτε ὀργισθῇ
     κύριος
verse 12a: δράξασθε παιδείας δράξασθε μήποτε ὀργισθῇ
     κύριος παιδείας δράξασθε
Teretism
verse 12a²: μήποτε ὀργισθῇ κύριος
  'Αλληλούια ἀλληλούια

The rigid nature of the 'tripartite' scheme has been shattered
by pushing back the teretism into the body of the Psalm text
itself. But unlike the text treatment in the 'complex' examples,
the interpolation of phrases from other verses is not yet evident.

The three structural procedures ('tripartite,' 'intermediate,'
and 'complex') fall under a general heading of 'through-composed.' This designation serves to point out that each chant
represents the work of one composer only. To this 'through-
composed' category belong twenty of the kalophonic settings
in MS. 2622: seven by Koukouzeles, six by Koronis, three by
Glykys, and one each by Thivaios, Ethikos, Tzaknopoulos, and
Dokeianos. A chart of these twenty 'through-composed' settings also reflects the distribution of the three sub-classifications.

From this chart it is evident that not all the 'through-composed' chants in MS. 2622 fall clearly into one structural category or another. A few partake of certain features which belong
to two procedures. Setting 6 by Glykys, for example, while
basically a 'tripartite' scheme, nevertheless contains within
the Psalm text a second teretism, which is followed by two

N

Chart I

'Through-composed' Kalophonic text settings for Psalm 2
Athens MS. 2622

Composer	Number of text lines	Setting in MS	Folio	Psalm text represented in setting	Structural procedure
1. (Glykys)	one-line	1	f. 25^r	v. 1	Tripartite
2. Koukouzeles (No. 1, 2458)	multi-line	2	f. 26^r	vv. 1, 2a, 2b, 2c	Complex
3. Koukouzeles (No. 2, 2458)	multi-line	3	f. 27^v	vv. 1, 2a, 2b, 2c	Complex
4. Koronis	multi-line	4	f. 29^r	vv. 1, 2a, 2b, 2c	Complex
5. Koronis	multi-line	5	f. 30^v	vv. 1, 2a, 2b, 2c	Complex
6. Glykys	one-line	6	f. 32^r	v. 2a	Tripartite/ Intermediate
7. Koukouzeles (nearly identical to No. 3, 2458)	multi-line	7	f. 33^r	vv. 2a, 1	Complex
8. Koukouzeles (No. 6, 2458)	multi-line	12	f. 42^r	vv. 4a, 4b, 1, 2a, 2b, 2c	Intermediate/ Complex
9. Koukouzeles (No. 7, 2458)	multi-line	15	f. 46^v	vv. 5a, 5b	Complex
10. Koronis	one-line	16	f. 47^v	vv. 5a^1, 5a^2	Intermediate
11. Koukouzeles (No. 8, 2458)	multi-line	18	f. 50^v	vv. 8a, 7b, 7c	Tripartite
12. Glykys	one-line	19	f. 52^v	v. 9a^1, 9a^2	Intermediate
13. Koronis	multi-line	22	f. 57^r	vv. 11a, 12a^2	Intermediate (Text only. No teretism or Alleluia)
14. Koronis	multi-line	23	f. 57^v	vv. 11a, 11b, 12a^2	Tripartite
15. Koukouzeles (No. 9, 2458)	multi-line	24	f. 59^r	vv. 11a, 12a^2, 10a, 10b	Intermediate/ Complex
16. Thivaios	multi-line	25	f. 60^v	vv. 11a, 12a^2	Complex
17. Koronis	multi-line	26	f. 61^v	vv. 11a, 11b, 12a^2	Tripartite
18. Ethikos	one-line	28	f. 64^v	v. 12a	Intermediate
19. Tzaknopoulos (No. 10, 2458)	one-line	29	f. 65^v	v. 12a	Tripartite
20. Dokeianos	multi-line	31	f. 68^v	vv. 12c, 5a, 5b, 12a, 12b	Intermediate/ Complex

restatements of v. 2a. Koukouzeles' setting 12 contains a restatement of v. 4a immediately before the Alleluia, which gives
its overall 'complex' scheme the characteristic feature of the
'intermediate' type of setting. The same is true for setting 24.
The twenty-second setting by Koronis, however, is unique

among the 'through-composed' settings since it contains only a chant for the Psalm text with no teretism or Alleluia to follow. This peculiar example may be simply a fragment from still another type of kalophonic structure which I shall explain below.

In addition to the twenty 'through-composed' settings in MS. 2622 there are also eleven examples of a structural procedure which was not attested in MS. 2458. This type of setting I shall label 'composite', simply to distinguish another difference in structure from the 'through-composed' examples. Whereas the 'through-composed' examples are each the work of only one individual, the 'composite' settings consist of two parts—a simple Prologos with the Psalm text and a Kratema[23] —which may be the work of two different composers. In the example illustrated below, however, both the Prologos and the Kratema are by Koukouzeles.

The most significant feature in the structure of the 'composite' style of kalophonic chant is the complete separation between Prologos and Kratema. The characteristic break of continuity in examples which cite two different composers for Prologos and Kratema may possibly be the result of grafting together compositions to form a single kalophonic chant. One is also confronted with the possibility that the 'composite' procedure may have been the result of an assembly-line method of turning out kalophonic chants. Of the eleven Kratemata which serve as teretisms for the 'composite' settings in MS. 2622, eight are by Koukouzeles; three of these are labelled by the names 'Ethnikon,' 'Viola,' and 'Trochos,' which can be identified in Akolouthiai manuscripts outside of the kalophonic repertory for the second Psalm.[24] Not only does this seem to indicate that these Kratemata were appropriated from other contexts to serve as kalophonic teretisms for Psalm 2, but the absence of the Alleluia at the end of the teretism is also noteworthy. All of the 'through-composed' kalophonic settings contain an

---

[23] A Kratema is a Byzantine church melody on the syllables τε ρι ρεμ, νε να, τι το, requiring an extraordinarily beautiful voice and great technical skill. N. I. Kakoulides, 'Κράτεμα,' Θρησκευτική καὶ ἠθικὴ ἐγκυκλοπαιδεία, vii (Athens, 1965), col. 957.

[24] For the appearance of these three Kratemata outside the service of Great Vespers, see Athens MS. 2406: 'Ethnikon': ff. 298ᵛ, 329ʳ; 'Viola': ff. 330ᵛ, 354ʳ (Lampadarios embellishment); 'Trochos': f. 344ʳ.

'Composite' structure. Athens MS. 2622 (Setting 9, ff. 36ʳ–37ᵛ). (For a transcription of the Prologos, see Ex. 4).

I. PROLOGOS (Koukouzeles, f. 36ʳ):

verse 2b: Καὶ οἱ ἄρχοντες συνήχθησαν ἐπὶ τὸ αὐτὸ
οἱ ἄρχοντες κατὰ τοῦ κυρίου συνήχθησαν
οἱ ἄρχοντες ἐπὶ τὸ αὐτὸ

II. KRATEMA (Teretism: Koukouzeles, ff. 36ʳ–37ᵛ)

Chart II

'Composite' kalophonic text settings for Psalm 2

Athens MS. 2622

	PROLOGOS				KRATEMA (teretism)	
Composer	Number of text lines	Setting in MS.	Folio	Psalm text represented in setting	Composer	Epithet
1. Anonymous (?)	multi-line	8	f. 34ʳ	vv. 2a, 2c, 2b², 2a²	Koukouzeles	
2. Koukouzeles (No. 4, 2458: Prologos only)	multi-line	9	f. 36ʳ	vv. 2b, 2c	Koukouzeles	'Ethnikon'
3. Koukouzeles	multi-line	10	f. 37ᵛ	vv. 2b, 2c, 1	Koukouzeles	'Viola'
4. Kontopetris	multi-line	11	f. 40ʳ	vv. 3a, 3b	Koukouzeles *	
5. Koronis	one-line	13	f. 43ᵛ	v. 4a	Koronis	
6. Anonymous (?)	multi-line	14	f. 45ᵛ	vv. 4a, 4b	Koukouzeles	'Trochos'
7. Ethikos	one-line	17	f. 49ʳ	v. 6a	Dokeianos	
8. Koukouzeles	multi-line	20	f. 53ʳ	vv. 9b, 9a	Koukouzeles	
9. Thivaios	multi-line	21	f. 55ʳ	vv. 10a, 10b	Koukouzeles	
10. Koronis	multi-line	27	f. 63ʳ	vv. 11a, 12a²	Koukouzeles	
11. Panaretos	multi-line	30	f. 66ᵛ	vv. 12a, 12b	Koronis	

* Kratema ends with Alleluia.

elaboration of the Alleluia refrain found at the end of the simple settings. The omission of the Alleluia in the teretismatic sections of all but one of the 'composite' settings (Setting 11,

Kratema by Koukouzeles) certainly indicates that these Kratemata were not originally intended for the kalophonic repertory
of Great Vespers, but were simply appended to the Prologos
with the Psalm text to form a kalophonic chant. Only further
study of the vast kalophonic repertory of the fourteenth and
fifteenth centuries will reveal how widespread this practice was.

The problem of the origin of the Prologoi also arises. Were
these taken from the text of the simple verse settings or were
they composed separately? Since each simple setting consists
of not more than one line of text (and very often of only a
fragment of a line), it is apparent that the majority of the Prologoi which utilize a multi-line Psalm text were composed
apart from the 'classical' settings. The texts of the Prologoi,
despite their brevity, were probably constructed and the chants
composed especially for a kalophonic setting, while Kratemata
were appropriated as terestismatic filler. It is possible that
Koronis' setting 22 may be the Prologos of a 'composite' setting
whose Kratema has, for one reason or another, been omitted.

If we compare the tabulation of the composer's use of one-
line and multiple-line texts with the historical order of kalophonic Kontakia composers as cited in a treatise by mid-fif-
teenth century composer Manuel Chrysaphes,[25] it can be seen
that two of the older composers (Glykys and Ethikos) display
an exclusive preference for a Psalm text of one line. Koukouzeles, on the other hand, who follows Glykys and Ethikos in
chronological order and who, as Levy suggests, may have been
a younger contemporary of the two older men,[26] reveals an
exclusive predilection for a multi-line text. Xenos Koronis,
who may have been a younger contemporary of Koukouzeles,[27]
is represented by two settings in the one-line style of Glykys
and Ethikos and also by five multi-line settings not unlike
those which were preferred in the Koukouzeles schemes.

This comparison suggests that the one-line settings by
Glykys, Ethikos, and Tzaknopoulos may represent an older,
less highly developed tradition than the multi-line versions of
Koukouzeles and others. If Xenos Koronis were indeed a
younger contemporary of Koukouzeles, the ambivalent nature

---

[25] The order of names cited by Chrysaphes is Aneotes (Ananeotes), Glykys,
Ethikos, Koukouzeles, and Ioannes Lampadarios. Tardo, *op. cit.*, pp. 233-4.

[26] Levy, *op. cit.*, p. 156.   [27] *Id.*

of his settings could be explained as the work of a composer whose own art eventually fell under the sway of 'the Master'. Koronis, then, appears to be an imitator whose text treatment started first in the older tradition but later, under the influence of Koukouzeles, came over into the multi-line treatment. This comparison leads to the conclusion that Koukouzeles may have been the key-figure—perhaps even the innovator—in the switch from the one-line setting to the multi-line scheme.

From chart I we can see that all 'through-composed' settings which employ only one line of text belong either to the 'tripartite' or to the 'intermediate' arrangement. While the multi-line settings occasionally use the 'tripartite' and 'intermediate' procedures, most of them fall into the 'complex' category. It is then tentatively possible to link the simpler text with the first two structural procedures—hence with an earlier style—and to associate the multi-line text with the 'complex' procedure and with a later development.

The major question raised by this study of the kalophonic repertory for Psalm 2 in MSS. 2458 and 2622 is the precise meaning of a variety of kalophonic text settings. Do these actually represent a chronological sequence in the development of the kalophonic style? It would certainly appear that the simple verse settings existed prior to the kalophonic ones and that the latter developed after the former. The most perplexing point, however, concerns the procedure which represents the next stage of development after the simple setting. Was a Kratema, without an Alleluia, appended to a Prologos to form a type of kalophonic chant; or did there follow the foresquare 'tripartite' scheme, a symmetrical shape which, after all, did retain the Alleluia of the simple model? Since the type of kalophonic chant with separate Prologos and Kratema appears only in the later manuscript (MS. 2622), this may indicate that the 'composite' scheme either did not exist in A.D. 1336 (the date of MS. 2458) or was not yet widely used.

Whatever the precise sequence of kalophonic text development may have been, it would appear that the simple setting was the original form of verse setting which was eventually supplemented by the free kalophonic versions preserved in the fourteenth century Akolouthiai manuscripts. Likewise, the 'complex' text adaptation would seem to represent the kalophonic setting at its most mature and sophisticated level. Such examples by Koukouzeles as settings 2 and 3 from MS. 2622 display an unusually imaginative and uninhibited treatment of the text. Exactly what role the 'composite' type of setting played in the development of the kalophonic tradition is not clear at present.

If this study of the kalophonic textual structures in Psalm 2 has succeeded in raising more questions than it has been able to answer at the moment, it has, nevertheless, outlined five principal techniques used by late Byzantine composers to manipulate and rework a Psalm text for kalophonic treatment. It has also revealed that there was a variety of structural procedures (with variants) for Psalm verses which were used in one particular kalophonic repertory of the fourteenth century. The procedure observed in MSS. 2458 and 2622 can be summed up in the following outline:

I. Simple setting is composed of not more than one line of a Psalm text followed by the Alleluia.

II. Kalophonic settings
    A. 'Through-composed' type indicates that each setting is the work of one composer.
        1. 'Tripartite' structure is a rigid three-part procedure composed of text, teretism, and Alleluia.
        2. 'Intermediate' structure contains a restatement of the initial line of text which intrudes between the teretism and Alleluia of the 'tripartite' procedure. The teretism is thereby pushed back into the Psalm text.
        3. 'Complex' structure denotes a thoroughly homogenized text treatment in which numerous lines or fragments of lines are interpolated and in which internal teretisms are introduced into the text. The seams of the 'tripartite' structure have been erased.
    B. 'Composite' type has a two-part shape composed of a Prologos with Psalm text and a Kratema, which serves as a teretism. The two parts may or may not be by the same composer, and the Alleluia is attested at the end of the Kratema in only one instance.

The analysis of the various textual patterns in selected kalophonic chants of the fourteenth century has revealed the increasing range with which late Byzantine composers handled the underlying Psalm verses in their kalophonic texts. The freedom with which a text was adapted apparently both conditioned and matched the freedom of the musical idiom which it served.

EXAMPLE 3

a) Athens MS. 2622 Prologos (Koukouzeles, setting 9) f. 36ʳ

b) Athens MS. 2622 Kratema called 'Ethnikon' (Koukouzeles, setting 9), f. 36ʳ

EXAMPLE 4

'Intermediate' structure. Athens MS. 2622 (Setting 28, Ethikos), f. 64ᵛ

Index 1

Byzantine Musicians

Index 2

Byzantine Musical Manuscripts Cited